"Mark Smith has given us a firs* ___
matter of the Old Testament. T
attentive to the conversation wi
that always confront us when w
necessarily written as a textboo.
the Old Testament, this would b ___ ___ ..AtuuoK."

— Patrick D. Miller
Professor of Old Testament Theology
Princeton Theological Seminary

"Mark Smith's new book should be required reading for every student of
Scripture, no matter how proficient. This is a *theo*-logy (study of God) for
ordinary searching people as well as for scholars. Smith deals clearly and
sensitively with difficult and ambiguous issues such as God's anger, God's
gender, and human suffering. His questions lead us to reflect on our own
situation, and his conclusion is truly profound."

— Irene Nowell, OSB
Author of *Pleading, Cursing, Praising: Conversations
with God through the Psalms*

"Mark Smith has done it again! A major biblical scholar and prolific author,
Smith has gathered up significant elements of his work to address some
of the essential ways in which the Bible, especially the Hebrew Bible, has
understood God, and then, through the Bible, how modern readers may do
so. Aiming at an American Roman Catholic audience, but embracing also
Christians more generally and Jews, he does not stint on the scholarship
he draws on, and a rich set of notes and bibliography guides the reader,
both nonprofessional and professional, to more detailed analysis. But the
scholarship is not obtrusive; it only enhances what is an unusually open
conversation between Smith and especially his nonprofessional readers: a
chatty, lucid, and very personal effort to make sense of the biblical witness
and its present impact. Smith makes clear that the Bible is not uniform in its
treatment of God and his ways, and among the biblical views are some that
he is honest to admit are dark and difficult, even close to impossible to crack
open. Yet this variety leads to no despair but serves Smith as a rich source
of stimulus for his own reflections about God and ourselves. To be sure,
one will not always agree with Smith's interpretations—how could it be
otherwise with the Bible!—but readers will regularly come away challenged
to think more deeply and differently about issues and passages and the Bible
as a whole than they have done before.

— Peter Machinist
Hancock Professor of Hebrew and Other Oriental Languages
Harvard University

"Smith not only asks questions that we all have about God, and some excellent ones most people have probably not imagined; he also offers answers with theological and pastoral sensitivity and depth. All kinds of readers will find themselves enriched by Smith's clarity and his sensible, yet learned, reflections."

— Jacqueline E. Lapsley
Associate Professor of Old Testament
Princeton Theological Seminary

"After earlier forays into the study of 'God' (cf. *The Early History of God, The Origins of Biblical Monotheism, God in Translation,* and *The Memoirs of God*), Mark Smith has now turned his considerable expertise and scholarship to the question of *How Human Is God?* Certainly a challenging subject to attempt to write about and interesting to read about! In this study Smith provides what may be characterized—in something of an oxymoron—as an anthropology of God combined with an anthropology of humanity. Smith delves not only into gender and sexuality but also into areas such as anger, suffering as punishment, the demonic, and so much more. In these areas his approach is reflective, even sometimes philosophical. The book is easy to read because the impressive scholarship on which it rests is largely contained in the copious footnotes rather than argued in the text."

— Joseph Jensen, OSB
Professor Emeritus of Scripture
The Catholic University of America
Monk of St. Anselm's

How Human Is God?

Seven Questions about
God and Humanity in the Bible

Mark S. Smith

LITURGICAL PRESS
Collegeville, Minnesota

www.litpress.org

1	2	3	4	5	6	7	8	9

Library of Congress Cataloging-in-Publication Data

Smith, Mark S., 1955–
    How human is God? : seven questions about God and humanity in the Bible / Mark S. Smith.
        pages   cm
    Includes bibliographical references.
    ISBN 978-0-8146-3759-3 — ISBN 978-0-8146-3784-5 (ebook)
    1. God—Biblical teaching—Miscellanea.   2. Anthropomorphism.   I. Title.
BT103.S59   2014
231.7—dc23   2014007738

In memory of Charles (Charlie) Jay Smith
(November 18–22, 2013)

"You formed my inmost being;
you knit me in my mother's womb"
(Psalm 139:13)

"Before I formed you in the womb, I knew you"
(Jeremiah 1:5)

"A story is a letter that an author writes to himself, to tell himself things he would be unable to discover otherwise."

"A book is a mirror that offers us only what we already carry inside us"

—Carlos Ruiz Zafón, *The Shadow of the Wind*

Contents

Invitation to Thinking about God in the Hebrew Bible

In this book, I invite you to think more about God. When it comes to God, we often focus on our *feelings*, or perhaps our *experience*. However, less *thought* tends to go into what and who God *is*. Of course, our emotions are critical for our religious experience, a point suggested not only by the writings of religious persons but also by recent neuroscience.[1] Yet we have minds as well as hearts, and they affect one another: how we feel affects how we think, and how we think informs how we feel—and also what we do in the world. So in our efforts to know and serve God and humanity, it is important to use our God-given ability to think.

The church draws from the Bible and tradition for a deeper sense of God. Yet, in churches week in and week out, little insight is offered about the nature of the God in whom the church believes so steadfastly. When we hear Bible readings in church or read our Bibles at home, we may be drawn to images of God that move us or comfort us (such as God the shepherd in Psalm 23). Sometimes, though, we do not really use our brains very much in thinking about God.[2] The Bible uses different expressions for God designed not only to move our hearts but also to challenge our minds. It is important to think more about God.

Thinking about God in the Bible is a matter of human language. We cannot escape or "get around" human language and experience in order to "get to" God; this is not a biblical idea.

Indeed, the Bible came to us in human language. The Bible's
language for truth about God is figurative or metaphorical. A huge
amount of the Bible's language for God is poetic—for example,
the prophetic books and the psalms. Poetry in the Bible can be
hard for people to understand. Biblical language for God is not
always obvious; sometimes it requires our patience, a willingness
to linger over words and images. Metaphor and poetry are the kind
of language that help people to think about what is not human,
including God. In using various sorts of metaphorical and poetic
imagery, the biblical writers tried to tell us about God. An effort at
understanding God through a deeper awareness of the varied uses
of human language can lead beyond, to undiscovered territory.

Understanding God in the Bible, however, is not limited to the
question of the human language. The Bible's sense of God is tied
to its visions of humanity, in all its great wonder and with all its
severe limitations. For Christians, God's very nature includes God
in human form in the person of Jesus Christ. The world and humanity are also focal points of the Holy Spirit's presence and activity.
God's working in the world is also a central concern in what Christians call the Old Testament and Jews call the Bible or Tanakh.[3] In
biblical writings, God and humanity are locked together, both in
an embrace of love and in conflict over their differences.

This book explores several questions about God in the Bible
that I invite you to think about more, and more expansively. As you
go through this book, I invite you to think about your own sense of
God. This is a topic for which no scholarly expertise and reflection
can suffice. By its very nature, it is an open-ended pursuit, and I
encourage you to engage in the effort. My goal is to ask you to
think from the heart. By this, I mean intellectual exploration that
is touched by the heart and also touches on matters of the heart.

God in America

For those of you who are believers, God is of central importance. Yet even for those of you for whom belief is not important,

an effort to understand God in the Bible should be important, because God is important in America.[4] At present, the historical importance of the biblical deity in this country is clear. Jewish, Christian, and Muslim tradition, faith, and practice attest to this fact.[5] The question of the biblical God is obviously significant for adherents of these traditions, which taken together constitute the majority of Americans.

The Bible and its God are also central to the American story. Over and over again in our history, the Bible has shaped American public life, whether one considers the Liberty Bell (1752, 1753) with its quotation from Leviticus 25:10 ("Proclaim Liberty throughout all the Land unto all the Inhabitants Thereof");[6] or "The Battle Hymn of the Republic" by Julia Ward Howe (1819–1910), with its echoes of Isaiah 63's vision of the Lord "trampling out the vintage where the grapes of wrath are stored" (see Isaiah 63:2-3). Biblical language resonates in our national motto adopted in 1956—"In God We Trust"—which itself derives from "In God is our trust" (perhaps inspired by the fourth stanza of the Star Spangled Banner).[7] In 1968, the power of biblical language was wonderfully evoked by Dr. Martin Luther King Jr. when on the night before he died he expressed the wish of the prophet Amos: "let justice roll down like waters, and righteousness like a mighty stream" (Amos 5:24).[8] Dr. King's dream is, I think, in many ways a biblical dream. These and other well-known textual monuments of our society echo biblical passages, often deliberately but sometimes less consciously.

Today the Bible seems to have less force than it once did in this country; this is a lament commonly heard in religious circles. As a sign of this apparent decline, many people today would describe themselves as spiritual but not religious. The religious sensibility of many people seems weaker as the tide seems to have turned from strong forms of faith and institutional identification to more fluid forms of religious seeking. At the same time, the Bible and its God continue to exert a powerful, if sometimes quiet, influence in our society, well beyond the doors of our churches, synagogues and mosques. While the Bible is certainly not *the* main spiritual source of inspiration for many people today, it remains an important source of inspiration in the religiously fluid situation in which we find ourselves.

To get a sense of the current situation about God in America, I turned to that most scientific of instruments, the Internet. What does the Internet show us about current interest in God? For book titles, we have *The Case for God* (Karen Armstrong), *The Language of God* (Francis S. Collins), *The God Particle* (Leon Lederman and Dick Teresi), *The Reason for God* (Timothy Keller), *The Misunderstood God* (Darin Hufford), *Facing the Abusive God* (David R. Blumenthal). There are the pairs of titles that sound as if they cancel each other out: *There Is a God* (Anthony Flew and Roy Abraham Varghese) versus *God: The Failed Hypothesis* (Victoria Stenger and Christopher Hitchens); *The Evolution of God* (Robert Wright) versus *The God Delusion* (Richard Dawkins); and *Evidence for God: 50 Arguments for Faith* (edited by Michael Licona and William A. Dembski) versus *36 Reasons for the Existence of God: A Work of Fiction* (Rebecca Goldstein). After these two titles, you may need the book *Is God a Mathematician?* (Mario Livio). There is also the God "not" books, for example: *God Is Not Great* (Christopher Hitchens) and *God Is Not One* (Stephen R. Prothero). And not too positively, there are *God's Lunatics* (Michael Largo), *The Stillborn God* (Mark Lilla), and *God Hates Us All* (Hank Moody). There are also the two I thought I might like to read: *The Complete Conversations with God* (Neale Donald Walsh) and *God According to God* (Gerald L. Schroeder). And then there are the one-word titles: *God?* (William Lane Craig and Walter Sinnott-Armstrong) and, simply, *God* (Timothy A. Robinson). Then, there's my personal favorite, Simone Weil's classic *Waiting for God*.

Maybe you've read one or another of these, and there are many others. We could easily do a similar exercise for movies or plays or other cultural forms.[9] These many works discussing God—and I think this is often really the biblical God—involve serious matters, and they are somewhat indicative of the place that God currently holds in our culture, not to mention the difficulties felt by many people about how God fits—or doesn't really fit—into their understanding of reality.

The current debate in our culture about God and atheism is cast in terms of biblical notions or categories about God. In a 2009 essay called "God in the Quad," James Wood in *The New Yorker* suggested this very point, and he went on to claim: "Atheism is structurally related to the belief that it negates."[10] I suspect that Wood's point runs deeper for discussions about God in the United States. When it comes to God, both sides of the debate often assume the idea of a personal God who relates to human beings, a notion that goes back to the Bible. So atheists arguing against religion may share with their believing opponents the very terms of their disagreement. It seems that we can't really understand the United States (even its unbelievers) without some sense of God in the Bible.

Finally, there is another reason why we should try to grasp something of the biblical God: the emergence of the understanding of God within ancient Israel was a redefinition of divinity in its time. This ancient redefinition of God may also be particularly worthy of interest now, as the change in ancient Israel's sense of God may anticipate changes taking place today. I suspect that today we are witnessing a profound paradigm shift * 2015 in the understanding of God and reality.

God and the Church

The question of God is not only an important matter in America; it is obviously a matter of central and critical concern for the church. In an address delivered at a number of American universities in 2009,[11] Walter Cardinal Kasper emphasized: "It is time, it is the right time, to speak of God." He refers in this context to the doctrine of the Trinity as having passed from "a period resembling the sleep of Sleeping Beauty" to a time now of having "regained actuality once more, in regard to historical research and systematic analysis alike."[12] Similarly, the feminist theologian Janet Martin Soskice, in a beautiful book entitled *The Kindness of God*, points to a great stirring prompted by biblical kinship language for God:

> for many centuries and until relatively recently, kinship titles and related imagery (father, brother, being 'born' again) was little remarked upon background noise of Christianity—the common and effaced coin of Christian speech . . . metaphors worn smooth, like an old marble staircase, through centuries of stately liturgical ascent until their original figurative potency was lost. It was left to a later day for kinship metaphors to disturb and scandalize, but also to reawaken us to the promise of what we may become.[13]

Here, both a Roman Catholic churchman, Cardinal Kasper, and a feminist theologian, Janet Martin Soskice, sense the change.[14] God has been taken for granted, I think. We've settled for distillations from the biblical or Christian tradition, yet we need more than summaries. We need to return to the sources in order to nourish our vision of God. We are ready to wake up to a powerful sense of God.

To be sure, there are grave limitations of ancient sources such as the Bible. I am acutely aware of the compelling critique of the Bible's patriarchal metaphor for God, leveled by many scholars such as Sallie McFague. By the same token, I don't feel able, as a Christian, to dispense with the Bible (which McFague's intellectual project largely comes down to).[15] While there is much that is appealing in her own reconstructive theology, for me it gives up too quickly on how we should struggle with the Bible, warts and all. The Bible still—always—calls to us, and it offers hope of renewed knowledge of God. The understanding of God in the Bible has not received sufficient reflection and communication broadly within the church; this discussion tends to be limited to theologians and biblical scholars whose voices reach too few. *academic*

About God and the Bible, now is the time to speak. Indeed, a recent Catholic document, *Verbum Domini*, refers to a world that often feels that God is "superfluous or extraneous." It states, "There is no greater priority than this: to enable the people of our time once more to encounter God, the God who speaks to us and shares . . . love so that we might have life in abundance."[16]

God seems too abstract to many people, and even believing people (myself included) often feel that our faith in God hangs but by the barest of threads. But this faith is not to be dismissed; it is perhaps by such threads that the world sometimes hangs. While great faith, perhaps even faith with a sense of certainty, has been granted to some people, perhaps more people experience faith marked by both hope and uncertainty, especially in the face of difficult realities.[17] Christians are told not to doubt God or what God can do (James 1:6-8), yet we may have uncertainty about the inexplicable matters around us in the world. Uncertainty can ✳ be good for faith; it can help keep us open. From a psychological perspective, uncertainty has been thought to be healthy:

> Andrew Gerber, a psychiatrist at Columbia University, notes that just as our brain is wired to help us when we're faced with fearful situations, it is also wired to help us with uncertainty. "Our lives are a balancing act between making decisions based on the information we have, the information we don't know, and our desire to make sense out of the world around us," he says, adding that the better we make peace with life's uncertainties, the better off we are. "The biggest mistake people make is not to accept uncertainty."[18]

Uncertainty, we might say, is good for faith, as it is true to life's complexities and inexplicable difficulties. It can help open up people to an ever-deepening sense of God. While readers of the Bible today may marvel at the faith-filled experiences of God attributed to Abraham or Moses or the prophets, it is certainly the case that most ancient Israelites had to struggle with the apparent absence of God.[19] We have to struggle as well. Like their time (perhaps like all times), ours is a time of great need, and of great purpose; ours is a time to reflect on God and the Bible.

I also think we need to get out of our routine thinking. We tend to go on autopilot when it comes to religion or God. We need to change this. I say this, as we stand at a time when the inherited wisdoms about God require rejuvenation, and perhaps more. In the words of the French thinker Roland Barthes (1915–1980):

> The old values are no longer transmitted, no longer circulate, no longer impress; literature is desacralized, institutions are impotent to defend and impose it as the implicit model of the human. It is not, if you will, that literature is destroyed; rather *it is no longer protected*: so this is the moment to go there. . . . Our gaze can fall, not without perversity, upon certain old and lovely things, whose signified is abstract, out of date. It is a moment at once decadent and prophetic, a moment of gentle apocalypse, a historical moment of the greatest possible pleasure.[20]

And, I would add, of hopeful and loving possibility.

Inspirations for This Book

To explain the sensibilities that informed this book, I would like to mention a few sources that have inspired me over the years. The first is an old and beautiful study by Jean Leclerq, OSB, *The Love of Learning and the Desire for God: A Study of Monastic Culture* (which resonates for me, largely thanks to my Benedictine schooling at Saint Anselm's Abbey in Washington). The main title of Leclerq's work, I think, captures the ultimate goal for this book, what we may call the "performative" character of study. In recreating the world of monasteries, this book performs the goals of learning and love of God that monastic life sought to infuse in monks. Leclerq's book reminds us that our labor of learning about God is to help us cultivate our love and desire for God. For this pursuit, the Bible is an essential resource. Christians ought to be, to use Leclerq's term for monks, "word-possessed."[21]

Another author whose words have inspired me is Simone Weil (1909–1943). Weil is famous for her writings of social criticism and political activism, but her life was also an inspiring and inspired search for God. A Jew who developed a deep Christian faith without becoming a Christian, Weil expressed her vision in these terms: "Our love should stretch as widely across all space, and should be as equally distributed in every portion of it, as is the very light of the sun. Christ has bidden us to attain to the perfection of the heavenly by imitating his indiscriminate bestowal of light. Our intelligence should have the same complete impartiality."[22] Weil is calling Catholics to be both catholic in our "love across space" and Catholic in our faith—and also in our intelligence. At the same time, I am also reminded of one of Weil's cautionary sayings about intelligence: "The intelligent man who is proud of his intelligence is like the condemned man who is proud of his large cell."[23] The God-given gift of intelligence requires us to be truly modest and honest not only about ourselves but also about what we really know about the Bible and about what the Bible does and does not tell us about God. It tells us what we need for salvation, but it does not tell us everything (cf. Proverbs 25:2, "It is the glory of God to conceal things").

A third inspiration comes not from a particular author but from my intense engagement with many Jewish scholars and communities in America and Israel over the past three decades. This experience has led me to view my work on God in the Bible through what I would call double lenses: my life and identity as a Roman Catholic Christian on the one hand, and on the other hand, my many rich experiences with Jews. Professionally I have taught in Catholic theological faculties, and now for nearly fifteen years I have served in a department of Jewish studies. Personally I am a committed Catholic, while my wife and I have raised three wonderful children in a Jewish home. If children are in any sense one's destiny, then I have, in a sense, cast one dimension of my destiny with the Jewish people. These personal and professional experiences have informed my study and love of Scripture.

At this point part of being Catholic for me means both to reflect from a Catholic perspective and to ask how such reflections might sound in a "Jewish key." It is not only an effort to make amends for the wrongs that the Catholic Church did to Jews before, during, and after the Shoah (sometimes called the Holocaust), although this remains a critical duty.[24] And it is not only an effort to rethink Christian theologizing on the Bible in light of the Shoah, a task that has been admirably taken up by many people much more qualified than myself.[25] It is to realize that whatever claims we Christians make about the Hebrew Bible (Old Testament), they are not only for and about ourselves. The Hebrew Bible lies at the heart of both Jewish and Christian traditions, and from a Christian perspective God chose the Jewish people before Christians for divine disclosure. We do well to think about how we are heard and received by others, especially Jews, especially as we reflect on biblical themes important to the Jewish people such as the covenant, which they were granted first and eternally (Genesis 17:7; see also Isaiah 55:3). We Christians may feel that we have learned this crucial lesson, but in fact we still have quite a way to go. We need to realize that our hope in God and our study of God in the Scriptures do not belong only to ourselves and were not meant only for us. You will see in this book references to admirable Jewish sources and scholarship alongside Christian sources and scholarship. As a scholar, I need both; and I think that as believers in the living God, we need each other.

My Approach in This Book

In what follows, we examine God in the Bible—or more accurately, human understandings of God. But how shall we approach questions of God and the Bible? At this point, all I can tell you is where I am. As a scholar and as a person, I am inclusive and wide ranging. At the heart of the task is the Bible, which is not one text but scores of texts stretching out over a period of about fifteen hundred years (ca. 1150 BCE/BC to 120 CE/AD). It contains a multiplicity of voices espousing views that sometimes can't be harmonized.[26] I often think of the Bible not as a book of answers to life's problems, and not only as a book that raises fundamental questions of life and reality; it is also the record of Israel's great voices debating and discussing the nature of God and reality for Israel. In our study, we get to join in this discussion and debate.

In addition to biblical texts, I use information from outside of the Bible that helps illuminate the biblical world. For studying the Bible, I sometimes take a literary approach, or I note historical and cultural aspects of the biblical world. My thinking is further informed by the study of religion and theology. Still other fields offer valuable resources for thinking about God. This book draws on feminist and Jewish studies, linguistics and anthropology, and even neuroscience, of all things! Overall, my approach is rooted in one way or another in the Bible's historical context. The mystery of the incarnation, which unfolded in time, requires Christians to consider what is historical.

About the Format

As you may have noticed, I sometimes do not use the term Old Testament, but Hebrew Bible. Old Testament is a specifically Christian term. However, this book has been written not only with Christians in mind but also for others interested in the subject. I recognize that the term Hebrew Bible is hardly ideal.

xx   *How Human Is God?*

A good amount of what is in the Hebrew Bible is not in the Hebrew language, but in Aramaic. The Hebrew Bible includes what is in Jewish and Protestant Bibles, but the term does not cover the books in Greek included in Catholic and Orthodox Bibles. Despite these drawbacks to the term Hebrew Bible, my desire to be inclusive (to be catholic) on this score overrides my need to use the traditional Christian label of the Old Testament.

In this book, I generally stick to the widely used translation, the New Revised Standard Version (NRSV). I don't think that this translation always captures the wording of the original Hebrew, Aramaic, or Greek. So sometimes I use other translations, such as the New American Bible Revised Edition (NABRE) or the New Jewish Publication Society (NJPS). At other times, I offer my own translations.

In the endnotes I provide the names of the germane sources, but the citations are hardly comprehensive. Some endnotes mention information from outside the Bible, but I don't always provide a lot of background information. You may want some further background as you read this book, so I have included recommendations for further reading at the end. In addition, there are many fine introductions to the Hebrew Bible that you might consider consulting if you wish. I have found one rather useful: Lawrence Boadt's *Reading the Old Testament: An Introduction*, revised and updated by Richard J. Clifford and Daniel Harrington.[27]

You don't have to deal with any of these matters if you don't want to. Some of you might agree with how our 22nd and 24th president felt about biblical scholarship. Grover Cleveland (1837–1908) stated: "The Bible is good enough for me, just the old book under which I was brought up. I do not want notes or criticisms or explanations about authorship or origin or even cross-references. I do not need them or understand them, and they confuse me."[28] Every now and again in this book, I mention details. So I would beg your patience when I tease out specific features. God in the Bible, after all, is often in the details.

Questions about God

Questions about God

❦ 1 ❦

Why Does God in the Bible Have a Body?

I'd like to open our consideration of God in the Bible with a question that might seem unusual. Christians might expect a discussion of God to start with Jesus or the Trinity. By contrast, Jewish readers might suppose that a look at God in the Bible would begin with divine mercy and forgiveness.[1] In later chapters, we'll touch on these subjects, but I want to raise a different question: why does God in the Bible have a body?

This question of God's body might seem odd to many of you (not to mention an unusual way to start off a book about God). Yet for Christians, the image of the divine body is central to the mystery of God. Jesus was God embodied and incarnate (literally, "in the flesh") as a human being. God the Father has often been thought of in terms of a human body, for example, as an elderly king enthroned in heaven. In Jewish tradition, the divine body becomes a subject of considerable thought, especially in mystical works. For these reasons, God's body in the Bible is actually an important question. God's body is also important because God's anger and God's gender and sexuality are bodily matters that we will be examining in subsequent chapters.

At the same time, it might seem that God shouldn't have a body. After all, the Bible reminds us that God is not human (Hosea 11:9).[2] According to other passages, God transcends the human, bodily condition. In Deuteronomy 4:12 and 15, God

3

has no form.[3] Church fathers agree. Origen (ca. 185–254) says about God: "He cannot therefore be understood to be a body."[4] To support this view, Origen cited Colossians 1:15: "He [the Son] is the image of the invisible God."[5] In the year 325 AD/CE, the "invisible God" would become official doctrine in the Nicene Creed.[6] A little-known church father, Arnobius (died ca. 330 AD/CE), devoted a long discussion to the impossibility of God having a body.[7] He also says: "divine bodies do not eat the food of men."[8] This claim, as we will see shortly, receives an interesting challenge from the book of Genesis.

Both Jewish and Christian traditions largely agree with this view. For Philo of Alexandria (a Jewish philosopher roughly contemporary with Jesus), God's body or body parts in the Scriptures serve to teach people about God, but they do not reveal God's actual self.[9] This approach would be expanded by Maimonides, a great Jewish philosopher of the Middle Ages. For Maimonides, biblical passages describing God in human terms do not refer to God's actual nature, but to divine "attributes of actions, or as assertions of God's absolute perfection."[10] Maimonides denied any bodily nature for God, a view that influenced a good deal of Jewish thought in the same period, when Jewish mystical literature was also focusing on the divine body.[11] Maimonides would be followed in large measure—though not entirely—by Thomas Aquinas.[12] Modern rationalist thought has also questioned the idea of attributing human characteristics or form to God.

The technical word in English for this kind of attribution is "anthropomorphism,"[13] which derives from two Greek words, *anthropos*, "humanity," and *morphos*, "form." The Greek philosopher Epicurus used *anthropomorphos*, "of human form," for *theos*, "God."[14] For the first modern use of the term, *The Oxford English Dictionary* cites the 1753 Supplement to the work of Ephraim Chambers (ca. 1680–1740), called *Cyclopeadia; or an Universal Dictionary of Arts and Sciences*. Hardly a household name today, Chambers was a major figure in the encyclopedia movement of the eighteenth century and a particular inspiration to Denis Diderot. "Anthropomorphism," according to Chambers, is, "among divines, the error of those who ascribe a human figure to the deity."[15] As this quote suggests, the modern philosophical tradition called for stripping away anthropomorphism from the notion of God.

From the perspective of Jewish and Christian traditions (not to mention the modern rationalist tradition), the idea of God having a body would seem impossible. In the *Catechism of the Catholic Church*, the issue is not even mentioned. For what the Catholic Church believes can be said of God, the *Catechism* (paragraph 42) has a list of what God is not: "the inexpressible, the incomprehensible, the invisible, the ungraspable."[16] Similarly, *Yigdal* (meaning, "He is great"), a Jewish song sung toward the end of Friday night Sabbath services, cites Maimonides in proclaiming that God "has no likeness of body nor body."[17] Bible scholars have largely accepted this view.[18]

So what are we to make of anthropomorphism? Is it simply a projection on the part of wishful human beings? I think it is fair to say that projection is involved to some extent. Many, if not most, people today would acknowledge human projection when it comes to ancient gods and goddesses outside of the Bible.[19] So why not when it comes to the biblical God? Believers may rush to defend the special case of the biblical God, but there is no denying the vast amount of human language used for God in the Bible. So what are we to make of human language for God?

At this point, it may be helpful to shift the discussion from this theological question and turn to the fields of psychology and anthropology, in order to help us reframe the question: what does anthropomorphism do for people? Psychological studies going back to Jean Piaget[20] suggest the importance that anthropomorphism plays in children's efforts to make sense of the nonhuman:

humans need models

for actions or thoughts to be understood, the unknown must be related to life as humans know it. Thus anthropomorphism as an

attempt to deal with the unknown is a psychological process. In
children it represents an effort to deal with a largely unknown
world (i.e., a child gives human qualities to a favorite toy).[21]

Anthropomorphism helps children move from the known to the
unknown. In a more recent study, the psychologists Justin L.
Barrett and Rebekah A. Richert demonstrate the flexibility that
children use in applying anthropomorphism to God.[22] Children
sense that God is different from humans even as they use anthropomorphism to understand God. In other words, when it comes
to anthropomorphic expressions about God, children sense the
difference about God beyond God's similarity to humans.

For adults as well as children, the anthropologist Pascal Boyer
suggests that human representations help them to draw inferences
about reality that have "salience."[23] Anthropomorphism offers a
way not just to bring order to perceptions or provide "a more
complex organization on the available stimuli."[24] "Salience," in
Boyer's terms, suggests recognition of the difference behind
the similarity. Boyer goes on: "Religious representations would
probably not be acquired at all if their counter-intuitive aspects
did not make them sufficiently salient to be an object of attention
and cognitive investment."[25] In other words, anthropomorphism
helps us to organize information, and it also helps to provide
insight into this information beyond its surface meaning. Anthropomorphism of the body in particular offers ways for people
to process, categorize, and gain insight into nonhuman aspects
of the world. The body and its parts provide a means for sorting
out and understanding nonhuman things. This point applies to
God's body. The body was one of the basic pattern recognition
tools that ancient people used for organizing their intuitions about
God and for gaining insight into God.

So how does the Bible use the human body to understand
God? We can start by noting that the Bible presents three sorts of
bodies for God.[26] One is a natural body, human in scale, which
appears to people on earth. It is presented as physical,[27] like a

human body. A second is a superhuman body; this divine body was not thought of as regular physical material; it may consist of light or fire. It too appears to people on earth. A third is not made up of regular matter either, but it is cosmic in its scope, and its location is in or even above the heavens. It is this third sort of body that ultimately became the divine body for Jewish and Christian tradition, and perhaps for early Islam as well.[28]

God's Natural "Human" Body in the Book of Genesis

The clearest examples of God's human body all appear in the book of Genesis: Adam and Eve in the Garden of Eden (Genesis 2–3); Abraham and Sarah in the Sodom and Gomorrah story (Genesis 18–19); and Jacob wrestling with God (Genesis 32). After we look briefly at these passages, I will say something about the significance of these naturalistic depictions appearing only in Genesis.

The first time in the Bible that we meet God with a body is in the Garden of Eden in chapters 2–3. In Genesis 1, God speaks and creates. However, there is no bodily representation of God until God forms the human from the ground in Genesis 2:7. At this point, God "breathed into his nostrils the breath of life." God here is breathing breath into the human person—God has breath! Divine creation of the human person here sounds like ~~kiss~~ mouth-to-mouth resuscitation.[29] In Genesis 2:8 God plants a garden, a rather physical activity that humans do. While this is not explicitly physical, it sounds rather like human activity. It is still possible at this point to imagine God without a body, until we see God "walking in the garden" (Genesis 3:8). Here God is out for a stroll. The conversation that follows in Genesis 3:9-19 sounds as if God is standing in the presence of the man and the woman.

It is quite possible to read much of Genesis 2–3 without thinking of God as really having a body. Certainly, some of the divine acts could be imagined without a divine body, such as making and talking. (After all, God speaks and creates in Genesis 1, and there does not seem to be a divine body there.) By contrast, God "walking in the garden" suggests a body. Christian art often provided God with a body in the Garden of Eden. For example, in Hieronymus Bosch's *Garden of Earthly Delights*, Lorenzo Ghiberti's gilded bronze of *The Creation of Adam and Eve*, and Michelangelo's painting of Adam and Eve in the Sistine Chapel (to name only a few examples), God's body is slightly larger than the bodies of Adam and Eve. In Genesis 2–3, God—being God after all—would be somewhat larger than the two humans. The picture of God strolling in the divinely made garden conjures up depictions of the gardens of kings, who themselves are not uncommonly represented as taller than their royal subjects in ancient Near Eastern art.[30] It would seem that God would be at least as tall as ancient monarchs.

If Genesis 2–3 is not so clear about whether God really has a body, doubts should be dispelled by the Sodom and Gomorrah story. According to Genesis 18:1, "the LORD appeared to Abraham." In verse 2 "the LORD" is one of the "three men standing near" Abraham (the other two are "the two angels" mentioned in 19:1).[31] Genesis 18:16 refers to the three figures simply as "the men." The very fact that the figures are called "men" suggests a bodily appearance on their part, and this in fact is one of the rare passages in the Bible that refers to God as "man."[32]

In Genesis 18:3 when Abraham "saw them, he ran from the tent entrance to meet them and bowed down to the ground." Abraham then offers them hospitality: water for washing "your feet" and "rest under the tree" (verse 4), as well as food (verse 5). To judge from the mention of "your feet," Abraham sees the bodies of three men, who seem to be human in scale. This impression fits the description of the meal that Abraham serves them in verse 8: "he stood by them under the tree *while they ate*."[33]

This scene was a problem for later commentators who were used to God being without a body. A medieval Jewish commentator such as Rashi would presume that "they appeared to be eating."[34] As you may recall from the discussion earlier, the church father Arnobius denied that God eats, but the passage here could hardly be clearer. God does indeed eat with the two other figures identified as "two angels" (Genesis 19:1). As Arnobius realized, eating suggests a human body. The scale of this body also seems rather human, since God and the two angels sit under the tree while they eat (verse 8).

After their meal, the three figures ask Abraham: "where is your wife Sarah?" (Genesis 18:9). It might be supposed that the question is merely rhetorical and that the three figures know where she is, but it is also possible that these "men" don't really know. Perhaps God in this passage is not understood to be all knowing, as some scholars have surmised.[35] "The LORD" converses twice with Abraham, first with Sarah in the picture (Genesis 18:19-15) and then without her (18:23-32). Between these two conversations is a remarkable interlude with God speaking to God's self (Genesis 18:17-21).

Many readers focus on Abraham pressing God and managing to get God to spare Sodom if ten "righteous" persons can be found. It is a remarkable picture, and it is without parallel in the entire Bible.[36] For many readers, the passage offers a model of spirituality where humans can take the initiative in talking with God and nego- *open view of God* tiating with God. What is also remarkable, and often overlooked, is that God exceeds the terms of the deal reached with Abraham.[37] In chapter 19, ten righteous people are not found in Sodom. Lot's family adds up to six people: Lot, his wife, his two daughters (Genesis 19:30), and the two sons-in-law (Genesis 19:12). And even these six do not leave Sodom, because the sons-in-law don't believe Lot and they remain behind (Genesis 19:14). So only four people flee from Sodom, and even one of these—Lot's wife—turns back and looks at Sodom and turns into a pillar of salt (Genesis 19:26).

According to this math, God could have destroyed these members of Abraham's family along with the city of Sodom. Yet God manages to exceed Abraham's demands for mercy without

consequences of Sodom's choices

sacrificing justice. God renders justice by destroying the city, but God also shows mercy in saving its few, considerably less than the ten that Abraham had bargained for.[38] God even saves Lot, who does not seem righteous in this story, since he offers his own daughters to be raped by the townspeople of Sodom (Genesis 18:8), and later Lot and his daughters commit incest (Genesis 19:30-38). In this story, we have a remarkable meditation on God's ability to exceed human expectations about justice and mercy. In addition, the picture of Abraham and the Lord is nothing less than two men who walk together and share a conversation. Here is a God who walks and talks, eats and drinks. This is perhaps the Hebrew Bible's most explicitly human depiction of God.

Another passage that refers to God as "a man"[39] is Genesis 32. The story begins with Jacob sending gifts to his brother, Esau, whom he fears (Genesis 32:3-8). Jacob prays to God for deliverance (verses 9-12) and sends yet more presents ahead to his brother's camp (verses 13-21). Jacob hopes that the gifts will mollify Esau when "I shall see his face" (verses 20-21). After sending his family across the river Jabbok (this name punning on the name of Jacob), Jacob is alone (verses 22-25). Without any introduction, it is said: "a man wrestled with him" (verses 25-26). Here the verb (*wayye'abeq*) also puns on the name of the Jabbok River in the story and on the name of Jacob (itself evoking his own tricky character back in Genesis 26 and 27). The struggle continues inconclusively until the mysterious figure strikes Jacob's hip socket (verse 25). The unnamed figure then asks to be let go "for the day is breaking" (verse 26), perhaps suggesting a figure powerful at night but not by day; it is unclear. Jacob refuses the request without the figure's blessing (verse 26). After asking Jacob his name (verse 27), he offers a name change from Jacob to Israel, "for you have striven (*sarita*) with God/gods (*'elohim*) and with humans, and have prevailed" (verse 28). The first verb puns in Hebrew on the name of Israel. Jacob in turn inquires about the name of the figure (verse 29), who instead "blessed him" (verse 29).

At this point, the "man" drops out of the story just as inexplicably as he had entered it back in verse 24. Jacob names the place Peniel, a known locale that puns on the word *panim* in his statement that "I have seen God face to face (*panim'el-panim*), and yet my life is preserved" (verse 30). This line not only connects back to Jacob's earlier mention of seeing Esau's face (in verse 20), but it also anticipates Jacob's later statement when he meets Esau (Genesis 33:10): "for truly to see your face is like seeing the face of God." Genesis 32 then relates how at sunrise Jacob passed by the place, now called Penuel, at this point limping because of his hip (verse 31). The episode closes with an explanation that "to this day the Israelites do not eat the thigh muscle that is on the hip socket, because he struck Jacob on the hip socket at the thigh muscle" (verse 32).

Several elements about this story are unclear, in particular the nature of the mysterious figure. According to verse 31, Jacob recognizes him as *'elohim*, which may be translated as "God" or "gods." The word *'elohim* here is translated by New Revised Standard Version as "God" (also in the New American Bible Revised Edition), and many commentators follow this approach. Others translate the word as "a divine being," for example, the New Jewish Publication Society Version. The word could originally mean "divine being" or "divinity,"[40] in keeping with the problem mentioned by the figure himself: "Let me go, for the day is breaking" (verse 26). This does not sound like God or an angel. While the divine figure remains a bit mysterious, he is understood as none other than God in the larger context. The chapter refers to Jacob seeing Esau's face before the wrestling scene (Genesis 32:20), and after the wrestling scene Jacob compares seeing Esau's face to seeing God's face (Genesis 33:10). In this way, Genesis 32–33 connects Jacob's struggles with his brother, Esau, with his struggle with God.

This story illustrates the message that it is Jacob's destiny to become Israel, to wrestle with God and people alike, to return to

the land, and to keep the dietary customs.[41] It would be tempting
to read in this story Jacob wrestling with himself; it is perhaps a
conflict between the side of himself that he cannot overcome and
the side that cannot overcome him, in other words, between who
he is up to this point and who he is to be from now on. Such a
psychological reading, however, is not suggested clearly by the
story. What is clear is that the wrestling with God is emblematic
of Israel's identity, and it points to a very physical human sort
of divine body.

With the story of Jacob, we reach the end of the depictions
of God's human body. Genesis is the only book of the Bible with
such naturalistic depictions of God. This divine body was traditionally associated with divine visitations made to people. This
sort of depiction, after Genesis, came to be applied to angels, as
we see in Judges 6 and 13. With the biblical cases that we have
noted, the human-like depictions of God in Genesis also appear
only with famous figures, namely Adam and Eve, Abraham and
Sarah, and Jacob. These episodes perhaps show a progression,
moving from a natural coexistence of the human and the divine
(the Garden of Eden), to an easy visit of the divine with the
human (the Sodom and Gomorrah story), to a problematic in-
teraction between the human and the divine (Jacob wrestling).
Adam and Eve live in the garden of God. Abraham walks and
converses with God, and with Sarah's help, he serves God a meal.
Jacob struggles with God, as befits his name. The progression
perhaps suggests that such interactions with the divine in human
the form were considered less and less common. The authors of
the Bible saw God's body as a human experience that occurred
only in the distant past, and only with the famous figures of that
past. Even the great figure, Moses himself, has interactions with
God that point to a different sort of divine body, as we see in
the next section.

God's Superhuman "Liturgical" Body

In the book of Exodus, we first meet a superhuman body of God in chapter 24. Moses, Aaron and his two sons, Nadab and Abihu, along with seventy of Israel's elders, are initially summoned to worship at a distance; only Moses is to ascend the mountain (verses 1-2). Then a covenant ceremony follows (verses 3-8),[42] ending with Moses' declaration: "See, the blood of the covenant that the LORD has made with you in accordance with all these words." It is a striking drama of covenant ritual. Yet the passage takes a further, stunning turn.

Verses 9 to 11 return to the figures of Moses, Aaron, and the others mentioned back in verse 1. Rather than remaining at a distance as before, they go up the mountain to further formalize the covenant with a meal. There "they saw the God of Israel" (verse 10). This is an unqualified statement of seeing God, and it is not only Moses who sees God here; all these persons do. This is remarkable, because as many readers of the Bible know, people in the Bible are not supposed to be able to see God. The popular fear about seeing God and dying as a result[43] is clearly expressed elsewhere in the Bible. We saw this earlier with Jacob after he wrestles with the divinity (Genesis 32:31; see also Judges 6:22-23; 13:22-23).[44] With Moses and the other leaders, God acts with grace: "God did not lay his hand on the chief men of the people of Israel" (Exodus 24:11).

Exodus 24:10 provides a unique glimpse of God's body: "Under his feet there was something like a pavement of sapphire stone, like the very heaven for clearness." The feet are God's, and they are evidently perceived by the human figures through what looks "like a pavement of sapphire stone." From descriptions of the temple on the divine mountain known elsewhere, the pavement is the temple's flooring. Nothing else of the divine temple or divine body is mentioned, and the passage here barely evokes the divine body. The divine body in this passage is mysterious, and it is not clear from this description how large it is. The context seems to presuppose the traditional idea that the superhuman-sized God is enthroned in the divine palace, with God's feet perhaps resting on a divine footstool.[45] Moses and the leaders in this passage see God, but with the bare mention of the divine feet there is only a glimpse of God. We are left wondering about this divine body, as perhaps we should. The passage ends with the covenant meal of the human figures on the mountain (Exodus 24:11).[46] All in all, this is a remarkable episode.

Another Exodus passage with the theme of seeing God is in chapters 33–34, where God tells Moses: "you cannot see my face; for no one shall see me and live" (Exodus 33:20). Unlike the passage in Exodus 24, Exodus 33–34 "splits the difference" with the manifestation of the divine body: Moses can see God's back but not his face. God says to Moses, "while my glory passes by I will put you in a cleft of the rock, and I will cover you with my hand until I have passed by; then I will take away my hand, and you shall see my back; but my face shall not be seen" (Exodus 33:22-23). The next chapter then narrates God passing before Moses and pronouncing his name and attributes (34:6-7).

One of the notable features of the scenes in Exodus 33–34 is how, as I would put the point, it "splits" the divine body. On the one hand, Moses cannot see God's face and live. As we noted earlier, this seems to be a response to a common fear expressed elsewhere about humans seeing God or an angel. On the other hand, God offers a unique self-presentation in showing Moses the divine back, perhaps as an expression of divine concern to preserve Moses' life. Showing the divine back in this manner is unique in the Bible. To achieve this, the passage offers an unprecedented picture of God's hand to cover Moses in the cleft of the rock as God passes by.

The question is: what sort of divine body is this? First of all, it is large. It is large enough that God's hand can cover Moses as God passes by. So it would seem that the hand is the size of Moses himself. If God's hand covers Moses, it suggests a hand that is the size of a human; God's body, by implication, is huge (I'd guess about seventy feet in height). This is on an entirely different scale compared with what we saw with Adam and Eve, Abraham, and Jacob. Second, God's body in this scene is not as naturalistic as what we see in the Genesis story. God is not walking. This God "passes by" Moses standing in the cleft of the rock of the mountain. The picture seems to be like the divine presence or "glory" sweeping by the side of the mountain where Moses and the cleft of the rock are. Perhaps purposefully, the narrative has left out details of God's passing by. Third, this mysterious and unique manifestation of the divine does not seem to be physical, as God's body seemed to be in Genesis.

To better understand the divine body on Mount Sinai, we may turn to Isaiah 6. This passage is perhaps best known for its line in verse 3: "Holy, holy, holy is the LORD of hosts; the whole earth is full of his glory." As many Christians will recognize, these words appear at a central point in the Christian Mass. This verse also occurs at a crucial moment in Jewish services on Saturday morning, in the prayer known as the Qedushah (meaning, "holiness"). In echoing Isaiah 6:3, Christians and Jews are acknowledging God, much as the prophet does. In the beginning of this passage, the prophet recounts in his first-person voice how "I saw the LORD sitting on a throne, high and lofty; and the hem of his robe filled the temple" (Isaiah 6:1). It is this verse that I want to focus on.

First of all, the prophet saw God. This is stated in a straight-forward way. This may be because this human who can see God without such a problem is a prophet (although, as we shall see in the next section with the prophet Ezekiel, his visionary experience is more complicated). Isaiah does not see a literal, human body for God. It is a visionary experience of a divine body with a garment that fills the temple and a glory that radiates throughout the earth: "the whole earth is full of his glory" (Isaiah 6:3; see also Numbers 14:21 and Jeremiah 23:24). What the prophet sees of God is a seated body enthroned "high and lofty." The prophet is having this experience in the Jerusalem temple according to verse 1 (reflected also in the mention of the doorposts and the "House" in verse 4) and not in heaven (as in 1 Kings 22:19; cf. Jeremiah 23:18, 22).

The temple's physical structure implies some measurements ✳ to God's body as seen by the prophet. According to 1 Kings 6:23-28, God's temple throne consists of two cherubs, each one measuring ten cubits in height. With a cubit coming to about a foot and a half,[47] the cherubs are about fifteen feet high. In other words, God is imagined as sitting fifteen feet high. To put these measurements in perspective, let me compare the seat I sit on in my study. The seat of my chair is eighteen inches high, in other words, a biblical cubit. So in the vision of Isaiah, God seated is about ten times my size. (If I stand up, I come to a little under six feet; and if God were to stand up, God might come to about sixty or seventy feet in height.) Now recall my calculation about the size of God when God passes Moses in Exodus 33–34. I suggested that it might be about seventy feet in height. What we seem to have in Isaiah's vision and Moses' experience of God's body are fairly similar sizes for the divine body.

The idea of the supersized body of God enthroned in the divine palace on the cosmic mountain was quite traditional in ancient Israel.[48] This vision of God was grounded in the temple experience, as we see in Isaiah 6. It is also reflected in the ritual context of people visiting temples on pilgrimage.[49] It is for this reason that I call the second divine body God's "liturgical" body.

God's Cosmic "Mystical" Body in Later Prophetic Books

The third divine body is expressed as a heavenly or even super-heavenly reality. Unlike God's human and superhuman bodies, it is not manifest on earth. A good example appears in the final chapter of the book of Isaiah, written in the late sixth century (about two centuries after the prophet Isaiah himself lived). This passage contrasts the cosmic temple with the earthly temple (Isaiah 66:1):

Thus says the LORD :
Heaven is my throne
and the earth is my footstool;
what is the house that you would build for me,
and what is my resting-place?

Here God is seated over the heavens and the earth, in other words, over the whole universe. This is the cosmic body of God.[50] An allusion to this cosmic body is found in the question posed by the anonymous prophet of the exile in Isaiah 40:12: "Who has measured the waters in the hollow of his hand and gauged the heavens with a span?" The answer is God; this is the divine hand that is so large that it can take in the cosmic waters and the heavens. Similarly, Psalm 113:6 describes the enthroned God on high who "condescends to see what is in heaven and on earth" (see also 1 Kings 8:27: "the heavens, even the highest heavens, cannot contain" God).

We meet an elaborated version of the cosmic body in the call story of the sixth-century prophet, Ezekiel. The first chapter of Ezekiel recalls Isaiah's call story (in Isaiah 6, discussed in the preceding section). It includes Ezekiel seeing something of the divine body on a divine throne (Ezekiel 1:26-27), and it describes creatures with faces, wings, and legs (Ezekiel 1:5-12). The figures are also characterized in terms of fire, a bit like the seraphs (or seraphim, "burning ones") in Isaiah 6.[51] In Ezekiel 1:4, there is a divine appearance, beginning with "a stormy wind," "a great cloud with brightness," and "a fire flashing forth continually, and in the middle of the fire, something like gleaming amber." In these details, the presentation of the divine in Ezekiel 1 may have been inspired by the prophet's vision in Isaiah 6.

The similarities between the two prophetic visions end there. Perhaps most conspicuously, the two descriptions differ tremendously in their length. In seven verses Isaiah describes what he sees of the Lord and the seraphs with their six wings, as well as their praise of God ("Holy, holy, holy . . .") and the shaking of the temple (verses 1-7). By contrast, Ezekiel 1 takes twenty-eight verses to describe three matters: the four-winged cherubim[52] with four faces (verses 4-14); "a wheel on earth beside the living creatures" beneath the dome of the world (verses 15-25); and "the appearance of the likeness of the glory of the LORD" on a throne above the dome of the universe (verses 26-28). Unlike Isaiah, Ezekiel sees the heavens open and then sees visions of God above (Ezekiel 1:1). Ezekiel's vision moves from the winged creatures on earth, up to the world's dome (often called the "firmament"), and finally to the divine body on top of the universe. This is why I characterize this third divine body as "cosmic."

Another major difference between the two prophetic call stories involves the perception of the prophets. Where Isaiah sees God without qualification (Isaiah 6:1), what Ezekiel sees are not the things themselves. Instead, he sees their "appearance" (1:5, 10, 16, 26, 28 [2 times]). The descriptions of what Ezekiel sees are also studded with the expression "something like" (Ezekiel 1:5, 13, 16 [2 times], 22, 26, 27 [3 times]). In other words, he sees approximations of the appearance of things, hardly the things themselves. Ezekiel 1:28 ends the description by characterizing what the prophet sees of God as "the appearance of the likeness of the glory of the LORD." Where Isaiah "saw the LORD" (Isaiah 6:1), here Ezekiel's language shows three qualifications, not only "appearance" and "likeness," but also "glory," traditional language that we saw earlier for God's appearance in the storm (for example, in Psalm 29). As another, important element of Ezekiel's description, it is marked several times with fire (1:4, 13 [3 times], 27 [2 times]).

A final difference involves the size of God's body. In contrast to Isaiah's vision, Ezekiel's provides no precise sense of the size of this body. We know only that it is cosmic in scope, given its location at the firmament. Ezekiel's description of God's body in verses 26-28 begins with a throne, or, more accurately, "something like a throne, in appearance like sapphire; and seated above the likeness of a throne was something that seemed like a human form" (Ezekiel 1:26). This "human form" is the divine body, but apart from its form, this divine body is not like a human body. According to verse 28, this divine manifestation had "the appearance of splendor all around." There is no doubt that a human form lies at the heart of this description of the divine appearance (Ezekiel 1:27). This is also the only description in the Bible that explicitly locates this divine appearance above the firmament. Here, God is enthroned on top of the firmament, evidently in the heavenly palace.

Third, this is the only description that describes divine travel on four creatures, each with four faces (verse 10), each with its own chariot wheel (verse 15), each one with eyes in the wheel rims (verse 18), and each wheel animated by "the spirit" (verses 12, 20, 21). In effect, the chariot is alive. So not only is God alive; God is active in the world, as conveyed by the divine chariot. With the faces of the creatures in all four directions and with the eyes in the wheel rims, the divine in heaven sees all on earth.

With its baroque detail, the description in Ezekiel 1 is without parallel in the Bible. This unusual description of the divine body is suggesting that, fundamentally, humans cannot grasp the reality of God. At the same time, the fiery God in the heavenly throne room would become a standard representation of God. For example, in Daniel 7, "the Ancient of Days" takes up his throne to sit in judgment (verse 9a).[53] "His throne was fiery flames, and its wheels were burning fire" (verse 9b). This body is fiery in nature: "A stream of fire issued and flowed from his presence" (verse 10). God enthroned in heaven is the picture in depictions of the Last Judgment (see Revelation 20:11-15).

Before probing the three bodies of God more, there is one last aspect of God's cosmic body that we should note: the playful side of God. When God made the world, God included Leviathan and Behemoth as superhuman-sized creatures of divine play. Psalm 104 describes all of God's creatures, saving Leviathan for last in verse 26. The New Revised Standard Version translates this line: "There go the ships, and Leviathan that you formed to sport in it." In this translation, Leviathan was made for play by God. Yet this line in the translation may conceal a more playful side of God as well. The New Jewish Publication Society translation instead reads: "Leviathan that You formed to sport with." In this translation, God made Leviathan as his very own pet. Job also refers to Leviathan in this way. In Job 41:1, 5, God asks Job if he can do as God does with Leviathan: "Will you play with it as a bird . . . ?" God can play with Leviathan; Job certainly can't. In Job 40:15, God alludes to the play of the divine creation: "For the mountains yield food for it (Behemoth), Where all the wild animals play." God made the wild animals to play.

If God has Leviathan to play with and God's wild creatures play, what about human beings? An answer is intimated in Proverbs 8:22-23, 30-31, a description of when God first created Wisdom (personified as a female):

> "The LORD created me at the beginning of his work,
> The first of his acts of long ago,
>   . . . then I was beside him, like a master worker;
> and I was daily his delight,
> rejoicing before him always.
> rejoicing in his inhabited world
> and delighting in the human race."

The word "rejoicing" in this translation comes from the Hebrew word, "to play" or "to laugh." The word here may mean that Wisdom was playing before God. Wisdom, this playful wisdom of God, is also "in his inhabited world"; it's there for people.

So what's the point for people? Wisdom is a model for human beings; human beings are to take in the wisdom that this personification of wisdom offers in the book of Proverbs. We may discern that as we become wiser following the lead of Woman Wisdom, we too may join in the cosmic play offered by the

freedom
estatic experience

mystical God. We too may rejoice and delight in what God has called us to be and do; this, in the cosmic scheme of things, can be joy and play.

The Meaning of the Three Divine Bodies

At this point, it is time to probe God's three bodies a bit further. The form of the first divine body is basically like a human body. We may say that the first sort of divine body that we discussed is the most human-like, as it is human in form, scale, and substance. With the superhuman and mystical bodies of God, we move away from the human scale and concrete flesh of human bodies. Still the form remains.

The first, natural body of God characteristically appears in family settings (in Genesis 18–19 and 32).[54] God enters human spaces sometimes as a guest.[55] Yahweh appearing in the family contexts of Abraham and Jacob probably originated in traditional storytelling, which then developed into literary masterpieces, with their theological probing about God. These stories offer some of the most intriguing and meaningful narratives in the Bible. By contrast, the second, supersized body of God has its roots in ancient temples.[56] This is most clearly the case with Isaiah 6, where the prophet sees God in the Jerusalem Temple. The meeting of Moses and others with God on Mount Sinai in Exodus 24 and 33–34 also comes out of a temple worldview. This superhuman-god was thought of as living in his palace on his mountain.[57] The model for this second divine body understands God as a king giving an audience to his human subjects in his palace.

While the first two bodies were traditional to Israel and its immediate neighbors, the third body may not have been. Recently, scholars have proposed that Mesopotamian ideas about the universe issued in a corresponding view in Ezekiel 1 and Genesis 1.[58] In these two biblical chapters, a heavenly vault or dome (or "firmament") enclosed the earth and sky (Ezekiel 1:22, 23, 25, 26; Genesis 1:6-8, 14-15, 17, 20). This is unlike what we saw with the home of the superhuman-sized God in the heavens on top of his mountain (for example, Exodus 24:9-11). In Ezekiel 1, the place of God's enthronement was considerably higher, above the heavenly vault. Pictorial art shows Mesopotamian genies supporting the firmament; above it is part of a human-looking deity.[59] (Sometimes in Mesopotamian texts the heavens also have multiple levels or spheres for the homes of the gods.[60]) Like the Mesopotamian idea of the human-looking body at the top of the firmament, God's body in Ezekiel 1 is located at the cosmic level.

In several biblical works of the seventh and sixth centuries—such as the priestly work of the Pentateuch (Genesis 1), Deuteronomy, Ezekiel, Jeremiah, and Second Isaiah—monotheism emerged as one of those core beliefs or ways of understanding God.[61] The development of monotheism in ancient Israel corresponds to the development of the third, "cosmic" or "mystical" divine body. We see the diminishing of God's human and superhuman bodies in the Bible, as the cosmic body became the assumed norm in late biblical times and also in Judaism and Christianity. The trend, informed generally by astronomical learning and particularly by the concept of heavenly spheres, would continue in ideas about multiple spheres or heavens during the Greco-Roman period (for example, Paul's ascending to "the third heaven" in 2 Corinthians 12:2).[62] Perhaps similar shifts in understanding the cosmos and God are underway today, thanks to new scientific discoveries about the universe dramatically unfolding in our own time.

All three bodies of God are in the Bible, and they provide readers with different ways to think about God. To recall Pascal Boyer's comments discussed earlier in this chapter, biblical anthropomorphism about God's body provides insight into God. The first, human body of God occurs in situations of wrong leading up to potential conflict: Adam and Eve's disobedience of the divine rules in Genesis 3; Abraham's conflict over the innocent among the wicked in Sodom in Genesis 18–19; and Jacob's fear of his brother, Esau, for the wrongs that he had done to him, in Genesis 32–33. The human body of God does not signal that God resolves and redeems such conflicts. Rather, God comes to people as troubles unfold. This first body may also represent a challenge for both Christians and Jews today: Christians may readily identify this body with the Christian mystery of the incarnation, despite some significant differences, while Jews may be expected to have some difficulty with this notion, preferring other terms that maintain a distinction between the first body of God and the Christian notion of the incarnation.

The second, superhuman body marks a different sort of divine involvement with the human condition. The superhuman body signals the privileged access to God. Moses and Isaiah enjoy a particular experience of God. This manner of the divine body appearing to humans seems restricted to Israel's leaders and righteous. Yet people could hope for the experience of seeing the divine body. For example, Psalm 17:15 says: "As for me, I shall behold your face in righteousness; when I awake I shall be satisfied beholding your form" (New Revised Standard Version: "likeness").[63] The superhuman body offers the hope that experience of God is possible for people more broadly.

The third, cosmic God is not focused on an earthly experience. Instead, it entails God's connection to human beings within the larger structure of reality. In the picture of God in Ezekiel 1, we see the divine body potentially moving over the vast expanse of the universe. The mystical divine body conveys the mysterious reality that all in the universe is somehow permeated by the reality of God. In the Greek version of the biblical book known as Ecclesiasticus (Sirach), God is "all in all" (43:28); in the parallel Hebrew version of the same book (known in Hebrew as Ben Sira, 43:27), God is "the all." For Albert Einstein, such mystery is central not simply to religions but to humanity: "The fairest thing that we can experience is the mysterious. It is the fundamental emotion which stands at the cradle of true art and true science."[64] People may sense this divine reality. Christians and Jews may be, in a sense, mystics, even if we don't have mystical experiences.[65] We use mystical language in our liturgies and prayer, and in these we may sense the threads of reality binding us together with this God. While the first two bodies of God in the Bible express special divine presence that may inspire us, God's mystical body is for us to contemplate and to help us sense the divine working in our lives and in our world.

❧ 2 ❧

What Do God's Body Parts in the Bible Mean?

I n the preceding chapter, we saw how divine bodies in the Bible are both like and unlike human beings. The Bible uses not only the human body as a model for the divine body; it also uses body parts to express different aspects of God. They constitute physical aspects of God in some biblical passages, while in others they signal nonphysical features of God.[1] Just as we experience our human emotions, passions, desires, ideas, and memory in and through our bodies and body parts,[2] so too these aspects of the divine are expressed in and through God's body and body parts. And just as people communicate with and through their bodies and their body parts, so too God's body parts generate a divine body language that communicates with people. As the biblical scholar Andreas Wagner has suggested, God's body parts show God as a communication partner with humans.[3] These ideas about God lead to additional questions: what kind of person is God in the Bible, and what sorts of attributes does this god have? These questions are not easy to answer. As we make our way through God's body parts, I will try to address them.

Before we go any further, we should note that no biblical Hebrew word precisely matches the English word for person. This English word goes back to the Greek word *prosopon*. This Greek word means "face" in *The Iliad* (Book 7, line 212; Book 18, line

414) and *The Odyssey* (Book 19, line 361). In Greek theater, it came to mean "mask," or the dramatic part or character in a play, a character in a book, and a person.[4] It was used later in the Christian notion of the three persons of the Trinity.[5] It did not refer to the modern idea of self-consciousness associated with "person" and "personal."[6] Since the biblical writers didn't exactly have a word for "person," what terms did they use to express it? What did they mean by these words? In the discussion that follows, we will touch on these questions. We begin with the external body parts of God and then move to the internal body parts of God.

[handwritten margin note: individuate?]

God's Face

The Hebrew word that comes the closest to the modern word "person" is *panim*, literally "face." "Face" is part of a person's outer appearance, and it may also reflect the interior disposition of a person being communicated to another person. It may show happiness, when the face shines (Psalm 104:15); or it suggests sadness, when the face is fallen (we might say "downcast," for example, Cain's in Genesis 4:5-6), or literally "evil" (the two servants of Pharaoh in Genesis 40:7). Once she receives a blessing from the priest Eli (1 Samuel 1:18), Hannah's "countenance was sad no longer" (literally, "she no longer had her face"). Facing another person denotes giving attention and favor to that person (1 Kings 2:15), while turning away the face may denote refusal (2 Kings 18:24). As these passages suggest, a person's "face" communicates her or his feelings to others. In other words, it is body language.

[handwritten margin note: Greek mask]

These aspects of the word "face" apply also to God. Jacob compares seeing his brother, Esau, to seeing the face of God (Genesis 33:10). At Mount Sinai, Moses famously asks to see God's face (Exodus 33:20). God sees Moses "face to face" (Exodus 33:11); in other words, the two parties see one another. The unnamed speaker of Psalm 17:15 hopes to see the face of

[handwritten margin note: perceive?]

God (see also Psalm 42:3). God may refuse to show the divine face, thus signaling divine disapproval (Jeremiah 18:17): "I will show them my back, not my face, in the day of their calamity." Hiding the divine face is troubling to humans: "When you hide your face, they are dismayed" (Psalm 104:29).[7] God may issue a blast of the divine face as an expression of divine anger (Psalm 80:17; Psalm 21:10; Isaiah 65:3). God's face (sometimes translated "countenance") is also said to have light[8] ("in your light we see light," Psalm 36:9). In the New Testament (1 John 5), this notion applies to God: "God is light." This is the positive experience of God's favorable presence.

Throughout the Scriptures, we see different references to God's face, or we might say, to God's many faces. The face is central to how God appears as a communication partner with people.[9] Traditionally God's "faces" are understood as revelatory. A Jewish work offers a beautiful reflection on God's revealing face: "The Holy One, Blessed be He, revealed himself to them at Sinai with many faces: with an angry face, with a downcast face, with a dour face, with a joyful face, with a smiling face, and with a radiant face."[10]

God's Eyes, Ears and Nose

God's other body parts appear across the books of the Bible. Sometimes these body parts are explicit; sometimes they are implicit. An implied image for the divine head appears in God's words quoted in Psalm 60:8 = 108:8: "Gilead is mine; Manasseh is mine; Ephraim is my helmet; Judah is my scepter." Ephraim as God's helmet and Judah as his scepter are two parts of God's outfit. The helmet calls to mind God's warrior clothing and the scepter evokes God's royal insignia. Together, the two symbols stand for God's body as this warrior-god goes into battle. This sort of imagery carries over into the next verse: "Moab is my washbasin; on Edom I hurl my shoe; over Philistia I shout in triumph."

God wears and uses objects that are metaphorically identified with various tribes of Israel and its enemies. The superhuman-sized God here captures an essential element of God's relationship to Israel, namely, that God battles for Israel. In this passage, the divine body parts metaphorically express divine support in Israel's clash and conflict with its enemies.

Compared with God's head, God's eyes are common in the Bible. In a moving description of God's creation of the human person in the womb, Psalm 139:16 says: "Your eyes beheld my unformed substance." Divine sight generally denotes God's favor (see Psalms 33:128; 34:6); here it conveys that and more—God's intimate knowledge of this human being. God knows the speaker so well that their relationship begins even in the womb. The next two verses of Psalm 139 include another aspect of God:

> How weighty to me are your thoughts, O God!
> How vast is the sum of them!
> I try to count them—they are more than the sand;
> I come to the end—I am still with you.

Here God's thoughts are weighty and numerous. However, God is not just the brainiest person around! The verse is expressing wonder. On the one hand, God's thoughts show how God is totally different (or "other") from human beings (see also Psalm 92:6; Isaiah 55:8-9). On the other hand, these divine thoughts somehow extend to lowly people, such as the speaker of this psalm (see also Psalm 40:5).[11] The description of God's eyes and thoughts here in Psalm 139 culminates in an expression of how God relates to the human person: "I come to the end—I am still with you." This passage is remarkable. It uses God's body to express an essential mystery: God is really different from human beings, yet somehow intertwined intimately with human beings from womb to tomb.

The eyes and ears of God likewise express God's relationship with people. According to Jeremiah 32:19, God's "eyes are open to all the ways of mortals, rewarding all according to their ways and according to the fruit of their doings."[12] The divine eyes signal divine knowledge of human activity. So too God's ears hear as well. Second Kings 19:16 = Isaiah 37:17 asks God to "incline your ear . . . and hear; open your eyes, and see" (see also Daniel 9:18).[13] Here these body parts express the speaker's wish to be seen by God and for his prayer to be heard. The eyes and ears evoke a picture of God paying attention to people in a manner that is sympathetic. God is a sympathetic person.

If the eyes and ears evoke God as a sympathetic person, the nose may convey destruction, aimed often against Israel's enemies. When the Israelites cross the Red Sea, God's nostrils blow a wind that creates a tsunami: "At the blast of your nostrils the waters piled up" (Exodus 15:8). The words in Hebrew for "the blast of your nostrils" may be translated "the wind (or life force, *ruah*) of your nose" (see also 2 Samuel 22:16 = Psalm 18:15). This divine *ruah* is another part of God, which we will discuss later in this chapter.

The nose is the bodily locus of anger, both human and divine. When "Jacob became very angry with Rachel" in Genesis 30:2, the Hebrew words literally say, "the nose of Jacob burned." Anger is considered bad behavior in Proverbs 22:24. Like human beings, God gets angry. In Exodus 4:14, "the anger of the LORD was kindled against Moses." This line reads more literally, "the nose of the LORD burned against Moses." This idiom of the burning nose for anger is used for God in many passages (for example, in Exodus 22:23; 32:10-14; Numbers 25:4; 32:13-14; Deuteronomy 9:19; 2 Kings 24:20). Exodus 22:21-23 is particularly notable ("my wrath will burn"), as it refers God's response to anyone who oppresses the widow or the orphan. God's anger is a divine response for helping the underdog.

We should also bear in mind that God is also famously "slow to anger" (Exodus 34:6; Numbers 14:18; Nehemiah 9:17; Psalms 86:15; 103:8; Joel 2:13; Jonah 4:2; Nahum 1:3), just as people

should be (Proverbs 14:29; 15:18; 16:32; cf. 25:15). We will discuss God's anger in some depth in our next chapter. For now we
may note that body parts are connected to emotions, and together
they are expressive of divine care and justice. We might say that
just as people experience emotions in their bodies and use body
language to communicate their feelings to other people, so God's
body language is a relational language on behalf of human beings.

God has other body parts. As far as I have noticed, God's
body in the Bible, unlike the human body, does not have flesh or
blood or bone. Nor is it described with eyebrows, teeth, throat,
joints, liver, kidneys, breasts, a penis or vagina, or knees.[14] The
hair of the divine head is mentioned in the description of "the
Ancient of Days" in Daniel 7:9 (cf. the heavenly Son of Man in
Revelation 1:14). More famously, God's mouth communicates
divine commands to people (literally, "the mouth of the LORD,"
for example, in Numbers 14:41; 22:18; 1 Samuel 15:24; Proverbs 8:29).[15] Truth is said to issue from the divine mouth (Isaiah
45:23). The mouth of the Lord commands heavenly beings to
level the ground for the Israelites to return more easily to Jerusalem (Isaiah 40:3-5). God says of his relationship to Moses
(Numbers 12:8): "With him I speak mouth to mouth, plainly
and not in riddles, and he beholds the likeness of God." Moses
is unusual in this regard; usually the mouth of the Lord has not
spoken to people (Jeremiah 9:11). When God appears with the
divine lightning and thunder, it is from his mouth that fire is said
to come out (2 Samuel 22:9 = Psalm 18:8). The divine word also
issues in creation (Psalm 33:6). In all these passages, the mouth
of the Lord speaks for the benefit of humanity and the world.

God also has a voice. The word "voice" may be used in a
general way as "sound." In Isaiah 6:8, the prophet Isaiah says:
"I heard the voice of my Lord."[16] The divine "voice" is also
used seven times to denote God's thunder in the stormy divine
appearance in Psalm 29:3-9, an idea that we also see for God
on Mount Sinai (Exodus 19:19; Deuteronomy 5:22). These pas-

sages play on the two senses of divine voice; it is both God's human-like voice and the "voice" of thunder (see also Job 37:2). A personal experience: When I was a child, I was once caught in a terrible thunderstorm and hid under a tree at the edge of the woods. Lightning struck, and I felt the power of the electricity surging through the ground where I was standing; I thought I was going to die. This power was real power! How much so its ultimate source.

The divine voice in 1 Kings 19:12 plays off the traditional idea of thunder as God's voice. The Lord was not in the wind, nor in the earthquake, nor in the fire; the Lord came to Elijah in a paradoxical way instead, in "a sound of sheer silence" (New Revised Standard Version), or perhaps somewhat more literally, "a sound—sheer, silent."[17] In the next verse, God's "voice" speaks. In these passages, the divine "voice" represents ways that God appears to human beings. Whether it is the thunderous voice experienced in nature or in "a sound—sheer, silent," the divine voice may yet speak to us.

God's Hands, Arms and Feet

God has yet other body parts, including hands, arms, and feet. In Exodus 33:22-23, discussed in the preceding chapter, we saw a literal yet supersized palm of God's hand. In this passage, the divine hand covers Moses in the cleft of the rock on Mount Sinai as God passes by. God also uses the divine hands to take hold of lightning and throw it: "He covers his hands (literally, "palms") with the lightning, and commands it to strike the mark" (Job 36:32; see also Habakkuk 3:4). In terms recalling the divine body in Ezekiel 1:26-28, the prophet Ezekiel describes how God physically seized him: "there was a figure that looked like a human being . . . It stretched out the form of a hand, and took me by a lock of my hair" (Ezekiel 8:2-3). This passage shows the divine hand that acts physically.

Metaphorical uses of the divine hand are common in the Bible. It can denote divine affliction: "You hem me in, behind and before, and lay your hand upon me" (Psalm 139:5). To withdraw the divine hand may denote relief from divine affliction (Job 13:21). The hand of God often refers to divine power, carrying the idea that the hand upraised carries a weapon in battle. This is the idea when Moses tries to get Pharaoh to release the Israelites from slavery; in effect, God has gone to war against Pharaoh (Exodus 6:1; 9:15; 13:3, 9, 14, 16). Like Moses (in Exodus 4:6), God may hold his hand to his chest, indicating that God chooses not to exercise power on Israel's behalf (Psalm 74:11). The upraised hand of God is also the instrument of divine judgment (Isaiah 9:11, 16, 20; 10:4).

The divine hand can also convey divine favor.[18] God's hand is said to strengthen the tribe of Joseph (Genesis 49:24). In a beautiful promise made to Israel, Zion "shall be a crown of beauty in the hand of the Lord, and a royal diadem in the hand (literally, "palm") of your God" (Isaiah 62:3). The "shadow" of God's hand may denote divine protection (Isaiah 49:2). The divine hand on someone occasionally denotes prophetic inspiration (2 Kings 3:15; Ezekiel 1:3; 3:22; 37:1; 40:1). At times, the people question whether the hand of the Lord is too short to help them (Numbers 11:23; Isaiah 50:2; 59:1).

The divine finger is an instrument used for writing the commandments (Exodus 31:18; Deuteronomy 9:10).[19] The divine finger also writes signs in the world pointing to acts of God. Pharaoh's magicians interpret the plague of gnats sent by God in this way: "This is the finger of God!" (Exodus 8:19). The divine creation of the heavens is called "the work of your fingers" (Psalm 8:4). The verse evokes a picture of God as creator making the universe with his hands. God leaves a mark in and on the world through the divine finger.

Like the divine hand, God's arms denote divine power (Deuteronomy 4:34; 5:15; 26:8; Ezekiel 20:32, 34; Psalm 136:12). God asks Job: "Have you an arm like God, and can you thunder with a voice like his?" (Job 40:9). Arm and voice together here denote divine power. The divine arm can strike a "blow" against enemies, such as the Assyrians (Isaiah 30:30). God carries the weak in his arms like a shepherd (Isaiah 40:11; cf. God's "arms everlasting" in Deuteronomy 33:27, according to the New Jewish Publication Society translation). The divine arms symbolize strength (Isaiah 40:10; 51:5) and help (Isaiah 33:2; cf. 53:1; 59:16).

Moving down past God's waist ("loins" in Ezekiel 1:26-28), God has feet. In the preceding chapter, we discussed the vision of God's "feet" that Moses and the other leaders see on Mount Sinai (Exodus 24:10). In the description of God's flying on the cherub in the clouds (2 Samuel 22:10 = Psalm 18:9), "thick darkness was under his feet." According to Zechariah 14:4, the supersized God will stand with his feet on the Mount of Olives. In an evocation of the cosmic body, God's feet rest on a footstool in his sanctuary.[20] In Isaiah 66:1 God declares: "Heaven is my throne, and the earth is my footstool." As we saw in the preceding chapter, these verses reflect the third divine body, the cosmic body of God as King enthroned over the universe.

The Heart of God

With God's heart (attested 28 times in the Bible),[21] we move to God's internal body parts. For both God and humans, thinking and emotions operate out of the heart.[22] Sometimes, the heart is used the way that we would use "mind," a word for which Hebrew has no corresponding term.[23] For example, the way to say that something did not come to mind is literally, "it did not ascend to the heart." This expression can be used of the human heart (Isaiah 65:17; Jeremiah 3:16) or the divine heart (Jeremiah 7:31; 19:5; 32:35; cf. 44:21).[24] The human heart can be expressive of one person toward another, like someone seeing her or his face reflected in water: "Just as in water the face (appears) to a face, so a human's heart to a human" (Proverbs 27:19).[25] Internal prayer to God is described occasionally as speaking to one's own heart (Genesis 24:45; 1 Samuel 1:13).

God's heart is also expressive of a divine emotional life. In the story of Noah, the divine heart suffers grief because of human wickedness (Genesis 6:6; see also verse 7): "the LORD was sorry that he had made humankind on the earth, and it grieved him to his heart." Later, in the time of the early monarchy, when Saul is guilty of not carrying out God's commandments, God expresses regret for making him king (1 Samuel 15:10).[26] This divine regret captures something of the human tragedy here: Saul's drama is so sad, it evokes emotion in God. Although Numbers 23:19 says that God does not change his mind, Moses indeed asks God to do so for Israel in Exodus 32:12.[27] Sometimes, the change of the divine heart is for good.

God's heart is stirred for Israel (Hosea 11:8): "My heart recoils within me; my compassion grows warm and tender." "To speak to the heart" of another person[28] suggests personal intimacy; it is used not only in communication of a man in love with a woman (Genesis 34:3). God too calls for such tender speech on the part of the angelic host in Isaiah 40:1: "Comfort, O comfort my people, says your God. Speak tenderly (literally, "speak to the heart") to Jerusalem." The divine heart can be an expression of divine tenderness.

As we have seen so far, the physical parts of God can be expressive of God's relations to human beings. We might think that such body parts are not supposed to be literal, but metaphorical for the different ways that God relates to people. However, sometimes the body parts are not simply metaphors, and in other cases, the body parts are used in metaphorical ways that still suggest a physical idea of God's body.[29] As we noted in the preceding chapter, modern people and medieval philosophers view God's self as totally unknown, and human language for God seen either as a human projection or simply as a way to express how God relates to people. From a biblical perspective, God's body parts do both. They disclose something fundamental about God: even as God is really different (or "other") compared with human beings, God somehow is also mysteriously relational to human beings.   *Incarnation*

God's "Self"

Body parts are not the only terms referring to God. The common word *nepesh*[30] refers to a human person, or self—that which makes a person.[31] It involves human vitality (or, "life force"), breath, or life in a person and the life of a person.[32] Underlying these meanings is the idea of a person's life being manifest in breathing. In referring to the throat,[33] the word *nepesh* can also express hunger (Psalm 107:9; Proverbs 27:7) and thirst (Proverbs 25:25).[34]

The word also applies to human desire for God. In Psalm 42:3, this desire may include the physical self, as expressed by the verse's simile: "As a deer longs for flowing streams, so my very self (*nepesh*) longs for you, O God."[35] Emotions too can be attributed to the *nepesh* of a person: weeping (Jeremiah 13:17), loathing (Leviticus 26:11, 15, 30, 43; Jeremiah 14:19), joy (Psalm 35:9), and love (Song of Songs 1:7; 3:1-4). Proverbs 14:10 refers to the *nepesh* of the human heart when it endures bitter suffering: "The heart knows the bitterness of its *nepesh* (or, perhaps, "its own bitterness")."

"Soul" is the English word often used to translate *nepesh* in Bibles today. We often hear the translation, "Bless the Lord, O my soul" (Psalms 103:1, 22; and 104:1, 34). This English translation follows in the footsteps of the older Greek translation of the Bible that used the Greek word *psyche*, "soul" (the basis for our English words "psyche" and "psychology"), when it translates *nepesh*.[36] Because of this translation, Bible readers may get the impression that *nepesh* refers to an individual, immortal soul.[37] We may like this translation because we are so used to it; after all, the idea of the soul has played a central role in Christian thought.[38] However, *nepesh* in the Bible is not really a soul. The death of the *nepesh* signals the death of the person (Psalm 78:50; Numbers 23:10; and Judges 16:30).[39] To make it clear that the *nepesh* is the living person, some priestly texts qualify the word as a "living *nepesh*." For example, in Genesis 1:20, God commands on the fifth day of creation: "Let the waters bring forth swarms of living creatures (*nepesh*)."[40]

People sometimes think of the soul as something in a person. When I was in sixth grade, I thought my soul must have been tucked under my ribcage because this is the only place in my body where I thought there was enough room for my soul. (Of course, I also thought that if I turned around fast enough, I would catch a glimpse of my guardian angel; it never happened.) However, the *nepesh* in the person is a living reality, not so much *in* a body, but *as* a body.

There is a further nuance to the human *nepesh* when engaged in prayer. The *nepesh* sometimes seems to be a way of mustering the entire self in praying to God. Yet at other times in the Bible more seems to be involved: the speaker calls on his *nepesh* to join himself in blessing God: "bless the Lord, O my soul (or better, "my self," *napshi*)" (Psalms 103:1, 22; 104:1, 34).[41] The same way of speaking is seen in a lament: "Why are you downcast, O my self (*napshi*)?" (Psalms 42:6, 12; and 43:6). This psalm also describes the speaker pouring out his *nepesh*, much as Hannah pours out her own *nepesh* in her lament in 1 Samuel 1:15 (compare Psalm 102:1).[42] This is what I would call the "lamenting self."[43] In passages where a person talks to her or his *nepesh*, the speaker is summoning up a kind of "second self,"[44] perhaps what we might call a "redoubled" or "reflexive" self.[45] Here the person redoubles not only her or his effort, but even the very self in prayer or lament.[46]   *bicameral mind!*

Now let's turn from human *nepesh* to God's *nepesh*.[47] Just as we see the human "lamenting self," there is a certain reflexivity seen in God when God swears by the divine *nepesh* (Amos 6:8; Jeremiah 51:14; see also Jeremiah 5:9, 29; 9:8). While people swear by God, God swears by his own self, that is, the divine life (Numbers 14:21, 28) or by divine holiness (Amos 4:2).[48]

Also like the human *nepesh*, God is an emotional *nepesh*, which shows God's involvement with people. The *nepesh* of God is exhausted because of people's suffering: "his *nepesh* was shortened by the trouble of Israel" (Judges 10:16).[49] God's *nepesh* takes delight in his servant (Isaiah 42:1; see also 1 Samuel 2:35). The divine *nepesh* may even include divine weeping (Jeremiah 13:17).[50]

When we look more closely at passages across the Bible, a remarkable range of emotions is expressed in terms of the divine *nepesh*: divine love (Jeremiah 12:7), divine disgust (Jeremiah 6:8; Ezekiel 23:18), divine impatience (Zechariah 11:8), and divine spurning (Leviticus 26:11, 30). God displays great emotional feeling for Israel. Human metaphor for God serves to explore more than the character of God. What is going on in Jeremiah and Ezekiel is perhaps what David Stern has noted about anthropomorphism in later Jewish sources.[51] Stern focuses on the striking image of God weeping for his destroyed temple in a work known as *Lamentations Rabbah*, a great collection of stories commenting on the biblical book of Lamentations. In this work, divine justice plays out with the temple's destruction but not without God suffering. The anthropomorphism here discloses a God affected and afflicted by the difficulties and tragedies of human experience. Stern adds: "to the extent that the Rabbis were intent upon characterizing God, it was precisely in order to make Him *more* of a God whom they could worship." When we read about God in the Bible, we enter into the complexity of God's emotional *nepesh*.

God's Life-Breath

Complementary to *nepesh* is the divine *ruah*,[52] often referring to force, life force, or breath.[53] It is the component of God that hovers over the waters just at the moment before God initiates creation in Genesis 1:2, and it is how God recreates Israel in the valley of the dry bones in Ezekiel 37:5. God is said to create the hosts of heaven "by the *ruah* of his mouth" (Psalm 33:6).[54] It is also a physical force that God has and gives to people (Psalm 104:29-30; Ecclesiastes 11:5), and which returns to God when they die (Ecclesiastes 12:7; see also 3:21; Psalm 146:4; Job 34:14-15). This *ruah* belongs to God: "No human has power over *ruah*" (Ecclesiastes 8:8; my translation). *Ruah* is a divine infusion placed in living beings at creation (Psalm 104:29).

Sometimes God bestows additional *ruah* on people,[55] for example, on the craftsman Bezalel (Exodus 31:3; cf. 1 Samuel 10:10). It is given to warriors, including the famous muscle man, Samson (Judges 13:25; 14:6, 19; 15:14; cf. 3:10 and 11:29). It also infuses prophets (e.g., Micah 3:8). Some political leaders receive not the *ruah* of the warrior, as we might expect, but the *ruah* of the prophet (1 Samuel 10:10 for Saul; 2 Samuel 23:2 for David). The unnamed prophetic voice of Isaiah 61:1 declares: "The spirit of the Lord God is upon me, because the LORD has anointed me: he has sent me to bring good news to the oppressed, and to bind up the broken hearted." The divine *ruah* inspires people to know God's presence in the world or to help bring it into the world.

Isaiah 63:10-11 recalls how Israel's rebellion grieved "his holy spirit," suggesting once again God's emotional response to the people. "The holy spirit" (which can also be translated "the spirit of holiness") represents for Christians the Old Testament roots for the notion of the Holy Spirit.[56] What we see in the Hebrew Bible and also in the Dead Sea Scrolls[57] is God's "spirit of holiness" that God can give to people. (We need to remember that Hebrew does not distinguish uppercase and lowercase letters.) This "holy spirit" or "spirit of holiness" is not a technical usage for a person of the Trinity, but an aspect of God that God chooses to bestow upon people. Psalm 51:10-12 mentions spirit three times (my italics):

Create in me a clean heart, O God,
and put *a new and right spirit* within me.
Do not cast me away from your presence,
and do not take your *holy spirit* from me.
Restore to me the joy of your salvation,
and sustain in me a *willing spirit*.

[handwritten: God in humanity before the Incarnation. what did the Incarnation do for man?]

The middle pair of lines refers to God's "holy spirit," while the other lines suggest a broad meaning for this spirit, one that is new, right, and willing. The three uses of spirit suggest a complementarity between God's regeneration of the human spirit for right and willingness on the one hand, and on the other hand, God's own "holy spirit" in the human person. God's "holy spirit" in this passage is like God's "good spirit": "Let your good spirit lead me on a level path" (Psalm 143:10; see also Nehemiah 9:20).

[handwritten: spirit of the mind Rom 12:2]

Unlike "face," "heart," and "self," "life-breath" (*ruah*) is something that God has and gives to sustain people's lives. In this capacity, God is called the "God of the spirits of all flesh" (Numbers 16:22; 27:16). "Life-breath" connects God and humans; their *ruah* comes from the divine *ruah*. With this term, the reality of the human person is inherently—yet mysteriously—connected to the reality of God the divine person. In Psalm 104:29-30, the divine "face" (*panim*) and "life force" or "breath" (*ruah*) are combined in an amazing expression of how people are fundamentally connected to God:

When you hide your face (*panim*), they are dismayed;
when you take away their breath (*ruah*), they die and return
    to their dust.
When you send forth your spirit (*ruah*), they are created;
And you renew the face (*panim*) of the ground.

The first and last lines here use the word "face" (*panim*) and the middle two lines use "spirit" (*ruah*). People not only depend on God for divine favor ("your face"), but they need God for their life "breath"; otherwise, they die. Together, these two words convey a subtle yet powerful picture of reality: the *ruah* of humanity comes from God's *ruah*, and it continues to depend on God's *ruah* to live. In other words, our being alive comes from the "life-breath" of God's own self.

Psalm 139:7-10 offers another remarkable passage about God's *ruah*:

> Where can I go from your spirit (*ruah*)?
> Or where can I flee from your presence (literally, face, *panim*)?
> If I ascend to heaven, you are there;
> if I make my bed in Sheol [the underworld], you are there.
> If I take the wings of the morning
> and settle at the farthest limits of the sea,
> even there your hand shall lead me,
> and your right hand shall hold me fast.

No matter how far away we may go, there God awaits us.[58] Somehow, mysteriously, incomprehensively, the universe is filled with the reality of God's spirit and presence. The psalm also refers to God's hands (see also verse 5), and earlier we noted in this psalm God's eyes (verse 16) and thoughts (verse 17). The psalm brings together the cosmic body of God filling the universe in a variety of divine body parts, all inexplicable expressions of God's intimate care for each person. As the extent of God seems more cosmic, it is, perhaps paradoxically, also more personal.

In this survey, we have seen how the divine body contains a number of emotional components including heart, *nepesh*, and *ruah*. Biblical thinking about the human person and the divine person is not dualistic (body-soul or body-mind), but it is not exactly a complete unity either.[59] Instead, the human person contains a number of bodily parts and centers, each contributing to the functioning person. (This view compares in an interesting way with recent theories on the human person.[60]) God, we might say, is similarly attributed various body parts.

greek masks

Beyond the physical centers of the human person, social roles also constitute who a person was in antiquity.[61] Personal identity includes the social roles that one acts in, not in the personal inner depths that modern psychology has identified for us. In other words, to some extent, one is one's behavior as is proper to one's roles in the family and society.[62] In a relationship with God, a person is, in a sense, one's fidelity to the covenant relationship; and in turn, so is God.

In these different dimensions, God is shown to be a person rather than a generic figure (or a "type" of deity).[63] Some aspects of God suggest more than similarity to human persons. Some express an inner connectedness between God and humanity—and to all God's creatures. As we have seen with Psalm 104 above, God's life force (*ruah*) is also in human beings. The divine breath (*neshamah*) is what God puts in human beings at creation (Genesis 2:7), and it is in all of God's creatures (Psalm 150:6: "Let everything that breathes praise the Lord!").[64] This divine breath and life force express how the very life and being of people come from God's self. In other words, we are not only fundamentally related to God; our very selves partake of something that is God's very self, which at the same time is totally different from human beings. How this can be is not only a great divine mystery but also a wonderful divine reality. This strange yet comforting reality extends to God's emotions of love and anger, the subject of our next chapter.

unified differentiation

the Spirit of the Lord is the candle of man

❧ 3 ❧

Why Is God Angry in the Bible?

The Problem of the Angry and Violent God

❧ **F**or people today, divine love and anger are two of the most polarizing aspects of God in the Bible. Today people see love and anger as opposites. Anger, to many modern people, reeks of personal abuse, cruelty, or a lack of care. In people's imaginations, anger does not seem too distant from hatred and violence. The same problem applies to God. Divine love is what people really want of God, while divine anger seems strange and inexplicable; it also seems to be beneath God, so much so that some people criticize the angry, violent monotheistic God of the Bible.[1]

When we turn to the Bible, we can find divine anger on many of its pages. In fact, many people believe that it is the primary picture of God in the Bible—and especially the Old Testament (Hebrew Bible). Some people were raised on the mistaken notion that the God of the Old Testament is a God of angry judgment, while the God of the New Testament is a God of love (for example, in the commandment to love one's enemies in Matthew 5:44; Luke 6:27). On the contrary: both love and anger are attributed to God in both testaments (see "the wrath of God" in John 3:36; Romans 1:18; Ephesians 5:6; Colossians 3:6; and Revelation 19:15).[2] Even Jesus is, on occasion, a source of violence: "Do not think that I have come to bring peace upon the earth. I have come to bring not peace but the sword" (Matthew 10:34).[3]

concept of Messiah

The angry, violent God of the Bible poses a great challenge, and several scholars have offered thoughtful responses. It is not enough to note that divine anger was a common notion in the ancient world of the Bible.[4] We need to do some thinking about the problem. In a probing essay entitled "The Beauty of the Bloody God," the biblical scholar Corrine Carvalho comments on the problem of divine violence in this way:

> Are some descriptions of violence always evil? Always beautiful? Certainly not. Violent images can simply be inflammatory, disgusting, and gratuitous. I would argue that language about violence, just like descriptions of sexual activity, are not inherently good or bad; erotic or pornographic; glorious or gory. Rather, violent images can be used to resist, recover, entertain, inflame or inspire. Therefore, while some violent texts provide an outlet for human violence or function as a therapeutic outlet for victims of violence, sometimes they pro- ? vide an aesthetic experience. Are they beautiful? That would depend on one's definition of "beautiful." However, I do know that for many readers these texts are moving, memorable, complex, fascinating, emotive, satisfying, and an appropriate revelatory experience of God.[5]

The argument, as I hear Carvalho, is that biblical representations of the violent God cannot simply be labeled as bad because they are angry or violent. In her view, that's just too simplistic. We need to go beyond our own visceral reactions to these images. As we try to understand God in the Bible, we need to think more deeply about what divine anger expresses and how it functions in the relationship that God has with Israel.

Carvalho's comments capture a paradox. On the one hand, images of the violent and angry God suffer in *their* limitations as they partake of *our* human language. On the other hand, these images capture helpful dimensions of what the divine is about. Carvalho ends her reflections in this way: "We can't get rid of sex or violence and remain human, and we can't remain human

without misusing them. We remain on this side of reality where
the grotesque is beautiful."[6] We cannot escape our human limitations and the limitations of our human language. For the moment,
we can try to set aside our own assumptions about anger and ask
instead about the sort of thinking that the ancient Israelites had
about the biblical God. My goal here is not to defend or justify
divine anger (I don't think anger is defensible); my goal is to try
to understand what it means in the Bible and its world.[7]

Two Social Models for Understanding Divine Anger

Before we explore the human models for understanding divine anger in the Bible, we first need to understand that our own
thinking about anger does not easily fit with what the writers
of the Bible intended. For the Bible, love and anger are not
the opposite of one another. At a very fundamental level, God's
anger and love are closely related in the Bible. This may not be
our viewpoint, and we don't have to accept the Bible's view on
this score, but whatever we may think, we need to know a little
about human anger in the Bible in order to understand the Bible's
communication of divine anger. Human anger is the model for
divine anger, of course, and while there may be some differences
between them, looking first at human anger in the Bible will
provide some perspective on divine anger.

There are two social models[8] informing the Bible's descriptions of divine anger. The first involves social authority, in many
cases exercised by the family patriarch or a king. In this model,
anger is considered a "natural" human response to an inappro-
priate challenge to someone of higher social rank, whether this
entails an offense against someone or an offense against others
of concern, especially to those in social or political authority. As
Deena Grant has shown in her important work on divine anger,[9]
biblical anger most commonly arises in struggles for authority,
and it is expressed by persons in positions of authority.

Grant observes that of the twenty-six individuals named in the Bible who express anger, twenty-one are kings, leaders, masters, or high-ranking family members. Kings are proverbial for their anger in the book of Proverbs (14:35; 16:14; 19:12; 20:2; see also Ecclesiastes 10:4).[10] The older brother Esau gets angry at Jacob, his younger brother, for stealing his birthright (Genesis 27:45). In the story of Esther, the wicked Haman gets furious over Mordecai's refusal to bow to him. In these and many other passages, people manifest their anger when they perceive that someone has violated their authority.[11]

Typically, Grant observes, anger compels individuals in authority to meet the threats to their authority. For example, the brothers of Dinah kill Shechem and all the males of his town (Genesis 39:19-20). By contrast, anger at family members is almost never lethal. Saul throws a spear at Jonathan, but Jonathan escapes unharmed (1 Samuel 20). Paternal anger is almost always benign (1 Samuel 20:30-34; 2 Samuel 13:21). David gets angry at Amnon for his rape of Tamar (2 Samuel 13:21), but David does nothing to Amnon. With brothers, the bonds are sometimes similar. Esau's anger subsides after he expresses his wish to kill his brother (Genesis 27:45). Later, when they meet, it is Esau who is ready to embrace Jacob (Genesis 33:4).

Now let's turn to the anger of God. Like human anger, divine anger is often set off by human disregard of divine authority. God is angered by idolatry (the Golden Calf in Exodus 32:20), or by religious violations, such as breaking the Sabbath (Ezekiel 20:13), or for infractions involving cultic purity norms (Leviticus 6:1-6). All are infringements on God's authority. Divine anger sometimes expresses God's care for others in situations of social injustice:

> You shall not wrong a stranger or oppress him, for you were sojourners in the land of Egypt. You shall not mistreat any widow or orphan. If you do mistreat them, I will heed their outcry as soon as they cry out to me, and *my anger shall blaze*

> *forth* and I will put you to the sword, and your wives shall
> become widows and your children orphans. (Exod 22:21-24)[12]

God's anger is sometimes, in Julia O'Brien's words, "a powerful claim of divine concern for human suffering."[13] A comparable motivation informs divine anger against other nations when they assault or oppress Israel.[14]

The ultimate aim of divine anger is not simply the restoration of divine authority. It can also entail an act of persuasion on God's part, to convince Israel that God is its rightful authority. God is the father of the Israelites, and when he gets angry at them, his anger is ultimately tempered, in contrast with his anger at the nations (which is lethal). The anger of God reminds Israel that Israel belongs to God as family, and his anger against others for the sake of Israel is an expression of divine love for Israel.

The second social model of divine anger is based on the human aggression of warriors, considered in ancient cultures to be a prized virtue in battle.[15] When it is applied to God, it shows the divine capacity to defend Israel. One term for this warrior aggression is "strength, might." At its core, this is essentially a physical quality. When used in the context of conflict, the word may denote fierceness, which combines the physical and the psychological. In modern terms, the word sounds like the effects of adrenaline produced by the "flight or fight" response in the face of a serious threat.[16] Fierceness is the response of readiness and disposition to fight. A related set of terms for divine anger revolves around "anger" (*'ap*, from the Hebrew word for nose or nostrils).[17] As we saw in the preceding chapter, the nose is combined with the verb "to burn" (**hrh*). The physical responses produced by anger include an increase in facial temperature accompanied by an increase in the rate of breathing.[18]

Yahweh's anger is manifest against the cosmic Sea in Habakkuk 3:8 and against peoples in Habakkuk 3:12 (cf. Deuteronomy 32:22; Psalm 110:5).[19] Used sometimes in conjunction

with the word "force" (*ruah*) (Exodus 15:7 and 2 Samuel 22//
Psalm 18:16), this expression of divine anger involves God's
forceful bodily response.[20] Related words include "wrath" (literally "overflow"), used for people in Genesis 49:7 and Amos 1:11,
and for God in Habakkuk 3:8; "fury," used of God as warrior in
Isaiah 42:13;[21] and "wrath" or "heat," used in Psalm 76:11 for
both God and humans.[22] The basic idea is the body "burning"
with "heat."[23] The warrior combines maximum physical adrenaline and emotional energy directed against a perceived enemy.

In the Bible, this "heat" is often unleashed on behalf of others. Human fierceness is for defending against human enemies.
For God, it is for fighting against cosmic enemies or for defending humans—especially Israel—against human enemies.
In this case, it is to defend others whom God recognizes. This
is the basic meaning of divine anger: God is willing to fight for
God's own. In the context of battle, these terms express a positive quality. To be sure, such aggression outside of the battle
context could get out of control, and it was recognized as a social
danger (see Genesis 49:6-7[24]; 2 Samuel 3:39).[25] In the case of
God the divine warrior, this quality too could be dangerous for
Israel (Psalm 74:1; Lamentations 2:3-4; 4:11). Yet when directed
against Israel's enemies, divine anger was prized (Isaiah 42:13;
Lamentations 3:66).

The Love and Anger of God

Now let's turn to the relationship of divine love to divine
anger. First of all, divine love is grounded in the covenant between God and Israel.[26] The book of Deuteronomy speaks of
God's love, and it also meditates on the necessity of Israel's
love in return. Deuteronomy 6 famously commands Israel to
love the Lord with all of its self (verse 5), and chapter 11 commands this love in connection with obeying God's laws, rules,
and commandments (verse 1). Love of God in Deuteronomy is

covenant love "defined by and pledged in the covenant."[27] Love of God in the covenant is not simply a feeling; it is a matter of sustained performance.

This notion of divine-human covenant love corresponds to human covenants made between persons unrelated to one another by blood. Covenant is "family substitute."[28] David and Jonathan make a covenant, and they share love, as beautifully described in 1 Samuel 18:1: "As he [David] finished speaking to Saul, Jonathan's self (*nepesh*) became tied to the self (*nepesh*) of David; Jonathan loved David as himself."[29] (Sound familiar? It is known to Christians from the citation of Leviticus 19:18 in Matthew 22:39; Mark 12:31; Luke 11:27.)

Kings of equal or near-equal status make treaties expressed with love: Hiram king of Tyre is the "friend" (literally, "lover," *'aheb*) to David (1 Kings 5:1). Kings make treaties with vassals, who are required to love them and to perform service and obedience to them. Kings commonly speak of their love for one another and call each other brother when they are in a relatively equal relationship; or, one party may refer to another as father when the relationship is not between relative equals. The king of Assyria required his vassals to take loyalty oaths, and these included the following requirement: "You will love Assurbanipal as yourselves."[30] (Sound familiar?) In another text the oath is recorded: "the king of Assyria, our lord, we will love."[31] In different social and political contexts, covenant and treaty are ways to establish relationships across kinship lines, and these relationships come with responsibilities.

So what does divine love have to do with divine anger? Anger is the divine response to attacks on Israel as members of God's family, or on Israel for its failures to keep the covenant. When divine anger is exercised against Israel, God in a sense is asking Israel why it is acting as if it does not wish to be members of God's family. Even if Israel's answer seems to be a rejection of God, God does not abandon divine love for Israel. Biblical family metaphors for God show divine anger and love: "When Israel was a child, I loved him, and out of Egypt I called my son . . . I led them with cords of human kindness, with bands of love" (Hosea 11:1, 4). Despite Israel's sin, God asks: "How can I give you up, O Ephraim? . . . My heart recoils within me; my compassion grows warm and tender. I will not execute my fierce anger; I will not again destroy Ephraim" (Hosea 11:8-9). This passage may remind us that God's compassion for Israel is understood in association with God's fierce anger. God may become angry at Israel, and yet God may also abandon divine anger.

The images of biblical poetry can offer to us a way to think and feel when we might think God is punishing us. The book of Lamentations implores God to give up his fury. In these images of Israel's suffering at God's hands, readers of the Bible may see expressions of their own suffering and pain. As Kathleen O'Connor has suggested in a very moving book on Jeremiah,[32] biblical images of divine anger allow people to face the suffering that they may feel is God's punishment and yet also allow God to be a part of their effort to heal. Accompanying expressions of divine anger are images of tremendously horrific violence that force people to look at themselves. In her study of imagery of horror in the prophets, Amy Kalmanofsky insightfully comments: "the prophets employ abject imagery to force their audience to confront and ultimately reject their monstrous, abject selves."[33] The Bible offers psalms and stories with images that people can soak in, a process that can help them face not only the suffering that they might feel is God's doing but also their own "abject" doings.[34]

For example, many Christians find consolation in Mary's psalm of praise known as the Magnificat (Luke 1:46-55).[35] This poem is consoling to many readers when they feel powerless. The Magnificat witnesses to God's aid to the weak who may feel that they have nothing left except God. The song sings of divine might and even violent divine judgment against the mighty (verses 51-52): "He has shown strength with his arm; he has scattered the proud in the thoughts of their hearts. He has brought down the powerful from their thrones, and lifted up the lowly." It is for God to set things right, and divine anger was the traditional way of God taking action. Yet the language of divine anger does more.

Biblical images can also give voice to people who feel they should challenge God after having suffered (or even before suffering) God's terrible anger. Moses in the Golden Calf story (Exodus 32) captures how Israel comes face to face with God's wrath. Furious with Israel's idolatry, God threatens to destroy Israel. But Moses implores God not to. Even as Israel is to be punished for its sin, it can—like Moses—turn to God and implore God to relent. Similarly, when God threatens to destroy the innocent with the wicked in the Sodom and Gomorrah story (Genesis 18), Abraham questions God about the divine punishment of the wicked. Moses and Abraham in these stories capture the side of our relationship with God—one that continues communication with God, even when God seems to hide the divine face and show divine anger. In the end, God's anger can be swayed by divine mercy. Moreover, divine anger can induce humans to acknowledge their need for human repentance and divine mercy. As humans respond to God, God at the same time is responding to humans. Human efforts matter; they can affect God's disposition and mollify the divine heart.[36]

In this push and pull between divine anger and mercy, the Bible shows the deeper reality of divine love, for example, repeated four times in Psalm 118 (verses 1-4): "his steadfast love endures forever." But God is not angry forever.

God cares; God cares enough to be moved by humanity. God responds with anger against people, and in doing so, God gets their attention so that they will know not only that they have sinned in God's eyes but also see that their behavior may have consequences extending beyond what they are aware of. God sees what we do not see, even of ourselves. But the divine response does not end with this punishment. When those whom God loves are defeated in the course of human history, God weeps for them (Jeremiah 9:8-9): "Upon the mountains I will take up weeping and wailing, upon the pastures of the wilderness, a dirge."[37] God's anger and love are remarkably two sides of a single divine person. This divine person loves Israel and expresses anger to help Israel come to life in God. This is a love that can be difficult to fathom.

How Divine Anger Is Tied to Human Pain in the Bible

The biblical scholar Julia O'Brien suggests that the modern reaction against the violence of God in the Bible says more about modern sensitivities than it does about the Bible. Our negative response to divine violence and anger in the Bible may reflect our own feelings, but they may overlook the message being communicated about God's justice or the responsibilities of the covenant, which for the biblical authors comes with real consequences if *yes !* they go unmet. We can't focus only on divine anger or divine violence and then miss what may be the deeper expressions of divine concern in the Bible. At the same time, we shouldn't ignore the violence; we should be critical of it, but we also need to think about it and ask why it made for a compelling image of God in biblical times.

Part of the difficulty in understanding divine anger and violence may be that many Americans don't have a comparable experience of violence as the ancient Israelites. Americans may experience awful domestic violence or terrible crime or devastating illness, sometimes with overwhelming loss and permanent personal damage; these are truly terrible. The world of the biblical authors had all these experiences and more. They experienced foreign invasions and terrible destruction at the hands of national enemies. On this score, few Americans have experienced what ancient Israelites experienced. To give only one example, after the fall of the city of Lachish, some Israelites were impaled on the stake, as seen in Assyrian reliefs housed today in the British Museum in London.

There seems to be a relationship between the intensity of Israel's national troubles and the intense, biblical expressions of divine anger. Deuteronomy, Jeremiah, Lamentations, and Ezekiel all occur in the time of Israel's oppression at the hands of the Assyrians and Babylonians—invasions, executions, sieges, and enslavement could and often did occur. In these biblical books, the depth of Israel's pain and suffering at the hands of its human enemies seems to correspond to the depth of divine anger directed against Israel. It is as if the intensity of God's anger in these biblical works and their expression of how bad things have gone for Israel are two sides of the same coin. This point may put into context the very furious anger of God seen in these biblical books. Otherwise, the angry God might otherwise seem downright abusive.[38] In fact, what we see is a profound effort to fathom historical tragedy and to face it as a national and religious problem. In effect, these literary works of the Bible represent efforts at facing up to Israel's major shortcomings. If and when national disaster overtakes us, will we do as well? And in the meantime, can't we do better?

The bitterness and anger expressed against Israel, especially in Ezekiel and Jeremiah, make Yahweh sound like an embittered, rejected spouse in a divorce (see Jeremiah 2–3; Ezekiel 16 and 23). This divine love has turned to bitter anger, perhaps even hate. Indeed, "wounds by a loved one are long lasting" (Proverbs 27:6; New Jewish Publication Society translation).[39] Anger and love are strong, powerful emotions that reflect how deeply one feels about another person. In Jeremiah and Ezekiel, this is God and Israel, husband and wife,[40] now suffering from their terrible breakup. Even anger, terrible anger, is part of this tragic love story. Yet even so, this story is never done, because God is never done; God recovers from the wounds inflicted by Israel, and so Israel does as well. Let me explore this biblical point about God a little more.

When Is God Angry and When Is Israel the Aggressor?

Many people think of divine anger as typical of God in the Bible. This thinking flattens out the biblical picture. It focuses on the book of Deuteronomy and a few other biblical works, and it does not recognize alternative views about punishment within the Bible. For example, according to Psalm 1, the wicked punish themselves by having their way separate from God: ungrounded in the reality of God, they are like chaff that blows away (verse 3); and their way simply perishes, unlike the way of the righteous whom God knows (verse 6). The wicked, in a sense, punish themselves. This model of self-punishment also informs a number of biblical stories, for example, in the book of Esther, where the wicked Haman arranges for gallows for Mordecai (Esther 5:14) that end up being used for Haman's own execution (Esther 7:9-10).

We see yet another idea of punishment in the prophets—Israel rejects God and so God is driven away. This, in turn, leaves Israel vulnerable to attacks by other powers, such as Assyria or Babylonia. For Ezekiel, Israel's sins make the temple impure, thus driving God into exile (see chapters 8–10). We see a parallel idea in Jeremiah. God says in Jeremiah 12:7-9:

> I have abandoned my house,
> I have deserted my possession,
> I have given over the beloved of my very self (*nepesh*),
> into the hand of her enemies;
> My own inheritance has become to me
> like a lion in the forest;
> she raised her voice against me;
> therefore I hate her.
> My inheritance acts towards me
> like a bird of prey or a hyena.[41]

In this passage, it is Israel that is the lion, the bird of prey, the hyena. Here it is Israel that is the animalistic aggressor that has acted against God.

My point in mentioning these passages is that there are different biblical models presented for the way things work out between God and those who reject God; divine anger is only one of these models. When thinking about God in the Bible, the model of divine anger may readily come to mind, maybe because it is simple. When we sin, God gets angry and punishes us. We think *gives us what we chose* of this idea perhaps because this is what we learned or heard as children; or, perhaps, it was what we could hear as children. This is, I think, a simple, even prosaic, answer to a mysterious problem often expressed in the Bible's poetry. The Bible invites us to explore and contemplate the mystery of the divine-human struggle with poetic images. Biblical poetry shows God and humanity locked together, in an embrace of love and in angry conflict. When God deals with humans, humans are dealing with a most human God.[42]

As we have seen, poetic images suggest complex ways of understanding divine love and anger. We need to be more poetic about God and God's anger. This extends to other representations of the divine. Another challenging set of biblical images for God is divine gender and sexuality, the subjects of the next chapter.

$$\approx 4 \approx$$

Does God in the Bible Have Gender or Sexuality?

The Gender of God as a Challenge for the Church

Up to this point in this book, we have explored God's body and body parts as well as divine emotions. The divine body and body parts raise the question of God's gender and sexuality. This is an important subject, as gender issues have come to the forefront of American religious life. They have become critical concerns in society and in churches, splitting some right down the middle. These are matters that need to be engaged in a thoughtful manner. The Bible has been central to this discussion, because it has been used to justify a male understanding of God. This male understanding of God is true of much of what we see in ancient Israel and in Israel's Bible, yet this is hardly the whole story.

To discuss divine gender and sexuality in the Bible, we need to be fair to the ancient evidence. We also need to be sensitive to the modern context. It is important to state clearly that the biblical past cannot be and should not be always the norm for the present. After all, the Bible supports or condones institutions or practices that neither society today nor the church would condone (slavery is a good example). The Bible is not a socially perfect document; it does not always support modern views that should be supported.

The question is how to explore what the Bible says about God in a manner that recognizes this gap between our present

55

and the biblical past and also discerns a disclosure of the biblical God that can speak to us today and perhaps even inspire us. To be honest, I am not sure that it can when it comes to gender and sexuality. Usually in the Bible, God seems to have a male body, but the Bible rarely focuses on features that distinguish God as male; we never see God's sexual organs or sexual activity. As it is, the body of God is not always so clear in many biblical passages, as we have seen already in Chapter One.

Whatever we may think of God's gender and sexuality, it leads to questions. Does it disclose some aspect of God? Is it a marker of some "essence" of God? The feminist theologian Janet Martin Soskice nicely captures the dilemma facing Christians on this score:

> We find ourselves to this very day torn between two positions which are each compelling, but seem at times incompatible. We must say that, Christologically speaking, women and men cannot be different, for "all will bear the image of the man of heaven." But we may also say that sexual difference is not, or should not be, a matter of theological indifference. Genesis 1 suggests sexual difference has something to tell us, not just about human beings, but about God in whose image they are made, male and female. The unresolved question then is: where, why, and how does sexual difference make a difference?[1]

These are hard questions, and perhaps our efforts to address them may not get us to intellectually satisfying answers that tidy up matters. As we will see, the process of pursuing the task itself teaches us about the difficulty of knowing God.

Gendered Images for God in the Bible

The Hebrew Bible clearly uses a good deal of male language for God. One central gendered image for the divine in ancient Israel involved God as a great king.[2] Many psalms praise God precisely as King (for example, Psalms 93, 97, 99; see also Psalm 74:12). The verbs for divine kingship used in these psalms include the royal functions of ruling and notions of might. <u>By contrast, there is no comparable language of Queen for God (cf. the Queen of Heaven in Jeremiah 7 and 44).</u>[3] When we look at God as divine parent, the picture is also heavily weighted—and freighted—to the male. The overall picture in the Bible shows much more language for God as male than female.[4] God is imaged as father in many passages.[5]

In an intriguing passage hinting at God's sexuality, Genesis 4:1, Eve says: "I have produced a man with the help of the Lord." The New Revised Standard Version translation, echoing the Greek translation (the Septuagint), renders the same line as "I have acquired a man through God." There is no word "help" in the Hebrew here, and it has been noted that the verb is also used for procreation. So a literal translation might go: "I have procreated a man with Yahweh."[6] This gives the impression of Yahweh as the biological father of a human being. (No wonder the New Revised Standard Version translation changes the wording!) However, what Genesis 4:1 suggests is not a virgin birth on Eve's part, but the idea of Yahweh as a creator god and divine aid to conception.[7]

Male language for God appears forcefully in the prophetic idea of God as the husband of Israel. Israel appears as God's wife in Hosea (chapter 2), Jeremiah (chapter 2), and Ezekiel (chapters 16 and 23).[8] The idea is that <u>the covenant is a marriage relationship.</u> *suzerainty (equals)* This biblical metaphor has inspired Jewish and Christian traditions to understand the Song of Songs as the love song between God and Israel or God and the church. The metaphorical imagery in Hosea and Jeremiah may seem beautiful, but the comparable images in Ezekiel turn ugly, pornographic, and even abusive in their rhetoric against Jerusalem. Whether beautiful as in Jeremiah and Hosea, or ugly as in Ezekiel, the imagery is problematic. Feminist scholars of the Bible have rightly questioned the normative character of biblical imagery so laden with male images of God and female language symbolic of human idolatry.[9] Even if the imagery of Israel as God's beloved spouse is viewed in positive terms, it still casts Israel in the subordinate role, and this may convey the sense that women should be like Israel: subordinate.   *Adamic mindset*

When we turn to female images for God, we see God imaged as a mother, as in Deuteronomy 32:18: "The rock who bore (*yld) you, you neglected, and you forgot God who gave you birth (*hwl)."[10] Isaiah 42:13-14 also combines male and female imagery in expressing God's acting for Israel: "Yahweh will go forth like a hero, Like a warrior he will stir up rage. He will shout; indeed he will roar. He will prevail over his enemies. 'For a long time I kept quiet; I was silent; I restrained myself. Now I will scream like a woman in labor. I will inhale, and I will exhale simultaneously.'"[11] Female language of God as midwife is used in Psalm 22:9-10: "You drew me from the womb, made me secure at my mother's breast. I became your charge at birth; from my mother's womb You have been my God."

In biblical texts, gender metaphors focus on Israel's *relationship* with God. The question still remains: how much of this gendered language was thought to be expressive of who God is? Some scholars suggest that the Bible offers no clear statement about God's motherhood in the same manner found for God's fatherhood. It might be thought that the picture is asymmetrical, with male metaphor more dominant. It is. The question is whether that matters and how. Passages in the Bible lacking divine gender also show how complicated the matter of God and sexuality is.

Passages Transcending Gendered Language for God

At this point, I would like to turn to two passages that transcend gendered language for God. The first is Ezekiel 1, a passage that we discussed in Chapter One. According to Ezekiel 1, over the firmament (verse 22) and above the heads of the heavenly figures (verse 26) was something like the appearance of a throne, with something like a human form that was the "likeness" of the glory of Yahweh (verses 26-28). The divine is imaged in neither male nor female terms, but in human terms; verse 26 uses the Hebrew word "human" and not "man" or "woman" (or, "male" or "female"). In this context God is but a likeness, "like" the appearance of a human. Here God transcends categories of gender or sexuality.

The second passage is Genesis 1. In verse 26, God proposes: "Let us make the human in our image, according to our likeness." We may notice the first person plural "us" and "our," like many earlier Christian commentators. Several considered this "us" and "our" to be an allusion to the Trinity. Modern commentators understand this language as a way of speaking by the royal head of the heavenly hosts to address the heavenly court. This is what we see in Isaiah's vision of God (Isaiah 6). After witnessing the heavenly hosts, the prophet hears the voice of God asking them: "Whom shall *I* send? Who will go for *us*?" (verse 8). Here the first-person singular with the first-person plural is a conventional way of the divine warrior-king speaking to his heavenly court. That's what seems to lie behind the divine "our" ("in our image") in Genesis 1:26.

So far, so good. Things get more complicated though when we get to the next verse in Genesis 1. In verse 27, the text narrates the divine act of creation:

> God created the human in his image;
> In the image of God he created him;
> Male and female He created them.

The first thing that makes this expression more complicated compared with verse 26 is that it is a small piece of poetry highlighting the importance of this divine act. In the poetry of biblical Hebrew, short lines are laid out usually in groups of two or three lines.

This verse has three lines. Hebrew poetry in the Bible doesn't use rhyme at the end of the lines or metrical patterns, like a sonnet. Instead, poetry in the Bible is all about the compact quality of the lines as well as the correspondences of words or phrases between lines (what biblical scholars call "parallelism").[12] The language of "image" is used in the first and second lines, as we saw already in verse 26, but the third line expands our vision: "Male and female He created them." In other words, the "them" is "male and female." Humanity is one, yet it is also two. This two together as one that procreates is like divine creation, and like the divine warrior-king, it has dominion over the world.

It has been asked how the human here can be in the image of God and still be a "them." It seems to be primarily a matter of analogy of functions and not of being (or "essence"). The poetic lines affirm that the human persons, male and female together, are in God's image, but they are also not like God by virtue of being gendered.[13] The passage reflects priestly theology in which God transcends gender. At the same time, it seems that the author thought of God primarily in male terms. The verbs used for God here are masculine. So the analogy between the divine and the human is asymmetrical when it comes to gender and sexuality: God is generally male and the divine image of humanity is male and female.

How did this sexual asymmetry come to be? What was the situation in Israel that this picture of God's sexuality may have been addressing? Is there a larger background that might provide some perspective on the situation? It is possible to identify the larger cultural context in ancient Israel for female metaphorical language for God. Crucial to the cultural context of gender language for God are three goddesses and the different sorts of impact that they had on ancient Israel.

Three goddesses in Israel

Early Israel was home to a number of gods and goddesses, though their "careers" differed significantly. Who were they? The

best-known goddess may be Asherah, poorly attested to in the
Bible, but known in other sources outside of the Bible as the wife
of El, the head god, and mother of the other deities. Two other
goddesses are also known in Israel's Bible. These are Anat and
Astarte, both famous for battling and hunting in texts outside of
the Bible.[14] However, Anat seems to fade from Israel fairly early
(her name preserved in proper names, for example, in Judges
3:31 and 5:6), and Astarte is mostly a figure of criticism (see
Judges 2:13; cf. the Phoenician form of this goddess denounced
in 1 Kings 11:5). It is the story of Asherah that is particularly
relevant to the question of divine gender and sexuality. While
she belongs to the Bible's story of idolatry, she is also important
in the development of biblical monotheism.

The first chapter in our story about Asherah in ancient Israel
begins with the title "Breasts and Womb," in Genesis 49:25-26
(the translation is mine, since most translations obscure this title):

> By the god of your father [or El, your father] who aids you,
> And Shadday who blesses you (with)
>> the blessings of Heaven above,
>> the blessings of Deep crouching below;
>> the blessings of Breasts and Womb,
>> the blessings of your Father, warrior Most High;
>> the blessings of the Everlasting Mountains,
>>> of the outlying Eternal Hills.

The passage here seems to acknowledge a number of divine
figures associated with blessing. The blessings are given by El
(also called Shadday). The blessings are then associated with
various deities. First comes Heaven and Deep, which are two
ancient divinized parts of the universe. Next there is the pairing
of "Breasts and Womb" with "Father, warrior Most High." If
"Father, warrior Most High" refers to a god, then it stands to reason that "Breasts and Womb" is a title for a goddess. It won't do
(as some interpreters would have it) to understand "Breasts and

Womb" simply as a vague, generic label for fertility. Certainly fertility was one of the important blessings, but the title "Breasts and Womb" sounds like a female figure, a goddess who is mother. The best guess for this figure would be Asherah.

The next chapter in the story of Asherah involves a number of inscriptions from ancient Israel. These inscriptions have profoundly affected the contemporary discussion of divine gender and sexuality of God in the Bible. One group of inscriptions was discovered at a site in the south of Israel called Kuntillet 'Ajrud (it may have been a stopover site for travelers). Visitors seem to have left wishes of blessings for other people. For example, there are the following four blessings involving Yahweh and "his asherah":

1. "may they be sated . . . be granted (?) by [Ya]hweh of Teman and by [his] asherah"
2. "I (hereby) bless you by Yahweh of Samaria and by his asherah"
3. "I (hereby) bless you by [Ya]hweh of Teman and by his asherah"
4. "by Yahweh of the Teman and by his asherah"[15]

The formula involving "his asherah" is of great debate among scholars. Should the word asherah be translated with a "capital a" as the name of the goddess, Asherah? Or, should it be understood as a common noun with a "small a" and thus the symbol of the tree thought to symbolize the goddess? Biblical Hebrew does not make a distinction between capital and small letters, and so "the A/asherah" with a "capital a" or "lower case a" is part of the matter of interpretation.

On one side, it has been argued that Asherah in these inscriptions was a goddess with a "capital a." Other scholars disagree, because of a basic point about Hebrew grammar: personal names in Hebrew do not usually take a suffix, but objects do. So it seems to be an object and not a name. And in fact there is just such an object mentioned in the Bible. From the biblical perspective, this is part of the story of idolatry, as this *asherah* is condemned. For example, in Deuteronomy 16:21, Israelites are told not to put up an *asherah* (tree or pole) next to an altar of Yahweh. Perhaps the object of the tree was the symbol of the goddess denoting her fertility or life-giving powers; so even if it is not her name as such, her object might refer to her. These different interpretations have their merits, and that is one reason why this debate remains unresolved.

My goal at this point is not to end this debate, although I can tell you that I do think Asherah was a goddess in early Israel. By the time of the inscriptions, her name seems to have turned into a way of talking about Yahweh's blessing.[16] After all, the inscriptions say "his *asherah*," and so it is something bearing on *his* divinity. Whatever the *asherah* is, it's his, not hers. It remains possible that even if this reading of the inscription is right, ancient Israelites might have sensed a female figure here.[17] So as you see, the ancient evidence can be difficult.

The final chapter in our story of Asherah/*asherah* involves its adoption and adaptation into biblical thought without the notion of a goddess. (By the way, the word for "goddess" does not occur *Holy* in biblical Hebrew, unlike the word for "god.") The asherah's *Spirit* transformation can be seen in the imagery of personified Wisdom. In Proverbs 3, Wisdom is called "a tree of life," much like the *asherah* tree symbol. More than this, verse 18 makes a clever wordplay on the word *asherah*.[18] Wisdom "is a tree of life to those who lay hold of her; those who hold her fast are happy." The first line of this verse shows the symbolism of the female Wisdom as a tree of life, much as the *asherah* is a symbol of blessing. The second line uses the word "happy," which in Hebrew, *'ashre*, puns on the name of the symbol, the *asherah*. Here the *asherah* symbol is transmuted into a metaphor for divine wisdom. It has changed from the goddess's name or object into the metaphor of divine wisdom. Yahweh, in a sense, has incorporated the goddess. A later wisdom book, Wisdom of Solomon (7:25-26), puts the idea of female Wisdom this way: Wisdom "is an aura of the might of God, a pure effusion of the glory of the Almighty . . . For she is the refulgence of eternal light, the spotless mirror of the power of God, the image of his goodness." Maleness may be the general understanding of the godhead for ancient Israel, but this godhead includes female wisdom.

This story of Asherah brings us back to Genesis 1, which we discussed earlier. In a passage such as this, the Bible expresses the fundamental paradox of gendered language for God. It is couched in masculine grammar and imagery, while at the same time this divinity lies beyond such gender-specific language. Tikva Frymer-Kensky puts the problem this way: "God is not a sexual male, and therefore even the erotic metaphor of passion reveals a lack of physicality. God is not imaged in erotic terms and sexuality was simply not part of the divine order."[19] In the end, in Soskice's words, "God is mystery, and woman and man in God's image are mystery."[20] The biblical sense of God's transcendence that accompanies gendered language for God in the Bible, in works such as Genesis 1 or Second Isaiah, relativizes human language applied to God. Such human language applied to God not only falls short; it only makes sense for God when it is recognized as being partial and falling short. The Bible leaves us with a mystery, a problem, a paradox: while God transcends categories of gender, male language for God is common in our church thinking ("I believe in God, the Father Almighty . . ."). Overall, the biblical tradition raises a central question for today: is this the best the Bible and Christianity can do when it comes to gender imagery for God?

Three Cultural Considerations

In approaching this question, it may help to understand that gender language for God in the Bible was a moving target. We can see this point better if we recall the changing cultural setting for gender metaphors about God. Let me mention three aspects

of this changing situation. First, gods and goddesses were traditional in early Israel. As we have seen, early biblical literature
shows traces of several gods and goddesses known also from
sources outside of the Bible. Contrary to modern expectations,
in early Israel these deities are often not condemned, nor are they
even recognized as foreign.

Second, the traditional language of these older gods and goddesses, including its gendered formulations, did not immediately
stop with the emergence of monotheism in Israel. Rather, it continued to show its imprint in Israel right up through the New Testament. Monotheism allowed for old myth; the myth of the past
informs visions of the future (for example, the myth of Leviathan
and the seven-headed dragon running from the Ugaritic texts
through Isaiah 27, Psalm 74, and the book of Revelation).[21] The
ongoing use of mythic imagery includes the traditional gendered
language for God, even in the face of the rise of the monotheistic
worldview in ancient Israel.

Third, female imagery for God in the Bible accelerated once
goddesses were no longer—or at least less of—an issue in ancient
Israel. As Elizabeth Bloch-Smith has brilliantly suggested, this loss
of goddesses in Israel may help to explain the relative proliferation
of female imagery for God in the sixth-century passages of Isaiah
42:14; 46:3-4; and 49:15 (cf. Isaiah 45:10-11; 66:9, 13).[22] The author of Isaiah 40–55 (whom modern scholars have called "Second
Isaiah") apparently was trying out a rhetorical strategy for understanding Israel's chief deity. This may not have been an option in
earlier periods in Israel's history when goddesses were still part of
the religious landscape. The new female language for God in Isaiah
40–55 seems to be a new way to tell a new story about an old God.

Divine Sexuality and the One God

As the preceding section suggests, some passages in biblical
literature seem to show that there is no male essence to God, but
God continued to be thought of as male. This maleness may have

conveyed for that culture the superior role of God, because male language conveyed that superiority. So, for ancient Israelites in general, did male language for God convey essence or roles (or both)? Was maleness—for them—a matter of God's essence or not? Linguistic theory on gender may help us explore these questions. According to recent work on gender and language, there has been a profound shift in approach. Ann Weatherall suggests the following:

> Traditionally in gender and language research, like elsewhere in the social sciences, language was viewed as a mirror; it reflected the shared essences about women and men. Language was also thought to reflect society's beliefs and values about women and men. Now language about women and men and the way men and women speak can be understood as part of the same discursive process, the social construction of gender. Sex/gender no longer has to be viewed as something that we are. Rather it is something that we do, an interactional accomplishment that we achieve over and over again, in different ways, throughout the course of our lives.[23]

function

Weatherall further characterizes the social construction of sex/gender through language in these terms: "gender is not an essence, but a form of activity . . . gender is a routine and joint accomplishment of situated conversational activity."[24] In this view, gender and sexuality are not simply a matter of essence, of what people simply are; they are also a matter of social activity, namely, what people interacting with them make them out to be within a spectrum of socially recognized sexual possibility.

This distinction between gender as "essence" and gender as social "activity" provides a way to probe the operating assumption of the (male) authors of the Bible. Rather than deciding between gender as "essence" and gender as "activity," the situation in ancient Israel seems to suggest a both/and approach. To use Weatherall's terms of sexuality/gender as "essence" versus

"role"

"activity," the traditional male gender of the national God in ancient Israel seems to have been understood as essence, reinforced
by male metaphor in various forms of textual "activity" about
God. Yet this was not the end of the biblical story when it came
to God. Israel's textual "activity" changed, with female gender
language for this national male god increasing in the seventh and
sixth centuries and later. This suggests an awareness that the male
essence of Yahweh was far from absolute. The later "activity" in
works such as Isaiah 40–55 relativizes the perceived "essence."
As we saw in the preceding section, God is imaged as father
and mother or as male or female—or as neither (Ezekiel 1:27).

So what is the norm to be derived from the Bible on this
score? Perhaps most importantly, there is no single norm that
can be derived from the Bible without ignoring its complexity.
Otherwise, we run the risk of flattening out the complexity of the
Bible's gendered language for God. As we have seen, God may
be represented as male in most passages, but several passages
complicate this picture either with female imagery or representation of God as beyond gender. So we should not, to paraphrase
Deuteronomy 32:18, "forget God who gave us birth."[25] If Isaiah
40–55 in its time tried to tell a new story about an old God by
reference to female-gendered language, then the church today
may also try to tell a new story about God without forgetting the
biblical God who gave us birth.

The Trinity and Gender in Biblical Perspective

This reconsideration of the Bible's gender language for God
has implications for the church's gender language for God. Before
I begin, let me say that it is not possible to provide a full treatment
of the understanding of God in Christian tradition. Still, it is important to note how gender language informing the three persons of
the Trinity remains central to any Christian understanding of God.
For many people, the language of the Trinity, namely, Father, Son,

and Holy Spirit, tends to reinforce maleness. Yet at a more fundamental level, it embodies the central importance of fatherhood, sonhood, and spirithood, and not simply maleness. According to the *Catechism of the Catholic Church*: "the real distinction of the persons from one another resides solely in the relationships which relate them to one another."[26] The *Catechism* also reminds us: "God's parental tenderness can also be expressed by the image of motherhood (citing Isaiah 66:3, Psalm 131:2) . . . God transcends the human distinction between the sexes. He [!] is neither man nor woman: he [!] is God. He also transcends human fatherhood and motherhood."[27] I have added exclamation points to this quote in order to highlight the male pronouns in this formulation—it can be hard for us in the church to get away from the maleness of God.

Some scholars have appealed to the Spirit as the "feminine" side or dimension of the Trinity. In this view, the word spirit (*ruah*) expresses femaleness as a mediating force and in terms of its grammatical gender.[28] However, this approach to the Spirit has been strongly criticized.[29] It is a problem, because divine spirit in Israel's Bible is not as clearly marked for gender as father and son.[30] While grammatically feminine, the divine spirit in its actions and imagery is presented little, if at all, in terms of what was considered female in ancient Israel. A possible exception to consider would be the mediating role of the Spirit, which might be thought to reflect a mediating role of a mother mediating between the patriarch and the children within the household. However, this would be a rather vague comparison with how the Spirit mediates, and no biblical passage makes a connection between God's spirit and the mediating role of mothers. Moreover, "spirit" in New Testament Greek is neuter in grammatical gender (*to pneuma*), and the New Testament shows little imagery that is distinctly female or male for the Spirit. In fact, spirit is the dimension of the Godhead that is most unmarked for gender or sexuality.[31] Spirit arguably challenges the notion of sexuality in the Trinity, since Spirit is barely (if at all) female in gender or imagery. Instead, it stands apart from—and arguably beyond—sexuality. The Spirit seems to signal the transcendence of God with regard to gender or sexuality.

The Father and Son too are to be reconsidered. These two terms stress the special relationship, not their maleness as such. The biblical basis for the relationship of the Father and the Son comes from royal psalms. For example, we have the expression of the patron-god as the father of the king, who is his son, in Psalm 2:7: "You are my son; this day I have begotten you."[32] Father and son form a particular expression of the relationship between the divine patron and the human king.[33] The Bible provided a culturally specific language derived from the idea of divine patronage of human kingship, which later came to convey the special relationship of the Father and Son. When the Gospel of John speaks of the Father and the Son together, it often stresses their relationship and not their maleness; indeed, these terms of relationship are a hallmark of John's gospel.[34] Jesus understands God as his heavenly Father, and so Christians follow suit as "children of God" in praying the "Our Father."

So what is the Trinity expressing about God, and how might we think of the gender language of the Trinity? Theologians of our times have struggled with this question. In the phrase of Najeeb Awad, the Trinity may be understood as a "reciprocal *koinonia*" (partnership or communion).[35] In Soskice's words, "to be" for the Trinitarian God is "to be related."[36] She continues: "according to the doctrine of the Trinity, this is precisely what God does, what God is, is through being-to-other, being related, that God is one." Soskice concludes her discussion of the Trinity:

> The doctrine of the Trinity tells us nothing about how men and women should relate to one another as males and females. It does not show that all men should be like the "father" and all women should model themselves on a feminized Spirit. But it does let us glimpse what it is, most truly to be: "to-be" most fully is "to-be-related" in difference.[37]

In other words, what counts in the Trinity are the relationships of the three persons, and more specifically, the relationship of love, not some sort of divine male essence (or ontology). Here we may note the relational model of the Trinity voiced by Augustine (*De Trinitate*, VIII:14, 8.12.14): "You see the Trinity when you see the eternal love, for the three are the one loving, the beloved, and their love."[38] This trinitarian love is also a matter of God's love relationship with the world, expressed in traditional theological language in terms of the procession of the Son from the Father and the Spirit from the Father and the Son. In other words, the Father is God eternally in heaven, the Son a definitive moment of God for and in the universe, and the Spirit God's ongoing, renovating presence for and in the universe.

filoque clause

As a Catholic Christian, I have no desire to dispense with the language of Father, Son, and Spirit, and I can affirm it as a creedal matter. For us Christians to sever our link to this language would be to deny who we are as Christians. At the same time, I can also regard this traditional language with a critical sensibility. I can recognize its historical background, and just as importantly, I can recognize not only that a full account of the biblical texts suggests no simple male God, but also that Christian tradition can grow in wisdom based on its continual return to its Scriptures. In light of the Old Testament, I can hear the relational language of Jesus in the New Testament without the reification of gender in itself. As the son of a father and the father of a son myself, I can sense the power of the biblical language for these relationships. At the same time, there is no need or basis for regarding the specific gender quality of male imagery as a matter of divine essence (after all, I am also the father of two daughters and a grandfather to a granddaughter). Nor is there any reason not to acknowledge the problem that it poses for the faith, especially for liturgy (such as the gender language for God in the lectionary's Bible readings). There is a biblical and theological basis for inclusive language in modern liturgy,[39] and arguably for much more. With Augustine, I

can ask: "What then are you, O my God? What else can I say but
the Lord my God? . . . what is all that any one can say, when he
is speaking of you?" (*Confessions*, chapter IV).

Our times are fractured over sexual and gender politics; when
it comes to gender language for God, it is not hard to see why.
Even as theologians explore the issues,[40] voices on different sides
of the questions are stubborn, and there is little sense that the
discussion is moving forward. I am afraid that I cannot arrive at
a point today that is religiously satisfying to me as a committed Roman Catholic and as a Christian committed to justice for
women and men in the church and beyond. This story is ongoing,
and perhaps it will end only with the *eschaton*. That the ending
is not yet written but open ended may be the best news at the
moment. There remains the possibility noted by Soskice of what
she calls the "mobility" of gendered symbolic language.[41] The
language may be fixed in creedal stone ("We believe in God,
the Father Almighty . . ."), but our sensibility about this male
language for God need not be as fixed.

The many fields of study offering new insights into personhood, sexuality, and language, undertaken by thinking people
willing to struggle with these questions, give me hope that we as
a church might arrive at more intelligible and more credible understandings of God. For the moment, for this moment, I would
say that there is not only a problem here. There is also an opportunity to reconsider not only what the question of sexual and
gender language for God discloses about God's transcendence
but also for what it hides. At the moment, with the church facing
deep confusion over sexuality and with its work on gender and
God seemingly at an impasse, one may sense God hiding the
divine face from the church. That, it seems to me, may be the
revelation about God and sexuality for our times.[42]

Questions about God in the World

PART II

Questions about God in the World

What Can Creation Tell Us about God?

The Bible and Human Language

≈ In trying to understand God in the Bible, we can't get beyond or around human language. It is impossible not because of God, but because of us. We are human, and all human understanding comes in the form of language.[1] We use metaphors to capture many different aspects of life, including what is most dear to us, such as love. We "fall in love," and "love is a red, red rose." Metaphor is not simply religious language. It is human language for all areas of human life, including the religious. "Because metaphor is a primary tool for understanding our world and our selves," write George Lakoff and Mark Turner, "entering into an engagement with powerful poetic metaphors is grappling in an important way with what it means to have a human life."[2] Like so much of the Bible, creation texts use human language to convey who God is.

What Do Creation Passages in the Bible Say About God?

In ancient Israel, creation was presented in different ways.[3] It is not only in Genesis 1–2. There are allusions to it in the prophets (for example, Jeremiah 10:12; Amos 4:13; 9:6; Zechariah 12:1), and it is recounted in various wisdom books (Proverbs

8:22-31; Job 26:7-13; 38:1-11; Ben Sira 1:3-4; 24:3-9). The creation story was also a topic in Israel's worship (Psalms 74:12-17; 89:11-13; 90:2; and 148). These passages show us that several different creation accounts existed in ancient Israel, not just one or even two;[4] and they told the story of creation in different ways.

The theme of creation served as a way to express notions about God, humanity, and the world. Creation texts are like medieval and Renaissance paintings that show the same religious scene in different ways. You may recall different paintings of the sacrifice of Isaac or the Last Supper or perhaps others involving major biblical scenes. Different paintings of the same scene by different painters show different emphases and nuances; they are efforts to communicate different interpretations of a given biblical scene. In their own ways, biblical creation texts offer different emphases and nuances in portraying the world. They tell different stories about the same ancient moment and they look at it from various perspectives, each revealing something a bit different.

Let's begin with what different creation texts of the Bible say about God. The Bible's various versions of creation show three different ideas about God: God created the universe by divine *power,* with divine *wisdom,* or with some form of the divine *presence.* In emphasizing these three ideas or models for God, I am not claiming that the Bible does not have other models. For example, creation by divine procreation enjoyed a long and venerable tradition in the ancient world,[5] and it lies in the deep background of Genesis 1.[6] Divine power, wisdom, and presence characterize the connection between God and the world.[7] These are all ways of expressing the fundamental connection of God to the world and to humanity.

The First Model of Creation: Divine Power   mimetic violence? pagan)

In this model, creation issues from God's powerful victory over cosmic enemies,[8] for example, in Psalm 74:12-17:

12 Yet God my King is from of old,
   Working salvation in the midst of the earth.
13 You—You scattered **Sea** by Your might;
   You smashed the heads of the **Tanninim** on the waters.
14 You—You crushed the heads of **Leviathan**, ʼ
   You made him into food for the work of sea-beasts (?).
15 You—You split open springs and brooks;
   You—You dried up mighty rivers.
16 Yours is the day, Yours also the night;
   You—You established the luminary of the sun.
17 You—You fixed all the boundaries of earth;
   Summer and winter, You—You fashioned.[9]

In this model of creation, the universe is the stage on which God engages in battle against cosmic enemies, whether they are the cosmic waters personified (Sea, in verse 13 above) or monsters dwelling in these waters (Tanninim and Leviathan, in verses 13-14). In the aftermath of the divine victory, creation emerges out of the defeated cosmic waters. This model sometimes uses verbs of making, but this is not the dominant way of expressing creation in this model; for example, Psalm 74:12-17 uses only one such verb. Instead, the verbs in this passage highlight God's power (see also Psalms 65:7-8 and 68:35).

In this first model of creation, God is primarily a warrior-king, and power is the primary idea in this divine reality (cf. Psalm 62:12: "might belongs to God"). From the divine palace (or temple), God marches to battle; God gloriously returns after the divine victory.[10] The proper human response is to honor the divine king as a servant would, by paying homage in the earthly palace. In religious terms, this translates into sacrificial cult and praise of the divine warrior-king at the temple. Offerings constitute the basic elements and procedures of the symbolic system that expresses this relationship. For example, the offering of

Leviticus 2 is often translated as cereal or meal offering, but it literally means "tribute." God is the warrior-king who receives the tribute of his human subjects. In this model, God also punishes enemies with acts of powerful violence.[11]

In ancient Israel, this first model sometimes involved the mediating figure of the human king. As God's intermediary, the human king drew his own power from the power of the divine king and functioned as mediator between the divine king and that monarch's human subjects. Here power is the term governing reality. We might say that the power of the human king draws on the power of the divine warrior-king. In some cases of this first model, it is through the human king that divine power is made manifest in the world. For example, in Psalm 89:9-12 divine creation occurs in a context concerned also with the king's power and his divine support (mentioned in verses 18-24).[12] In this psalm, the king derives his power from God's own power, as expressed by God in verse 25: "I will set his hand on Sea and right hand on River(s)."[13]

shadow of christ

The Second Model of Creation: Divine Wisdom

The second model involves creation accomplished by divine wisdom, as we see in Psalm 104[14]:

Psalm 104

Opening Invocation of the Creator of the Heavens
1   Bless Yahweh, O my soul!
O Yahweh, my God, You are so great!
In splendor and majesty You are clothed,
2   Wrapped in light like a robe.
Spreads the heavens like a tent-curtain,
3   Sets the beams of His upper chambers in the waters;
Makes the clouds his chariot,
Travels on the wings of the wind;

4   Makes the winds his messengers,
    Fire and flame his servants.

Praise of Earth's Creator

5   He established the earth on its foundations,
    So that it would never shake.
6   The ocean covered it like clothing,
    Above the mountains the waters stood.
7   At Your roar they fled,
    At the sound of Your thunder they hurried.
8   They went up the mountains, down the valleys
    To the site that You had established for them.
9   You set a boundary so that they would never cross,
    Never again cover the earth.

Praise of the Creator of Waters on Earth

10 You made springs gush in the channels,
    Between the mountains they flow.
11 They provide water for every beast of the field,
    Wild asses quench their thirst.
12 With them the birds of the sky dwell,
    Among the branches they sing.
13 Watering the mountains from His upper chambers,
    The earth is saturated by the fruit of Your works.

Praise of the Creator of Food

14 You grow grass for the beasts,
    Herbage for humanity's labor:
    To bring food from the ground,
15 And wine which gladdens the human heart.
    To make the face shine with oil,
    and food which sustains the heart.
16 The trees of Yahweh drink their fill,
    The cedars of Lebanon, which He had planted,

17   Where birds make their nests,
     The stork, her home in the junipers.
18   The high mountains are for wild goats,
     The cliffs, a refuge for badgers.

Praise of the Creator of Seasons and Days

19   He marked the seasons by the moon,
     The sun knows its setting.
20   You make it dark, and it is night,
     When every beast of the forest roams.
21   Lions roar for prey,
     Seeking their food from God.
22   When the sun rises, they retire,
     And lie down in their lairs.
23   People depart to their work,
     To their labor, till evening.

Praise of the Creator of the Seas

24   *How many are Your works, O Yahweh!*
     You made them all with wisdom,
     The earth is filled with Your creations.
25   There is the sea, great and vast,
     There with creatures beyond number,
     Living things, small along with large.
26   There ships go about, Leviathan as well,
     Whom You formed to play with.

**Creatures' Dependence on the Creator,
including Humans**

27   All of them look to You,
     To give them food in due season.
28   If You give to them, they gather,
     Open Your hand, they are fully satisfied.
29   But hide Your face, they are terrified,

Take away their spirit, they perish
And turn again to dust.

30 If You send forth Your spirit, they are created,
And You renew the face of the earth.

31 May the Glory of Yahweh endure forever,
May Yahweh rejoice in His works,

32 Who looks to the earth and it trembles,
Touches the mountains and they smoke.

33 Let me sing of Yahweh all my life,
Rejoice in my God while I live.

34 May my theme be pleasing to Him,
I—yes I—rejoice in Yahweh.

35 May sinners vanish from the earth,
And wicked be no more.
Bless Yahweh, O my soul!
Halleluyah![15]

Readers often note the wonder of creation in this psalm. Our basic impulse to feel wonder in nature is deeply supported by the psalm, as it is elsewhere in the Bible. We may sense God in some fundamental or even primordial way in and through nature. For the Bible, not only revelation, but natural experience can give a sense of God. For example, Psalm 19 balances nature and teaching as two ways of knowing about God.

In the middle of Psalm 104 is the basic point that God made creation by wisdom (verse 24). Wisdom is reflected in how the unruly waters at the beginning of creation (verses 6-7) turn into a source of life for God's creatures (verses 10-13), and how different parts of creation are made to help other parts (for example, the grass to feed animals and humanity, in verses 14-15). Creation is truly full of God's wise consideration. At the same time, Psalm 104 draws on the first model of creation in mentioning God's power against enemies who flee at his roar and thunder (verse 7). The image of God stretching out creation like a tent (verse 2) is an additional metaphor for creation (see also Isaiah 40:22).[16] As we will see below, the reference to God's "face" (verse 29) and "spirit" (verse 30) are common for the third model of creation. While wisdom is the basic idea of creation (verse 24), with all its parts beautifully fitted together in this psalm, we also see how it draws on multiple models and images for creation.

In other passages in the Bible, the second model presents creation as the work of the divine craftsman who works as a builder, an engineer, an architect (see Job 28:25 and 38:4-6), or a metal worker (see Job 37:18).[17] Isaiah 40:12-14 describes God as the wise craftsman of creation, in contrast to the human craftsmen who make idols in Isaiah 40:18-20. In Proverbs 8:22-31,[18] the wisdom of divine creation is embodied by Wisdom personified as a female figure who was with God at the beginning of the divine acts of creation (see also Wisdom 6:22). In this model, wisdom is the primary idea, in contrast to power in the first model.

In this second model, the human response to God builds on the first model's idea of reverence of God: "the fear of the LORD is the beginning of knowledge" (Proverbs 1:7; compare Psalm 111:10 and Ecclesiastes 12:13). Biblical texts in this second model call men (and often not women?!) to acknowledge the wisdom of the universe as created by God, to learn wisdom and understand it, and accordingly, to live a life of wisdom. If in the first model the king is the mediator of divine power, it is wisdom itself built into the fabric of the world that mediates between God and people. In order to become wise, a person is to learn God's wisdom in the world, or in the terms presented by Proverbs 1–9, to approach personified Wisdom herself and to learn from her. As a result, people gain wisdom, which helps them withstand challenges over time (Proverbs 24:16). In this model, sinners perish from their lack of wisdom, but not because of divine punishment. Instead, because of their foolishness the wicked put themselves on the way to the underworld (see Psalm 49), and it is hoped that they disappear from the earth (Psalm 104:35).[19] In other words, they reject God's teaching, and so they pass away.

The Third Model of Creation: Divine Presence

The third model offers a view of the created universe as the place of God's presence. This idea is expressed by various terms: divine holiness, name, splendor, light, and word. Like the first model, the third involves the notion of the divine palace-temple, but the emphasis with the third model of creation does not fall on divine power, with the warrior-king marching from his palace. Instead, for the third model, creation bears characteristics of God elsewhere associated with the temple or the divine presence in it.

Let's begin with the universe as the place of God's *holiness*. In Psalm 150:1 the heavenly divine home is referenced in terms of holiness: "Praise God in his sanctuary (holy place), praise God in the firmament, his stronghold!" The firmament is not only the divine fortress; it is also God's holy place, the divine sanctuary.[20] Eden

Parallel to the heavenly palace or temple is God's temple-palace on earth. It too is regarded as a sacred or *holy* place established by God in the wake of divine victory. The praises of Exodus 15 include a reference to the sacred space that God provided for the people (verse 17) after the divine triumph over the Egyptians:

> You brought them and planted[21] them
> on the mountain of your inheritance,
> The place for your dwelling that you made, O Lord,
> The sanctuary, O Lord, that your hands established.

Jesus/the Human Being

The divine temple, whether in heaven or on earth, is God's sanctuary or *holy* place that mediates divine presence.

Like divine *holiness*, the divine *name* occurs in both creation and temple contexts. Following its initial reference to creation, Psalm 8 discusses the divine *name* in the universe (we will look at this psalm at the end of this chapter). In depicting various parts of creation joining in praise of God (verse 5), Psalm 148 proclaims that the divine *name* and *splendor* are over all heaven and earth (verse 13). This creation idea of the universe as the place of the divine name may compare with the presentation of the temple elsewhere understood as the place where God chooses the divine *name* to dwell (e.g., Deuteronomy 12:5, 11, 21, etc.).

Similarly, God's *light*, prominent in the account of creation in Psalm 104:2 quoted above, is also notable in temple contexts, such as Psalm 36. In describing an experience of God in the temple, Psalm 36:10 declares: "In your light we see light." In Psalm 27, divine *light* is an element of the temple experience linking human worshippers to their deity: verse 1 calls God "my light," and verses 4-7 describe the speaker's desire to be in God's temple.

Finally, the divine *word* informs creation. Psalm 33:6 states that God made the world by the divine *word*. In addition, divine teaching (see Psalms 1, 19, and 119) is a manifestation of the divine *word* (see Psalm 33:6).[22] All of these features[23]—divine name, word, holiness, and light—are expressive of the divine presence associated with the temple. In other words, creation is like a temple.[24] These signs of divine presence stand in contrast to the stress on power in the first model and on wisdom in the second model.[25]

The human response in the third model builds on the first. It includes giving proper service to God. People are to acknowledge God's characteristics in the world through praise (see Psalm 33, especially verses 1-2). In addition, the divine name is a source of trust for the upright (Psalm 33:21), but the wicked honor neither God nor the divine presence in the world. In a sense, it is the self-inflicted punishment of the wicked to remain outside the upright community, which recognizes the divine presence in the world. So in the third model, with the divine characteristics built into it, creation is God's temple. Within this "temple," the divine presence is at work. Outside of this "temple" are threats of cosmic waters (see Joel 3:3-9), which correspond to the potential threats of violence to humanity, especially from the wicked.

this is the best model

I hope that this discussion does not give the impression that the Bible delineates these three models neatly. On the contrary, they were used with a great deal of flexibility, and they can overlap even in a single passage. Different biblical authors could combine motifs from different models as it suited their purposes. For example, Psalm 104 basically uses the second model text with its emphasis on the wisdom of God's creation (verse 24), but it also mentions the image of the cosmic waters in verses 6-7, echoing the first model of power. It also mentions the divine light (verse 2) and the divine presence or "face" (verse 29), recalling the third model.[26]

progression of revelation

These three models show us three different ways for understanding God's relation to the world. In the first model, God is *powerful*, a warrior-king deserving of human devotion. In the second model, God is *wise*, deserving of human admiration and respect. In the third model, God is *present* in the world, deserving of human gratitude. In short, God has an unrivaled and wise agency in the world.

You may have noticed that the Bible does not use every available image for creation. For example, there is no model of an agricultural God who plants creation like a seed. We might think that such a model would seem particularly suitable for an agricultural society such as Israel. Yet the lack of such a model might suggest that Israel (like the rest of the ancient Near East) derived its models from leadership capacities. God is viewed as an active creator with powerful and wise agency. At the same time, what—or better, who—God is in the Bible is not reducible to the picture of this agency. God is still beyond these models. God remains mystery.

These three models of God also reveal three aspects of who the human person is to be. First, the human person is capable of agency in the world, a point that needs to be heard today in a time when people feel as if they have—or can have—little impact on the world around them. Second, the human person is capable of participating in the wisdom that the creator built into the world. Again, this is an important message to hear in the "culture of distraction"[27] from which we suffer in the United States, including "the illusion of wisdom"[28] offered by our colleges and universities. Third, the human person is potentially capable of channeling divine presence in the world. Again, this is an important message to hear despite what American culture sometimes conveys about the flatness of human purpose. In short, like the creator, the human creation has the potential for an unrivaled and wise agency in the world; and more, humanity has a potential for offering some measure of divine presence in the world. God has put within our very selves the basis and reason for our hope in God.   we are His Temple

What Does the Creation of Humans Say about God?

The Bible's pictures of the creation of humans also tell us about God. The Bible's creation texts describe aspects of the human person that were thought to come from God. So what are these aspects of the human person? Let's begin with an old version of human creation, one that Israel shared with other ancient Near Eastern cultures. According to Genesis 2:7, the human person, in part, is made from the dirt of the earth. This way of creation was fairly traditional in the ancient Near East (including ancient Israel), for example, in Job 33:6: "You and I are the same before God; I, too, was nipped from clay."[29] In Jeremiah 18:1-6, the prophet is commanded by God to go to the potter's house and see how he handles his clay, and to see how the potter reuses the clay when a pot does not work out. God says to the prophet: "Can I not deal with you like this potter? . . . Just like clay in the hands of the potter, so are you in my hands, O House of Israel!" The account of human creation in the Mesopotamian text known as Atrahasis includes clay from the ground.[30] In yet another text from Mesopotamia, the goddess "pinched off its clay" to create the king.[31] The dirt of the earth is the basic physical material of the human person.

The creation of the human person in Genesis 2:7 begins this way:

> The Lord God formed the human (*'adam*) with dust from the earth (*'adamah*). He blew into his nostrils the breath of life (*nishmat hayyim*) and the human became a living person (*nepesh hayyah*).[32]

The verse makes nice wordplay on the words "human" (*'adam*) and "earth" (*'adamah*), or as we might say, "human from humus" (dirt). If words mark reality in some manner, then these words mark us as mortals. This idea is in Genesis 3:19, echoed in what Christians hear on Ash Wednesday: "For dust you are, and to dust you shall return.

Genesis 2:7 then adds the rather human picture of God blowing the "breath of life" into this material. Divine creation of the human person here sounds like mouth-to-mouth resuscitation.[33] Then Genesis 2:7 states that this creation makes the human into "a living person." This is not a body-soul dichotomy, but a living body. We are living markers of God's own life force. Every breath *christ* we take is a sign of God's act of animating us. God is the living *in every* God, the God who fully embodies life and offers it as a divine gift. *living*

Psalm 104 makes this point more explicitly, with the word *ruah* ("life force," usually translated as "spirit") in verses 27-30:

> 27 All of them look to You,
>   To give them food in due season.
> 28 If You give to them, they gather,
>   Open Your hand, they are fully satisfied.

29   But hide Your face, they are terrified,
     Take away their spirit, they perish
     And turn again to dust.
30   If You send forth Your spirit, they are created,
     And You renew the face of the earth.[34]

The human person is created with *ruah*, and in this psalm it returns to God when people die. This *ruah* is in some sense integrally related to divinity. The fundamental life force of human beings (as opposed to their material selves, that return to dust) is somehow divine not only in its origins but also in its ultimate destiny. God gives *ruah*, and it ultimately returns to God.

Now let's turn to the creation of the human person in Genesis 1:26-28. If I ask most Christians how God made the human person, they don't think first of Genesis 2:7 but of Genesis 1:28, where God made the human person in his image and according to his likeness. The language of image and likeness gets away from the more human picture of God in Genesis 2 as the divine potter who adds his human-sounding breath to the molded dirt or clay. It is sometimes thought that the author of Genesis 1 didn't care much for the anthropomorphism of Genesis 2:7, and so this passage offers a vision of the human person that moves away from this overly human language for God. But what do "image" and "likeness" mean?

The word "image" tells us that we are patterned after God, but by implication we are not God. The second word, "likeness," tells us that we are analogous to God: we are like God, but again, we are not God. Both Genesis 1:26-28 and Genesis 2:7 suggest that humans are deeply related to God without being God. The only place outside of the Bible that uses the terms "image" and "likeness" together is an inscription found on a statue of a local governor in ancient Syria.[35] The statue is the image and likeness of this governor. It signals his presence, without being him literally. The author of Genesis 1 may be drawing on this notion of the statue in order to express the idea that human beings are

Spirit of the Lord is the candle of man

reminders of God and that <u>in their human responsibilities they</u>
<u>may stand in for God</u>. The difference would be that we are the
living reminders of the living God.

[margin note: dominion]

In context, Genesis 1:26-28 is surrounded by two other commands, which also tell us about the nature of the human person.
Human creation includes the divine wish for humans to rule over
the other creatures (verse 26). The narrative following human creation presents a divine blessing that the human person, male and
female, shall increase and multiply and rule over the creatures of
the earth (verse 28). So the human person seems to be like God in
being given dominion in the world like the divine warrior-king, and
also like the divine creator in being given the ability to procreate.
On earth, humanity stands in for God. In other words, <u>we are called</u>
<u>to do what God made us to do—and that is to be and act like God.</u>

Many people today do not like the idea of a <u>hierarchical</u> re- *?*
lationship of humans over creation in Genesis 1, but this creation account may also be read as the creation of <u>responsibility</u> for
people. To be like God is to reframe our questions about suffering
and evil in the world (which we will discuss in chapter 7). To be in
the image and likeness of God means to shift the issues from God
to ourselves. The question of how a good God could let bad things
happen becomes the question, "why didn't we and why don't we
stop these things from happening?" Many bad things happen that
are beyond our control, but many are of humanity's own making.
Genesis 1 may remind us that what happens in the world are things
we may <u>do to ourselves, that often we have ourselves to blame</u>. It
is often up to us to change the situation of our world.

What is our place in this world? Psalm 8:5 poses this very
question: "What is the human being that You remember her,[36] The
human that you are mindful of him?" The question basically asks:
Who are we? Echoing this verse, the cosmologist Paul Davies
ponders this question about humanity:

> Through science, we human beings are able to grasp at least
> some of nature's secrets. We have cracked part of the cosmic

code. Why this should be, just why *Homo sapiens* should carry the spark of rationality that provides the key to the universe, is a deep enigma. We, who are children of the universe—animated stardust—can nevertheless reflect on the nature of that same universe, even to the extent of glimpsing the rules on which it runs . . . . *What does it mean? What is Man that we might be party to such privilege?* I cannot believe that our existence in this universe is a mere quirk of fate, an accident of history, an incidental blip in the great cosmic drama. Our involvement is too intimate. The physical species Homo may count for nothing, but the existence of mind in some organism on some planet in the universe is surely a fact of fundamental significance. Through conscious being the universe has generated self-awareness. This can be no trivial detail, no minor by-product of mindless, purposeless facts. We are truly meant to be here.[37]

"Are we?" responds the neuroscientist V. S. Ramachandran. He adds: "I don't think brain science alone, despite all its triumphs, will ever answer that question. But that we can ask the question at all is, to me, the most puzzling aspect of our existence."[38]

That we can even pose this question is, for Psalm 8, something that links humanity to God. That we can ask such questions speaks to who we are. Furthermore, the speaker seems moved by God's "remembrance" of the human person and the elevation of humanity near to the ranks of the divinities or divine powers. The text is remarkable, as it shows how in this world the human person is a sign of the divine ruler and thus a reminder of how great God is in the universe. Like the moon reflecting the sun's light to the earth at night, humanity is a reflection, a sign, about God, shining back to humanity. In Psalm 8, the human person points back to God. The paradox of the human person as divine yet finite is in turn a signal of the mystery of God. We humans are often mysteries to ourselves.[39] How much more so is God![40] Understanding that we ourselves are paradoxes takes us to the very edge of the mystery of God.

❧ 6 ❧

Who—or What—Is the Satan?

Satan Today

We don't seem to hear as much about Satan or the devil as we used to. Yet for over two thousand years this figure has been central to religious thinking about evil. In traditional Christian thinking, Satan or the devil is always trying to get people to sin. He is the head of a vast army of hellish demons working to lead humans to their eternal damnation. According to the *Catechism of the Catholic Church*, Satan is in "The Lord's Prayer" (sometimes called the "Our Father"): "rescue us from the evil one" (Matthew 6:13, New Revised Standard Version). The *Catechism*[1] understands this not as evil in a general sense, but as "the Evil One," in other words, Satan.[2] At Easter Sunday Mass, each year, Catholics are asked: "Do you renounce Satan? And do you renounce all his works?" In the *New York Times*, Pope Francis was quoted as exhorting Catholic cardinals: "Let us not give in to pessimism, to that bitterness that the devil offers every day."[3]

In popular movies, the devil has been quite a trendy figure. He is usually played by men, such as Robert De Niro in *Angel Heart* (1987), Jack Nicholson in *The Witches of Eastwick* (1987), Al Pacino in *The Devil's Advocate* (1997), and Harvey Keitel in *Little Nicky* (2000), with Rodney Dangerfield as "Grandpa Lucifer." Timothy Dalton is reportedly scheduled to serve as the devil's voice in a movie in production, *Ivan the Fool* (2015), which is based on Leo Tolstoy's 1886 short story by the same name. The devil has been played occasionally by women, such as Elizabeth Hurley in *Bedazzled* (a remake of the 1967 British movie by the same name) and Rosalinda Celentano in *The Passion of the Christ* (2004). The child actor Harvey Steven was the devil in *The Omen* (1976).

Many religious people take Satan very seriously. For example, Warren W. Wiersbe, in his book *The Strategy of Satan* (1979), offers advice for spiritual combat against Satan's attacks. Other people seem to regard Satan as a projection of the worst of humanity.[4] Satan may often seem more like us than God does. There is a fascination with Satan, as John Milton evoked in his famous epic poem, *Paradise Lost*. In this great epic poem, Satan is not only evil, but he is also more engaging than the ideal figure of Christ. Satan is well known in the New Testament as well, for example, in the story of the temptation of Christ in the wilderness.[5]

It is often assumed that Satan is not really a Jewish idea. Instead, Jewish tradition classically attributes evil actions of humans to "the evil inclination" that human beings have. This idea too has biblical roots, for example, in Genesis 6:5.[6] Contrary to the notion that Satan isn't a Jewish idea, the oldest references to Satan or "satan" as a malevolent figure do not first appear in the New Testament or other Christian sources but in pre-Christian Jewish sources (see Wisdom of Solomon 2:24; see also the longer version of 2 Enoch 31, as well as the much later Babylonian Talmud Sota 9b and Sanhedrin 29a).

For many Christians, it is assumed that the snake in the Garden of Eden is Satan. The idea is noted in the *Catechism of the Catholic Church*, 98, which cites Romans 16:20 ("the God of peace will soon crush Satan under your feet"), itself an echo of Genesis 3:15. The identification of the snake in paradise as the devil is not just a Christian notion. It also appears in Jewish sources.[7] Overall, Christianity got the notion of Satan as the devil from Jewish tradition, and yet as a name it is missing from the Old Testament (Hebrew Bible). It seems that Satan became a proper name in Jewish tradition only in the centuries around the time of Jesus.[8] For example, Jewish works (such as the Assumption of Moses 10:1) refer to Satan's name.[9] If the ideas of Satan as the evil head of Hell and as the snake in Eden did not come from the Hebrew Bible, where did they come from? And if *satan* is not a name in the Hebrew Bible, when did it become the proper name Satan? To answer these questions, we will start with the name of Satan in the New Testament and in the Jewish literature of the period. We will then work back to the evidence for the title, "the satan," in the Hebrew Bible.[10]

The Satan in the New Testament and Jewish Literature of the Period

Jewish literature from around the time of the New Testament mostly uses "the satan" as a title and not a name.[11] For example, the Jewish work known as the Book of Jubilees (10:11), dated by scholars to the second century BCE, mentions "the satan" at the time of Noah: "All of the evil ones, who were cruel, we bound in the place of judgment, but a tenth of them we let remain so that they might be subject to the satan on earth."[12] In this context, the satan is a demonic "adversary," which is the basic meaning of the word.[13] However, this figure has little identity of his own.[14] In 1 Enoch 40:7, the plural "satans" is a general term for demons that "accuse those who dwell on the earth."[15] As these passages show, the noun *satan* could be used in the singular or in the plural to denote demonic force(s).

In the Dead Sea Scrolls, the word *satan* likewise refers to a malevolent force,[16] but not to a particular demon, much less an important one.[17] The beautiful "Plea for Deliverance" in the great Psalms Scroll (found in Cave 11) asks God: "let not a satan have power over me, nor an unclean spirit."[18] This prayer sounds like

94   *How Human Is God?*

the formulation of the "Our Father" that we noted earlier, "deliver
us from the evil one" (Matthew 6:13). However, unlike the Plea
for Deliverance, the "Our Father" seems to have a major demonic
figure in mind. The Plea for Deliverance adds here a further request about "an evil inclination": "let pain and an evil inclination
not have control over me."[19] These requests ask for help "from
all evil that may afflict his person, physical and mental, external
'satan' and internal 'inclination.'"[20] "This prayer," writes Miryam
Brand, "presents a complex view of sin in which internal and
external sources of sin combine to cause iniquity."[21]

others in darkness

When we get to the New Testament, the picture is more dramatic, with the word satan appearing thirty-five times.[22] Satan, or
more specifically, Satanas, is an Aramaic form of the word that
survives in the New Testament Greek. By contrast, "the devil" is
good Greek (*diabolos*); it is also the basis for the English word
"diabolical." Generally, unlike Hebrew, Greek can use the definite article for a name. So "the satan" in the New Testament is
generally understood to be the name, Satan. Many readers of the
New Testament are familiar with Jesus' command to Peter: "Get
behind me, Satan!" (Matthew 16:23). This verse illustrates the
proverbial idea of Satan as a tempter, a role particularly famous
in the temptation of Jesus.[23] In the story, this adversarial figure
is called "the devil" (Matthew 4:1, 5, 8, 11; Luke 4:2), "(the)
Satan" (Mark 1:13), or "Satan" (without a definite article, in
Matthew 4:9).[24] In Matthew and Luke, this demonic figure holds
power over "all the kingdoms of the world" (Matthew 4:8; Luke
4:5). These kingdoms are his to give and he is their ruler. Satan
is also called "the tempter" (Matthew 4:3; see also Matthew 4:1
and Luke 4:2). In rebuking him, Jesus cites the Scripture about
tempting in Deuteronomy 6:16: "You shall not tempt the Lord
your God" (Matthew 4:7; Luke 4:12).[25]

bicameral alienated mind

Satan's hold over humans is acknowledged by Jesus when
he heals a woman on the Sabbath (Luke 13:16). The spirit that
is cast out of the woman is "a spirit of infirmity."[26] The problems

associated with evil spirits are not limited to the moral, social, or political spheres. The evil represented by Satan can have a palpable physical dimension. Satan[27] can enter a person, for example, Judas (Luke 22:3; John 13:27).

The mention of Satan in Luke 10:18 is quite special. In this verse, Jesus says: "I watched Satan fall from heaven like a flash of lightning." This passage shows Luke's optimistic view of victory over Satan (perhaps even the beginning of a post-apocalyptic perspective in the Christian canon). The view here is fairly unique to this gospel. By comparison, as we will see below, the book of Revelation is quite future oriented.

I add one final reference from the gospels. John contains a reference to "the devil," which shows how the Bible uses the idea of Satan or the devil with catastrophic consequences. John 8:44 literally demonizes Jews who do not accept Jesus. The verse is part of a speech of Jesus in which he argues against his Jewish interlocutors who tell him, "God is our father" (John 8:39; see also verse 41). Responding to their rejection of him, Jesus is presented as telling them: "You are from your father the devil, and you choose to do your father's desires. He was a murderer from the beginning and does not stand in the truth, because there is no truth in him."[28] While this passage does not refer to Satan, it was assumed later to refer to Satan as the father of Jews. Worse, Christians—including Catholic clergy—historically used this verse to condemn Jews.[29] While some Christians may wish to defend the Bible by suggesting that such a notion appears only very rarely in the Bible[30] or that John 8:44 really isn't anti-Jewish,[31] the fact of the matter is that it is there, and it has played a major role in Christians justifying terrible acts against others in direct contradiction to Christian ideals.

The earliest reference to Satan in the New Testament is in its oldest book, 1 Thessalonians: "and so we wanted to come to you—I, Paul, once and again—but Satan blocked our way" (2:18). This reference to Satan sounds like the angel acting as a satan in Numbers 22:23 who, as we will see, blocks the way of the prophet, Balaam. In this New Testament passage, this power is much more extensive in scope. Paul reflects a perspective permeating much of the New Testament: cosmic evil is present in the day-to-day existence of believers, as well as the world at large (see also 2 Thessalonians 2:9-10).

At the end of the New Testament, in Revelation 12:9 (see also 20:1-3), we stand closer to the picture of the cosmic power of Satan represented in later Christian tradition: "The great dragon was thrown down, that ancient serpent, who is called the Devil and Satan, the deceiver of the whole world—he was thrown down to the earth, and his angels were thrown down with him." In Revelation 12:10 this figure is also characterized as an accuser: "for the accuser of our comrades has been thrown down, who accuses them day and night before our God." This verse echoes the old role of the satan as the heavenly accuser that we will see in Zechariah 3. Here the Devil and the Satan are identified with one another and also with "that ancient serpent" that is the old cosmic enemy of God in the Hebrew Bible (see Psalm 74:12-17).[32] In the New Testament, we still do not have the idea of Satan as the demonic head of Hell. Instead, the underworld is the place where Satan is to be imprisoned (see also Luke 10:18).[33]

Some scholars explain Satan and demons from a psychological or social perspective. For one scholar of Satan, Henry Ansgar Kelly, the demonic is identified in the Dead Sea Scrolls with internal psychological tendencies.[34] According to another, the eminent scholar Elaine Pagels, Satan is a way to think and argue about inner-Jewish communal conflict.[35] No doubt, psychological and social approaches help us understand Satan and other demonic forces better: these influence social life and communal perception, a point that I will return to. Yet, the issue is not only a matter of social conflict: for many New Testament writers, a person who impedes Jesus' mission in the world may be under Satan's power, and satanic power extends over much of the world. It also is important to note how the evil represented by these powers was experienced. It was not only psychological or social. It was felt as a physical power in the world as well, manifest through other people, even in their bodies. It was perceived to be cosmic in scope. To remember that evil powers were thought to be powerful throughout the world helps to us to understand Satan in the world at the time of Jesus. This raises questions about thinking about Satan today, which we will take up after we look at the satan in the Hebrew Bible.

[handwritten margin note: as a man thinks in his heart so is he]

The Biblical Prehistory of "the Satan"

The Hebrew Bible uses the word *satan* a number of times,[36] but it does not yet refer to the devil. This satan is neither a figure of evil nor the head of Hell, nor the head of demonic powers. So who—or what—is the satan in the Hebrew Bible? In what seems to be its earliest uses of the word *satan* in the Hebrew Bible, it is a common noun that refers to a human opponent or adversary,[37] but not an evil spirit. In 1 Samuel 29, the Philistine commanders reject David's help in battle against Saul, because they fear that he may be loyal to him (verse 4): "he should not go down with us to battle, or else he may become an opponent (*satan*) to us in the battle."[38] In 1 Kings 5, Solomon declares that God has given him rest, that "there is neither opponent (*satan*) nor misfortune" (verse 4 in many English translations, verse 18 in the Hebrew). Here *satan* is a common noun referring to potential human opposition, while "misfortune" refers to nonhuman problems (see also 1 Kings 11; 2 Samuel 19:23).[39]

The word *satan* is used for a human, legal opponent in Psalm 109:6: "let an accuser (*satan*) stand on his right." This may reflect the position of an accuser in a courtroom setting.[40] Earlier, verse 4 refers to enemies with a related word: "they accuse me" (**stn*). The speaker seems to draw on the idea of false accusers in court to describe his problems with social opponents who speak against him.[41]

[handwritten note: temple officials – Satan Anti-Christ]

There are a number of biblical passages involving a divine figure called *satan*, but this is still not Satan or the devil. The first time a divine figure is called *satan* in the Bible is in the story of the prophet Balaam in Numbers 22. God has sent an angel to block the way of Balaam riding on his donkey. Verse 22 explains why: "God's anger was kindled because he was going, and the angel of the LORD took his stand in the road as his adversary (*satan*)." The angel is a divine agent carrying out God's anger against Balaam. The donkey can see the angel, but ironically, the great prophet Balaam cannot. Eventually God uncovers Balaam's eyes, and he sees the angel, who says: "I have come out as an adversary (*satan*), because your way is perverse before me" (verse 32). There is no Satan or devil here, but an angel acting on God's orders. In verse 34, Balaam responds to this angel: "I have sinned, for I did not know that you were standing in the road to oppose me." Here the phrase "to oppose me" illustrates what it means to be a *satan*, an "adversary" or "opponent."[42] In some respects, the angel in Numbers 22 sounds a bit like the heavenly satan in the passages that come up in the next section.

The Early History of the Heavenly Satan in Later Books of the Hebrew Bible

When we turn to later biblical texts, we see the beginning of the supernatural use of the word *satan*. Unlike Numbers 22, these texts do not use *satan* simply as a common noun for "adversary" or the like. Instead, it is a title or name for one of God's heavenly angels. According to 1 Chronicles 21:1, "Satan (or a satan) stood up against Israel, and incited David to count the people of Israel."[43] This passage explains the reason why David takes a census: it is a negative act taken under "satanic" instigation. Readers are not told why this divine figure does this, only that he does so. There is no definite article "the" before the noun, and so it could be a name, "Satan," but it could also be an indefinite noun, "a satan," as we saw in the Dead Sea Scrolls passages.[44] We can get a bit more insight into this passage by comparing the same story as it appears in 2 Samuel 24. In verse 1 of this chapter, it says: "Again the anger of the LORD was kindled against Israel, and he incited David against them." Here "the anger of the LORD" corresponds directly to "Satan" in 1 Chronicles 21:1. In other words, the divine anger in 2 Samuel 24:1 is replaced by Satan in 1 Chronicles 21:1.[45] Some scholars believe that this substitution was made so that God wouldn't seem malevolent.[46] *[handwritten: # or to bolster David's reputation]*

Still, what are we to make of Satan in 1 Chronicles 21:1? We may be tempted to think of Satan/a satan here as a personification of evil,[47] but this doesn't seem right when we look at God's anger in 2 Samuel 24:1 compared with 1 Chronicles 21:1. Evil is not what this passage is about. We may also recall from Numbers 22:22 that God was angry at Balaam, and it is for that reason that the angel is his "opponent." In this story, God's anger sets the angel into motion as Balaam's adversary; so in Numbers 22 there seems to be a *cause and effect relationship* between the divine anger and the angel acting as a satan. By comparison, Satan in 1 Chronicles 21:1 seems to *substitute* for God's anger (as found in 2 Samuel 24:1).[48] In both contexts, the divine opponent represents God's warrior fierceness or anger against human figures[49] (an idea we looked at in chapter 3). This connection between divine anger and the satan adds a new dimension that we do not see with satan as a human adversary. The satan as an embodiment of divine anger may be viewed as an attempt to rationalize divine anger.[50] Satan as divine anger might sound like the Satan of Hell as known in later tradition, but we should be careful: this Satan in 1 Chronicles 21 does not live in Hell. This is clear from the next two passages that we will examine. *[handwritten margin note: Wink Daniel]*

In the book of Zechariah, an angel shows the prophet a vision in chapter 3.[51] The high priest Joshua is standing before the angel of the Lord, and the satan is standing to Joshua's right in order to accuse Joshua (verse 1).[52] We don't get to hear the

the law, Adamic mind

accusation from the satan's lips, but according to verse 2, God re-
bukes him, rejecting whatever the accusation was against Joshua.
Several facts emerge from these verses. First, this scene takes
place in heaven. Second, the satan appears in this chapter with
the definite article "the." So the satan is not a proper name but
a title. Third, the title denotes his role here. As we saw earlier
with Psalm 109, the role that the satan plays here is a legal one:
standing at the right side to accuse Joshua. In modern terms, the
satan seems to function like a prosecuting attorney; in ancient
terms, he is an accuser in court, as we saw above with the same
word in Psalm 109.[53]

function

non-judgement of Joshua

After the Lord's rebuke of the satan, the angel orders the
heavenly attendants to replace Joshua's "filthy clothes" with
"festal apparel," including "a clean turban" (verses 4-5).[54] Perhaps the "filthy clothes" allude to the nature of the satan's accusation, namely that the high priest and perhaps the Israelites
more generally stand in a state of defilement.[55] In verse 4, this
scene mentions heavenly figures, "those standing before him"
(or as the New Jewish Publication Society Version translates it,
"his attendants"), the same figures who obey the angel's command (verse 5). Overall, we seem to have a heavenly courtroom
scene, with an accuser on the right side and God presiding as the
judge along with some other angelic figures. Within this scheme
of things, the satan plays an adversarial role within the heavenly
realm. He is not evil, and he is not the devil; he works for God
in the heavenly court.[56]   *the law! / Rom 8:28*

mind

Job 1–2 also describes the satan in the heavenly court.[57] Two
heavenly judgment scenes (Job 1:6-12 and 2:1-6) are parallel to
the earthly testing scenes (1:13-22 and 2:7-10). These are framed
by the earthly descriptions of Job's initial pious life (1:1-5) and
his life under divine judgment afterwards (2:11-13).[58] The story's
opening circumstances on earth are familiar to many readers:
"There was once a man in the land of Uz whose name was Job"
(verse 1). Job is said to be the greatest of the people of the East—

and not an Israelite (verse 3). He is "blameless and upright, one who feared God and turned away from evil." He is also abundantly blessed with children, livestock, and servants. He is so pious that he would make offerings to God just in case his children sinned (1:2-5).[59]

The scene shifts from earth to heaven in verse 6 when "the heavenly beings" come before the Lord,[60] and the satan comes among them. It seems that the satan is regarded here as one of the heavenly beings in 1:6 and 2:1 (cf. Job 38:7), a rather traditional usage known elsewhere (Psalms 29:2 and 89:7). A dialogue ensues between the Lord and the satan (verses 7-12). The Lord asks the satan where he's come from, and he answers: "From going to and fro on the earth, and from walking up and down on it" (cf. Zechariah 1:10; 4:10; 6:7). These minor divinities move between heaven and earth. Their job may echo the function of Persian officials who investigated matters for the king;[61] it might also echo the older expression for God going down to see how humans have acted (Genesis 11:5-7).[62] God asks the satan if he has seen his blameless servant Job. At this point the satan accuses Job of fearing God just to receive God's blessing. To test this premise, God allows the satan to take all that Job has. Once God's blessing ceases, will Job's piety likewise cease?

In Job 1:13, the scene shifts from heaven back to earth. Job learns of the disaster that has happened to his oxen, donkeys, and servants at the hands of people called Sabeans (verses 14-15). Then it is reported to Job that "the fire of God fell from heaven and burned up the sheep and the servants" (verse 16).[63] Job is subsequently informed that the Chaldeans raided his camels and killed his servants (verse 17). Finally, he is told that his eldest son's house collapsed on top of his children due to a great wind, killing all his children (verses 18-19).[64] Because of these events, Job goes into mourning and blesses God (verses 20-21) rather than "curse" God as the satan had predicted (verse 11). Job acknowledges these events as divine acts (perhaps even as omens[65]): "the LORD gave, and the LORD has taken away; blessed be the name of the LORD." "In all this," we are told in verse 22, "Job did not sin or charge God with wrongdoing." Job may seem cursed rather than blessed by God, but he imputes no bad to God.

The scene shifts back to heaven with the heavenly beings and the satan before the Lord in 2:1; this parallels the heavenly scene back in 1:6. The dialogue (2:2-3) once again begins with the Lord asking where the satan has been and if he has seen his blameless servant Job, just as in 1:6-7. The satan reiterates his claim that Job's piety would disappear, but this time if Job himself were the object of attack. The satan, quite like Job's three friends later, questions Job's piety. In response, God allows the satan to afflict Job's body (2:4-6).

The scene shifts once more from heaven to earth, with the satan inflicting sores all over Job's body, which he painfully scratches with a potsherd (2:7-8). Job's wife questions his devotion, and she further suggests, perhaps sarcastically, that he bless[66] God (2:9). He responds with the piety that he should accept the bad as well as the good (from God) (2:10). The section closes: "In all this Job did not sin with his lips."

What is the purpose of this prologue of Job 1–2? According to Alan Cooper,[67] it serves to voice three possibilities about divine will and human behavior, and reward and punishment. First, the satan embodies the view that there is predictable causality between positive human behavior and divine reward. He argues to God that Job is pious only because of the prosperity that he receives from God. The satan's actions anticipate the role of the friends when they suggest that negative human behavior on Job's part must have caused divine punishment. Second, the perspective voiced by Job is that there is causality, but no predictable reason for his terrible situation. In other words, God is the cause of calamity, but the reason is not clear. Third, God endorses neither view. God does not agree with the satan's reasoning, nor does God endorse Job's view. As this is a heavenly test of Job's piety, the disasters that he suffers are not caused by sin, nor are they predictable. Neither divine causality nor predictability is discernible on God's part; God is not reducible to such choices. We will return to this point later.

man-centered

After this point in Job 2, we never hear of the satan again. Job's three friends come to comfort him (2:11-13). After Job's own lament (chapter 3), they probe the meaning of his circumstances along traditional lines. The poetic speeches of the three friends and Job (chapters 4–31), followed by the accusatory speeches of Elihu (chapters 32–37), agree broadly on the terms of the problem as expressed by the satan: disaster that happens *consequences* to human beings is divine punishment because of their sin. While Job agrees with the relationship between disaster and divine punishment, he has not sinned and so he does not believe that divine punishment should apply to him.

The book ends with the two parallel dialogues between God and Job. God offers two answers to Job (38:1–40:3 and 40:6–41:34), each beginning with God appearing in a whirlwind (Job 38:1; 40:6). The whirlwind for a divine appearance is unusual. God usually appears in divine glory often associated with a rainstorm (see Psalm 29),[68] as expected of a beneficial deity providing rain for life.[69] The manner of God's appearance at the end of Job hints that this God operates beyond the system where human piety gains divine blessing and human sin issues in divine punishment. With different reasons given in the speeches of Job and others for his situation, God remains beyond human reasoning about God.[70] In the end, Job does not ask for a legal judgment between God and himself, as he had demanded in the dialogues with the friends. Instead, Job realizes the gulf between what he now sees and what he had heard before (42:5); this is the gulf between the divine and the human. This does not mean his combative position throughout the book was in vain; on the contrary! Job's persistent questioning about what he does not know of God (42:3) is now affirmed by God (42:7).[71]

In the end, human systems, calculations, or reasoning cannot box in God. Job does not get to fathom God's nature and intentions, or the reason for his suffering. Still God responds to Job, and Job hears from God about the divine wisdom imprinted on cosmic creation.[72] This experience not only shows Job that, fundamentally, he does not know everything, but also that this is a fundamental part of the human condition—a condition he can now accept. The book's exploration of these themes is difficult, which in turn suggests that God is even more difficult to understand.

The Meaning of the satan in Zechariah and Job

The divine dialogues in Zechariah 3 and Job 1–2 dramatize a divine debate or perhaps a divine paradox. The satan is a legal official, perhaps one that investigates the claims of the accused,[73] while God stands as the judge. The heavenly council, with both God and the satan present, seems to give multiple voices within the Godhead as a whole. Do these two figures in the divine council give voice to two perspectives on human nature, with the satan attributing Job's piety to his prosperity and with God withholding judgment on this score?[74] The traditional idea of God and other divine figures interacting in the heavenly council offered a religious or theological opportunity to explore the apparently conflicting and perhaps conflicted sense that people may have about divine agency in the world. In offering these two divine voices with their ambiguity for interpretation, the divine council scene is less about the reality of God and the satan as such, and more about the paradox and perhaps "the complete obscurity"[75] of human understanding of the divine realm.

Let me unpack this situation a bit. Post-exilic Israel became monotheistic in terms of the God over all, but at the same time the divine world did not become less complex but more. The great scholar Frank Moore Cross once compared the world of divinity in the Old Testament with the New Testament's in these terms: "When you come to the New Testament, you can't even swing a cat without hitting three demons and two spirits."[76] The multitudes of demons and spirits in the Persian period[77] and later periods all stand under the One God,[78] in what has been called Job's monotheism[79] (sometimes labeled the book's "practical monotheism"[80]). Scenes of the divine council serve as a vehicle for addressing issues as they arose for Israel. Zechariah 3 is explicit about the human issue at hand, namely the figure of the priest and his impurity. Job 1–2 names an issue as well: Job's reverence for God. In both instances, the divine council scene reinforces the picture of the One head god who has ultimate authority and control over all. The divine council is a way to signal the complexity of how the Godhead relates to humanity; it is not really to explain who God is.[81] This is signaled by the fact that the divine council scenes in Job 1–2 are not deep but actually banal in the information that they provide about God. Their real purpose is to provide readers with information that Job does not have so that readers can see the vast difference between what God knows and does on the one hand, and on the other hand, what humans know about God and God's doings.

The divine council in Job 1–2 has an additional purpose. The "sons of God" and the satan "among them" (Job 1:6; 2:1) differ from what we see in Zechariah 3 or 1 Kings 22. In these texts, the lesser divinities are a "standing" staff. However, in Job 1–2, the role of the "sons of God" takes them from God in heaven to earth and back again. They are all about the circuit they travel between heaven and earth. We should also be aware of the wordplay of the title "the satan" with the verb, *shût*,[82] as one who "goes about." So this figure performs one role with respect to humans in going about in the world, and another role in debating with God. The issue in Job 1–2 then is not simply about what happens in heaven among the figures in the divine council but about the circuit traveled between heaven and earth—and what gets lost on the way. In other words, Job 1–2 depicts the slippage in perspective between heaven and earth. There are two levels about what the divine entails with respect to human beings, namely divine perception known only in heaven, and human perception experienced only on earth. Job has not, as Job 15:8 makes the point, "listened in the council of God." And what humans perceive and what the satan thinks are not the same as what God does: God sanctions, even authorizes, what the satan does,[83] but God does not assume the worst of people.

Job's problems come from the satan, but this satan operates by the authority of God. God is the ultimate cause of Job's suffering. Job 1–2 also suggests a more basic fact that while God authorizes that side of divinity, God is not reducible to that side of divinity. When it comes to God, it's hardly the whole story; and more, we do not get to know the whole story. While good and evil ultimately are to be traced to God, this can be messy for people to understand on the human level. There is no final answer; it remains a mystery, which in turn calls us to be our best selves, and we should do so without expectations of divine blessing. Contrary to what we hear from some preachers in the United States, there is not necessarily a divine "payback" for good actions. Sometimes we are blessed and we should thank God, but if we experience tragedies that are not of our doing, we are not to blame God or think we are cursed by God. When you boil the whole problem down, it is the capacity to be and do good that is a divine blessing.

So What Are We to Do Theologically with Satan and the satan?

What are we to think about all this information about the satan from the Old Testament and Satan in New Testament, not to mention the satan in the Dead Sea Scrolls and other Jewish sources? In our contemporary context, it would not be hard to dump this idea (or complex of ideas) on the ash heap of outmoded and outdated superstitions, right along with demons. Why not? After all, in the ancient world demonic forces constitute the sources of what are understood today as physical or psychological problems.[84] We do not consult specialists for magical spells.

It seems to me, however, that the issue is more complicated. On the one hand, in the New Testament the demonic was experienced not only in social and political terms but also in psychological and physical terms. It was understood as a power that permeated much of the world. This makes for a real challenge regarding how we should think about demonic evil today. If we explain away the demonic as merely social or psychological problems, then we may lose something of the sensibility, even the palpable feeling, of malevolence expressed in the New Testament. On the other hand, mythic or cosmic ways of talking about demonic evil pose the opposite risk of creating a superstitious attitude toward evil and the devil. This can be dangerous for how people act in the world. If the world is considered to be under the control of demonic power, might this lead us to disregard it as our responsibility? New Testament writers would see it as our responsibility to resist; we can't surrender responsibility in the face of evil. And there is a greater danger for Christians as well. As we noted in our earlier discussion of John 8:44, demonization applied to other people, in particular to Jews, has led to terrible sins on the part of Christians. So the Christian use of Satan or the devil is our responsibility. Christians are called to serve God in service to humanity and to work against the demonization of others. So there are dangers in either extreme.

There is something in the way people operate in societies that can show palpable malevolence. Human abuse and manipulation of social, political, and economic systems infect people across these systems of life. Sometimes in individuals or groups, there is evil or hatred so strong that it seems to dictate people's actions. In the New Testament, Satan expresses this experience of the demonic in people. On the other hand, it is difficult to agree to a superstitious view blaming supernatural forces for the problems in the world. We have free will and we are called to exercise it for good. As we saw, even the satan works for God in Job 1–2 as well as Zechariah 3. So what is the question for us about Satan today?

To put this question in perspective, we should remember that in the Bible, Satan himself is a moving target, hardly the same thing in the Old and New Testaments. In the Hebrew Bible, he is not an agent of evil. In fact, as we saw, Satan is not even Satan in the Hebrew Bible but really "the satan" or "a satan." He is also a fairly minor character. As God's employee, the satan can help us think about the mystery of God's relationship to humanity. In the New Testament, Satan is an instrument of testing, more malevolent than what we see in the Hebrew Bible. In the New Testament, Satan is also the ruler over much, if not most, of this world, perhaps reflecting the awful control that the Romans seemed to hold over the world at the time.[85] But that empire is this world, not the next world of Hell. In the Old Testament the satan is not the problem but points to the problem: namely, our own human behavior and limited thinking, while in the New Testament Satan is the problem of our world. It's our world—and ourselves—that constitute the problem of malevolence. Satan may be a way of saying that this evil in the world is greater than any one of us and that we need to recognize our failures. The sense of our failures as sins should remind us not simply that we fail but that we are moral beings who have failed before other people, with negative impact on them.[86] When we recognize our failures as sins, we are also reminding ourselves that we remain linked to God.

We Christians need to focus not on a demonic Satan but on our own evil, manifest in all the complex ways we act in the webs of the world's systems. (We often don't even realize how deep our involvements are.) We are all participants in the great complexity of human interactions (political, social, economic), which are having terrible, evil effects on ourselves and on the physical condition of our world. In a real way, we are killing ourselves as well as our world. We have agency in the world, and FB ! we need to exercise this agency despite the dulling effects of our routines and environments. In our words and deeds, we need to express our deepest love and to act with the greatest imagination for the world. That will take care of Satan, and it will also help to take care of the world. It will also help us sense God.

Why Do People Suffer According to the Hebrew Bible?

The Problem of Suffering and the Bible

T he question for this chapter is perhaps the most basic one in all of human existence. The problem of innocent people suffering is often on people's minds and hearts, and books on the subject get a wide hearing. To take but one example, we have the well-known book by Harold Kushner, *When Bad Things Happen to Good People*.[1] The problem of suffering can be overwhelming. The desire to understand why innocent people suffer terrible calamities can gnaw at people's hearts. When people suffer for no good reason, it can be unbearable. In Kushner's case, the death of his son at age fourteen led him to write his book. The loss of such a child leaves a hole in a parent's heart, one that may never heal. The death of a parent leaves a child deeply alone, perhaps for life. Suffering due to a terrible tragedy can be deeply wounding; this suffering is the tragedy played out a second time, and it can kill the human heart. Some of us want to know why our elderly have to suffer so much as they move through their final years (Ecclesiastes 12:1-8). Whether in the wake of a tragic event or because of physical suffering, people can feel terribly alone ("The heart knows its own bitterness," Proverbs 14:10). Theologians,[2] as well as biblical scholars,[3] have struggled with the problem of human suffering. Why does God let these things happen to the innocent or the righteous? In a world created by a good God, how can there be such evil and suffering?

As we enter into this terrible topic, it is important to empha- size that the Bible is not a book of answers to life's problems.[4] The Bible is a book that raises fundamental questions of life and reality. The Hebrew Bible is the record of Israel's great voices debating and discussing the basic issues concerning God, Israel, and the world. The New Testament writers continued this im- portant discussion in light of their transformative experience of Jesus. When we study the Bible, we get to join this discussion and debate; we get to continue the conversation that the bibli- cal authors began. The Israelites wrote the Hebrew Bible amid their struggles to understand God. We draw on the Bible to try to understand God as well. With this in mind, let's turn to what the Bible says about suffering.

Suffering as a Result of Sin

Many passages in the Bible affirm that people who sin suf- fer and that people who don't sin do not perish. We therefore might think that when bad things happen to us, it may be divine punishment. When violence happens to us or to our loved ones, our homes are seriously damaged or destroyed, or we suffer real financial loss, we may go in a tailspin. We want to know, why do these things happen to us? Sometimes we have played some role in the situation, and we don't realize it. But sometimes we have done nothing wrong, yet we still experience trauma.

In the Bible, suffering is commonly understood as divine punishment for sin.[5] Yet we also need to understand that the Bible does not always regard bad things happening to people as pun- ishment from God. As we saw in the preceding chapter, several biblical texts (most especially the book of Job) do not connect human suffering and divine punishment. As we observed, the satan represents people's sense that disaster can occur as a result of divine punishment, while God stands above and resists this causal relationship. Together the two figures illustrate the problem of interpreting disaster as divine punishment. At the end of the book of Job, God affirms Job, not the three friends and not the satan who disappears after chapter 2 of the book. And who would you rather believe, the satan or God?

Just as suffering is not always a sign of punishment, prospering is not always a sign of divine approval. In the Bible the wicked sometimes prosper, and so the correlation between human sin and divine punishment does not always work. Jeremiah 12:1 asks: "Why does the way of the wicked prosper? Why do all who are treacherous thrive?" The answer given in Psalm 73 and Job 20 is that disaster awaits the wicked. Psalm 73 hints at an unspecified, ultimate reward for the righteous, one that for some commentators is suggestive of an afterlife with God: "afterward you will take me with honor."[6] While such ideas may have been floating around at the time,[7] it is not clear that this is what the psalm has in mind. Christians may like the idea of the afterlife as an "explanation," but it is not really an explanation for suffering in the first place. Job 21 (especially verses 22-26) refutes the view of the ultimate punishment of the wicked.

So the biblical writers did not so much answer the question of who suffers and why—they debated it. Even within the book of Job there are multiple views, as we have seen. In the end, there is often no clear system of people receiving reward for good behavior and getting punished for bad behavior definitively offered in the Bible. Instead, people may experience bad despite their good behavior. And while good people experiencing terrible suffering may eventually be helped by God, this hardly clears up the problem of suffering in the first place.

So what can we take away from biblical descriptions of divine wrath? They suggest the need for our careful discernment and confession about our own behavior. We are supposed to know how we hurt other people, but sometimes we do not see it. We can sometimes live inside our own bubbles. Sure, we think of ourselves as basically good people, but we often don't see how our actions have an impact on others. Sometimes we don't see how our inactions have hurt people around us, or how they have diminished our communities, or perhaps how they have even damaged our world. A process of discernment and prayer may help us to come to understand that when such things do happen, we can sense properly whether or not we are guilty.

Discernment is important. When God's anger seems relentless to us, we need to ask if our poor actions or inactions have stopped or not. The Bible seems to understand the relentless divine action taken against people as corresponding in some cases to the relentlessness of human inaction.[8] Yet once we have made a proper discernment, we should neither second-guess ourselves too much nor mercilessly blame ourselves. If we have worked at discerning our own sin, asked sincerely for mercy, and made proper amends, it would be superstitious to continue blaming ourselves. We can't attribute to God things that we are not sure of, and that may include our suffering; blaming God is unfair to God. And for a healthy life, we need not only to be discerning. In a real relationship, two people cut each other some slack. God cuts us slack; we need to do the same for God.

National Disaster as Punishment for Sin

One of the most common presentations of divine punishment in the Hebrew Bible involves Israel's enemies.[9] In chapter 3, we explored the relationship between divine anger and Israel's national disasters at the hands of its enemies. We saw how Israel suffered sometimes because of its violation of the covenant. In chapter 3, I suggested that there seemed to be a relationship between the intensity of Israel's national troubles and the intense, biblical expressions of divine anger. Deuteronomy, Jeremiah, Lamentations, and Ezekiel occur in the time of Israel's oppression at the hands of the Assyrians and Babylonians—invasions, executions, sieges, and enslavement. In these biblical books, the depth of Israel's pain and suffering inflicted by its human enemies seems to correspond to the depth of divine anger directed against Israel. It is as if the intensity of God's anger in these biblical works and their expression of how bad things have gone for Israel are two sides of the same coin.[10] What we see are Israel's profound efforts to fathom its historical tragedy and to face it as its national and religious problem. These great works of the Bible represent Israel's efforts at facing up to its failures so that God and Israel can face each other again. We too need to face up to our failures.

Even within these biblical books that probe human short-comings and divine punishment, we should be aware that they do not offer a one-sided or straightforward answer to a theoretical problem. Instead, within the same book we hear a variety of comments on suffering. As we noted in chapter 3, Jeremiah offers a probing examination of divine and human pain, not a simple explanation. The book of Lamentations cites divine punishment as the reason for Jerusalem's foreign conquest and destruction, yet other notes are heard. Lamentations 1 mentions Jerusalem's divine punishment (1:5, 14, 18, 21-22), but the larger context is a lament focused on its suffering, perhaps even its victimhood.[11] "Beyond chapter 1," Elizabeth Boase suggests, "the reference to sin being causal in the destruction becomes less frequent and more ambivalent."[12] It is the depth of the pain being expressed that overwhelms the rational explanation of its cause. Overall, we need to be sensitive to how the book presents the idea of divine punishment. In Lamentations, it is part of an emotional process to find a path back to God.

What we often don't see is that the case made for divine punishment is also connected to a case being made for God's help. Israel continues its covenantal attachment to God in the face of divine punishment, and God helps Israel in the face of its human inadequacy. Despite evidence suggesting that they should call it quits, both Israel and God hold on to their relationship. We need to do the same. Here we stand at the threshold of the mysterious process of how we move from divine punishment to divine help. Fathoming divine forgiveness in our lives, if we take it seriously, may require greater love for God, and that may mean more patience with ourselves as well as God.

International Disaster: The Coming of the Apocalypse

Suffering in the world is sometimes explained as a sign of the end of the world (the "end-times").[13] In this view, God has allowed evil forces of the world to reign free. Ultimately, God will triumph over evil, but in the meantime, until the final divine victory takes place, evil rules the world.[14] This view of the world is appealing to many Christians in the United States today.

The apocalyptic atmosphere of the Gospel of Mark and 1 Thessalonians 4:14-17, as well as several New Testament passages, suggests that Christians consider this apocalyptic explanation. Paul warns the church in Thessaloniki: "we beg you, brothers and sisters, not to be quickly shaken in mind or alarmed . . . to the effect that the day of the Lord is already here" (2 Thessalonians 2:2). In the Bible, one book in each testament has an apocalypse (Daniel and Revelation—actually, Daniel contains four, in chapters 7, 8, 9, and 10–12). So we might think that the apocalyptic idea of evil and suffering in the world has good scriptural support. At the same time, an apocalyptic worldview is not particularly common in the Old Testament overall.[15]

It is usually overlooked that this apocalyptic worldview seems to be especially operative in the Bible when great empires are operative (as we discussed in the preceding chapter). But people in America do not live under an empire. So what can we learn from the apocalyptic perspective for today's world? One lesson to be learned here for Americans today is that any dominant political power such as the United States could in fact be considered a cosmic evil due to its vast power. So the United States—and Americans—need a humility corresponding to its power. Otherwise, we may act like some of the empires that helped inspire the Bible's apocalyptic books in the first place.

Are Natural Disasters Punishment for Sin?

Perhaps even more vexing than the suffering humans cause one another is the problem of natural disasters. Why do natural disasters happen to innocent people? Different books of the Bible offer different responses. On the one hand, disasters are regarded as a divine curse; these may include pestilence or illness (Deuteronomy 28:20-22). In keeping with this idea, famine and drought are seen as divine punishments (Amos 4:6-10).[16] On the other hand, some natural catastrophes are not attributed to God. As we saw in the preceding chapter, Job attributes the fire from heaven to God (Job 1:16), but the audience knows that it is the satan who is the immediate cause of this fire. We might say that God is the ultimate cause in letting the satan do this, and one scholar would even say that God here is "sadistic," an "abusive victimizer."[17] Yet we do not see any attitude of this sort actually displayed by God in Job 1–2, and so this particular reading of God in Job does not strike me as right. Given God's praise of Job in 1:8 and 2:3, God might be viewed as sympathetic to Job. The issue is not, to my mind, about this specific characterization of God. The divine council here seems to be a stage drama that sets up the problem of the book. So, as we saw in the last chapter, the issue is whether or not divine causality is to be discerned from disaster. Instead, the point is that such events as those that befall Job are more complex than what humans perceive. I will return to this problem later.

Perhaps a better example involves the famines that are regarded as natural occurrences, not divine occurrences. The famine that takes Joseph's family down to Egypt is not attributed to

God (Genesis 41:53-57). Even when the plan of God is revealed later through Joseph (Genesis 45:5-6), the famine is something that God helps Joseph's family to survive, not something God caused (much less caused as a punishment). Again, we may regard God as the ultimate cause, but the biblical writers do not say even this. They emphasize instead the natural phenomenon of famine; this is the world that we have. The book of Ruth also begins with a situation of famine (Ruth 1:1-5). There is no sense in the book that this was some form of divine punishment. Nor is any reason given for the famine. It is simply assumed to be a natural phenomenon. The book of Ruth signals divine involvement only when it is said that God "had considered his people and given them food" (Ruth 1:6). In other words, God did not start the famine in the first place. Instead, God helps when things go badly.

From these passages, we can see that the Bible presents different views of God and natural disasters. Some writers affirm a correlation between divine punishment and human suffering due to natural disaster; others biblical authors don't. So there is a difference of opinion about natural disasters in the Bible. We may like balance and symmetry in the way we look at things, but natural disasters do not indicate who is good and who is evil. As the book of Job would suggest, this way of thinking may be our problem.

In the end, when it comes to the suffering of people due to natural disasters, we don't get to know and so we don't get to judge. What we are to learn from the suffering of others is that we get to help—in fact, we must help. Only a compassionate response will do,[18] not a judgment: "Do not judge, so that you may not be judged" (Matthew 7:1). In view of this biblical warning, it is difficult to understand how Christian preachers in America can interpret natural disasters as divine judgment on people they don't approve of. As Pope Francis was recently quoted as saying, it is God's job to judge.

Is Suffering a Test by God?

Another biblical idea about suffering is that God is testing people. This is the notion in Genesis 22. The very first verse of the chapter states the narrator's perspective that Abraham's sacrifice of Isaac was a test by God (see also Hebrew 11:17).[19] At first glance, this notion of testing might seem odd. Why would God test Abraham? Doesn't God already know what Abraham would do? One approach would be to think that in the imagination of the biblical author, God perhaps isn't quite all knowing, and so God tests people to see how they will do.[20] I think readers are supposed to sense Abraham suffering at the prospect of sacrificing Isaac, but Genesis 22 does not say that the goal of the divine test was to make Abraham suffer. If God is understood in this passage to be all knowing, then perhaps the test is to show Abraham himself the depth of his obedience to God.

In other passages we do see the idea of the righteous tested by suffering (Tobit 12:14; Sirach 2:1; 4:17; 33:1; Wisdom of Solomon 2:17-20; 3:5; 11:9; 4 Maccabees 9:7).[21] For the early Christians, testing may involve endurance (1 Corinthians 10:13), or trials for the sake of the faith (James 1:1-3, 12-16; 1 Peter 1:6).[22] Jesus' life and passion are understood as testing by suffering (Matthew 17:12; Matthew 16:21, parallel to Mark 8:31; Hebrew 2:18; see also 4:15).[23] While testing may involve suffering, its basic purpose is to demonstrate obedience to the will of God (see, for example, the temptation of Jesus in Matthew 4:1-11; Mark 1:12-13; Luke 4:1-13).[24] Testing of faith is a common New Testament motif, but often it shows little reference to suffering.

In the Hebrew Bible, testing is often a means of discovering the limits of a relationship. The wilderness crises test both the Israelites[25] and God.[26] When the Israelites are tested, it is to see if they will follow God's statutes (Exodus 16:4; Deuteronomy 8:2).[27] God is tested by the Israelites, in one case to see if God is present (Exodus 17:7). Testing seems to be a way to find out things about other persons. In 1 Kings 10:1 (paralleled by 2 Chronicles 9:1), the queen of Sheba came to Jerusalem to test Solomon with hard questions. Testing is all about discovering ("All this I have tested by wisdom," says Ecclesiastes 7:23). With God and Israel, it seems to be a way of testing their covenantal relationship.

So what should we think of the idea of testing? Suffering is not necessarily a test from God. Instead, new circumstances arise in a relationship between people, and that may test the relationship. Changes in life, with failures on people's part, may test a relationship. For example, friendships are tested: "when you gain friends, gain them through testing" (Sirach 6:7).[28] Testing in the Bible goes both ways in the covenant relationship: both God and Israel are tested. So suffering does not mean that God is directly testing us but that difficult situations may arise that test our relationship with God. So from this perspective, this idea of testing might sound fair.

Tests might even sound like a good idea at times. "Test everything," says Paul in his earliest letter (1 Thessalonians 5:21); this would include ourselves. We accept the idea that tests are part of human experience. High school and college involve series of tests, year after year. We accept the idea of entrance exams for college or for various professional schools. Sports competitions are public tests of our physical abilities, and tests are performed on our bodies for health reasons. While we may not enjoy taking tests, we might accept the idea that they provide opportunities for further learning, insight, and growth. (I certainly felt that way about my examinations in graduate school.) Tests may push us to achieve and be more.

While this sounds reasonable, there is a problem with tests when it comes to God. We may instinctively recoil at the idea of being tested by God. It seems to be beneath God. Worse, with God we really don't get to know why we're being tested, while with school tests and other sorts of tests in life, we know why. With God we have to guess at the apparent reason—we even have to guess if we are being tested at all. So in a way, that makes being tested by God a double test. Yes, the author of Genesis 22 conceived of Abraham's ordeal as a divine test (Genesis 22:1), but

that does not mean that we have to understand our ordeals in this
way. And as far as we know, Abraham didn't know it was a test.
We might also have the impression that Job 1–2 is to be read as
the testing of Job, yet this is never said.[29] Instead, it seems to test
us as readers about the assumptions that we make about God.[30]

In the end what if anything is wrong with thinking that some
bad things happening to us may be tests from God? One problem
is that it can lead into superstitious thinking. We can end up as-
suming that it all comes from God, when in fact God may have
no such intention about such things happening to people. It also
might presuppose that we have the kind of direct access to God
that Abraham is represented as having. He hears directly from
God and later from God's angel. Do we? How do we know what
God intends? History suggests that it can be very dangerous for
people to assume that they know what God is doing and intend-
ing. There is no foolproof way for knowing God's will.

So what can we take away from this discussion? My intuition
is that there may be a certain freedom for people in not knowing.
We are not God: "I am God and not mortal" (Hosea 11:9). It is
God's job to know everything, not humans', and that includes
our knowledge of God ("It is the glory of God to conceal things,"
Proverbs 25:2). We are in the same situation as Job: if we knew
why things are the way they are all the time, then our actions
might be dictated by calculations about how to please God at
every turn, and then God would be required to reward us. To not
know is to have the freedom to act well without our knowing or
calculating about God's reward. As a result, we are freed from
the burden of such calculations. Like Job, we perhaps become
more free by not knowing and still doing what we ought to do.

Are There Merits to Suffering?

There is another idea that has been taken as an explanation
for evil afflicting innocent people. It is the idea that suffering has

effects that are good for us. In one version of this idea, divine discipline and reproof is good for a person (Proverbs 3:11-12).[31] Elihu says (Job 37:13): "Whether for correction, or for his land, or for love, he causes it to happen." In Job 5:17-18, divine discipline is good: "How happy is the one whom God reproves; therefore do not despise the discipline of the Almighty. For he wounds, but he binds up; he strikes, but his hands heal." When people read passages like these, they might assume that divine discipline may require suffering (although many of the passages don't really go into that), and so when we suffer, it is discipline from God.

In another version of this idea, suffering is redemptive. The famous figure often called "the Suffering Servant" in Isaiah 53 suffers for the sins of others. This passage seems to be a way to interpret Israel's sufferings at the hands of the nations during the Exile as well as Israel's role in the world as a witness to God. Theologically, it is not constructed as a sort of explanation for evil but as an expression of God's capacity to bring good out of evil. The same may be said for the passion story of Jesus in the New Testament gospels, which is regarded sometimes as an example of redemptive suffering as a reason for evil.[32] Neither passage provides a rational or spiritual explanation for evil itself. Instead, they show the asymmetry of good and evil. In other words, God draws good out of evil; and so should we.

The good that may come out of such evil is not really an answer to people's suffering. I don't think of suffering as having a purpose or being part of God's plan for people. God's purposes for people, I think, work out through and despite such suffering. In Psalm 23, God leads "through the darkest valley" (verse 4). For the author of this beautiful psalm, God is not this darkness, and God did not cause this adversity. What is clear is that suffering has damaging effects. Sometimes these are insurmountable; sometimes they are not. If and when we can survive disaster, it may develop our resilience[33] and add to our sense of agency in the world. Sometimes in the face of adversity we can do things that really are hard. Perhaps most importantly, <u>adversity should help us learn and express compassion for other people as they face trag-edies in their own lives</u>. These are not explanations for suffering, but lessons that we may draw from the experience of suffering.

Is God Both All Powerful and Benevolent?

A more recent approach to human suffering has been to question God's power and benevolence. Harold Kushner's book, which I mentioned at the beginning of this chapter, suggests that to maintain belief in God one must reject either God's benevolence or God's omnipotence. This has also become part of the landscape of Jewish thought in light of the Holocaust.[34] Similarly, Christian "<u>process theologians</u>" have recast the biblical idea of God in light of the problem.[35] The New Testament scholar Bart Ehrman likewise finds that three basic presuppositions in the Bible cannot all be true: "God is all powerful. God is all loving. There is suffering."[36] Such a God is either not all powerful, or is not all loving; otherwise, there would not be so much innocent suffering. Even if one suggests that God allows such suffering but does not cause it, this is still a god who does not choose to alleviate a massive amount of suffering. In other words, God is not all loving. It is because of this argument that many readers do not find the book of Job satisfying: why does God allow Job to suffer so much? (And what of his original family that is destroyed?)

We certainly face a problem, perhaps even a contradiction. On the one hand, some biblical passages tell us that God is the ultimate cause of both good and evil. Job declares in Job 2:10: "Should we accept only good from God and not accept evil?"[37] Lamentations 3:38 puts the point this way: "Is it not from the mouth of the Most High that good and bad come?" Isaiah 45:7 expresses the idea: "I make weal and create woe." On the other hand, as I suggested in the last chapter, the book of Job imaginatively uses the alternating scenes of the divine council in heaven and the scenes of Job and his family on earth to show a gap between the heavenly situation and people's perception of the situation. In other words, we don't get to understand how the various levels of divine causality work.

Many people are dissatisfied and should be dissatisfied with this response to the question of suffering. At the same time, we should be careful. We think that we deserve an answer, but there are many things that we don't get to understand. We live in a wondrous time when we are just beginning to understand the human person, with new frontiers being crossed in neuroscience and related fields. We stand at a time when the discoveries of the universe are overwhelming us not only with their beauty but also for the prospects for future understanding. The universe is a wonder. God's responses to Job at the end of the book in chapters 38–41 make precisely this point. God's appeal to the mysteries of the universe as beyond human understanding offers a basic argument about our not knowing: if we do not fathom the creation of God, why should we fathom the Creator? We can extend the argument: we do not understand ourselves completely, so why should we understand our Maker?

Still, this line of reasoning may be unsatisfying. People can live without knowing the mysteries of the universe. Here no personal faith is involved. But with God, our personal faith is. With God, we may think that we need to know or deserve to know. But how do we know that this is right? In the end, Job does not get to know "the answer"; instead, he says, "I have uttered what I did not understand" (42:3). Still, God supports Job (42:7), precisely because he questions with integrity the human norms of old that he had learned about God (see Job 42:5). This is Job's situation, and it is ours too.

The Argument from Divine Presence

The Joban "answer" to human suffering is sometimes thought to be the fact that God appears and speaks to Job. As a result of

his dialogue with God, Job can now understand in a way he did
not before. At the end of the book, Job's experience of God in
the whirlwind trumps his experience of the world and specifically the problem of not understanding rationally why righteous
or innocents suffer in this world.

At this point, I want to be careful about one aspect of the
book's ending: Job's experience of God is fundamentally different from other divine appearances to people in the Bible. With
Job, there is a perception of God ("now my eye sees you," 42:5),
yet this perception is not of God's face or body (as we saw in
chapter 1) but of God in the whirlwind (Job 38:1, 40:6). This is
not the usual way God appears (as I suggested in the preceding
chapter). God's speaking from the whirlwind is decidedly "other"
than the way God usually appears.

Job's seeing God is not exactly an experience of comfort or
solace. Psalm 73 also tells of an experience that induces a new
understanding on the part of the speaker. This speaker could not
understand the problem of evil people prospering "until I went
into the sanctuary of God" (verse 17). Other psalms speak of the
urgent desire to see God or God's face (Psalm 63:1-2), which
may provide consolation (see Psalm 17:15) or even joy (Psalms
42:4 and 43:4). However, this is not the sanctuary experience
in Psalm 73. The psalm tells us instead that the psalmist had
a new understanding after entering the sanctuary. There is no
mention of seeing God in any form. The psalmist turns to God
in the traditional site of worship, "the sanctuary of God" (verse
17), and this induces the psalmist's new understanding: God
supports the psalmist ("you hold my right hand," verse 23) and
God remains "the strength of my heart and my portion forever"
(verse 26). Thus, "it is good to be near God" (verse 28). Even
without the mystical experience of seeing God, the psalmist
knows God as a support and "the strength of my heart." Divine
presence is not an explanation of evil. Nor is it particularly
common in the Bible.

Let's look at one last example of divine presence overcoming human suffering. When the prophet Elijah flees for his life, he heads to the wilderness (1 Kings 19:1-4). There an angel appears to him and provides food and drink to fortify him for a journey to Mount Horeb (verses 5-9). This mountain recalls Moses' experience of God on Horeb in Deuteronomy 4:15 (see also 4:10; 5:2; etc.). What happens next to Elijah echoes the divine appearance to Moses in Exodus 33:21-23 and 34:6.[38] The wind, the earthquake, and the fire all take place on the mountain as expected of divine appearances elsewhere in the Bible, but Yahweh is said to be not in them. Instead, there was "a sound of sheer silence," or more literally, "a sound—sheer, silent"[39] (verses 11-12). What Elijah experiences of God is a nearly imperceptible voice. Then the divine voice speaks to Elijah and questions him, "Why are you here?" (verse 13). In response, Elijah recounts his suffering (verse 14). But God does not answer or explain the reason for his suffering. It is clear that Elijah's suffering is due to his enemies (verse 14), not to his god. Rather than providing an answer, God commissions Elijah to return, and after God speaks, Elijah sets off to do as God commands him (verses 15-19).

Job, the psalmist, and Elijah do not provide a rational "answer" to the problem of suffering. In fact, it is fair to say that they do not provide an "answer" in any conventional sense of the word. Instead, the three figures offer an experiential response: the experience of God complicates or displaces the question of suffering. It also seems to overtake (perhaps even overwhelm) the human desire for an answer. In sum, the human experience of God may overcome the problem of personal suffering.

As all these various biblical answers to the problem of suffering suggest, the Bible devotes considerable attention to the question. In the end, though, "the answer" is that we don't get to know "the answer." Instead, the Bible presents suffering as the struggle of human existence and as a religious mystery inexplicably lying between immediate human causes and God, the ultimate cause. This, I think, is the awful truth. It may present a tragic disconnect for many of us, so much so that we might become inclined to lose faith. And it is little consolation to read the Bible and see that we are not the first people to suffer. At the same time, God in the Bible somehow offered hope in the past to people like Job, like the psalmist, like Elijah; and God offers it to us today.

Might there be any benefit not to getting to know the answers to our questions about suffering? I suspect there is. There is a certain grace in not knowing and in not having certitude. We are made for uncertainty, we are told: "Andrew Gerber, a psychiatrist at Columbia University, notes that just as our brain is wired to help us when we're faced with fearful situations, it is also wired to help us with uncertainty. 'Our lives are a balancing act between making decisions based on the information we have, the information we don't know, and our desire to make sense out of the world around us,' he says, adding that the better we make peace with life's uncertainties, the better off we are. "The biggest mistake people make is not to accept uncertainty."[40]

Faith should face the considerable uncertainties of our world, and this includes suffering. In the face of this mysterious world, we are to do what wonderful things we can; it is what God made us to do. In chapter 5, I suggested that Genesis 1 may be read as the creation of responsibility for people. To be like God is to reframe our questions about suffering and evil in the world. To be in the image and likeness of God means to shift the issues from God to ourselves. "How could a good God let these things happen?" can sometimes become the question, "Why don't we stop more of these things from happening?" Many bad things happen that are beyond our control, but several are of our own making, in whole or at least in part. In chapter 6, I suggested that the satan is, in a way, our very selves that we must overcome. To choose to be in the image and likeness of God—and not of Satan—is the challenge, reminding us that we have ourselves to blame for a good deal of what happens in the world, and it is up to us to change it. And as biblical responses to suffering suggest, the task of our lives should include prayer and protest to God. Whether we pray to God like Mary in the Magnificat or we complain to God like Job and the psalmists, God hears; and in the end, somehow, God is here.

God in the Bible and Beyond

O n *St. Elsewhere*, an old American television show about a hospital in Boston, there was an episode called "After Life" (it aired originally on November 26, 1986).[1] In this episode, there is a doctor, played by Howie Mandel, host of the NBC show "Deal or No Deal," and more recently a judge on the NBC show "America's Got Talent." This doctor is dying of a bullet wound and has an out-of-body experience. He goes to heaven and arrives at a beautiful picnic. He recognizes people there whom he had known in his life. As he walks around and talks to people, he asks, "Where's God?" He's told not to worry; God will show up. After a while, he sees a figure in the distance walking toward him. The figure comes up to him and greets him, and the doctor can see that he looks identical to him. Surprised, the doctor asks, "Who are you?" The mysterious figure answers, "Don't you recognize me? I made you in my image and likeness."

I tell this story, because it reminds me of what we have seen over the course of this book. I have talked about God's body and body parts, about some of God's emotions, and about divine gender and sexuality. I have also taken a look at God in the world, seen through the positive lens of creation and through the negative lens of evil and suffering. These ways of talking about God all draw on human language and ideas about humans, but they also show cracks in the façade of a purely human-seeming

God.[2] Through the cracks, sometimes expressed as paradoxes, we may sense something more, or we should say, someone more.

Thanks to the Bible, we think of God as both human-like and not human-like. Human images constitute a starting point for thinking about God. In other words, we have "analogical imaginations."[3] This is a beginning, not the end. In its ancient context, the Bible told new stories about an old God, because there were changes in the perception of God over the centuries. Because people change—we change—our discovery of who God is changes. Our own stories, the stories about how we've changed, inform our changing sense of God.

When we first probe what the Bible tells us about God, there might seem to be a sort of symmetry between God and humanity: God is God and humans are human. Yet when it comes to the human desire to know and love God, we also face fundamental asymmetries. We have seen the basic asymmetry between God's knowledge and our knowledge; between good and evil in the world; and between suffering and well-being. Unlike God, we human beings in our basic constitution are on the way, and our journeys in life can often be mysteries, even to ourselves.

People, whether good or bad, want more, and it is this desire for more that marks our many different paths. The ways that we make in our world are uncertain, since there is so much that we don't understand. Not understanding all things is the price of our finite human condition. Yet our lack of perfect knowledge and our uncertainty may also be helpful to us. Humans have the freedom to do right and become more, based on what we know and despite what we do not know. Thanks to what we don't know, we cannot calculate about God or compel God. We can do right for the right reasons. We can learn more and become more.

The nature of our limits also means that our paths move in one direction through time. We can't go back in time and change things; there are no "do-overs." We know each moment matters, and we have to do the best we can do in every moment. Parents know that for any given moment in their child's life, they get only one shot. We try our best; sometimes we fail, perhaps even tragically. But the point is that every moment does count, and so we try to be mindful and attentive. At moments, it can work out; we become more.

At times uncertainty can be a gift for us, especially when it may lead us, like Job, to aspire to know more. We are human. Leaving room for us, God checks divine power at our doors, when and as we meet. This often leads to uncertainty, but it also allows us to act freely. Our uncertainty about divine power and presence may lead us to pursue more, beyond ourselves and perhaps even toward God. Thus, we are human.

Uncertainty may leave us open to wander a bit, but also to wonder. Wonder is our sense of the vastly more beyond us—and in us and through us as well. Wonder is a signal of our human intuition that the universe is not empty and cold, but vastly and deeply full. Humanity too is a signal of the fullness of life: people have a vast and deep desire for more than what they have now and are now.

At turns in our history or in our lives, the negative looms much more—and much more devastatingly—than the positive. We do live on this side of reality, no less grotesque than beautiful.[4] Still a sense of presence and fullness is ultimately more compelling than an acceptance of absence or emptiness. This sense of more provides a better account of reality than a modern view (or "faith") that reality is little more than what we can rationally conclude based on our sense perceptions. Hope in our fellow humans is hardly rational, but neither is falling in love. Hope in God is a bit like falling in love. These experiences involve a faith in more than what we can see or hear. There seems to be more, not less.

At the same time, faith in God may go hand in hand with uncertainty about the world, leading to exploration and wonder. In my own wandering, I am often drawn to God in the imperfect set of human documents called the Bible. From its words and beyond, we may catch familiar-sounding, yet still strange signals about God. We may sense this seemingly chance mystery in moving moments with the Bible, as we can in our routine life with people or in rare encounters with nature.

This mystery sometimes breaks through the cracks in biblical images or through the surface of our lives (or even ourselves); *and our paradigms* and so it may shine a refracted light on our paths. It can bring us a certain joy, and sometimes it inspires love. In being human, we have set off on the journeys for which we were made, often facing negative experiences and inexplicable problems. At more graced moments than we probably know, we are touched by this terrible, wonderful mystery, this positive Inexplicable, which we name as God.[5] Just as we think we are looking around for God, God *FB* comes right up to us to be recognized, greeted, and embraced.

Notes

Prologue—pages ix–xx

1. See V. S. Ramachandran and Sandra Blakeslee, *Phantoms in the Brain: Probing the Mysteries of the Human Mind,* Quill edition (New York: Harper-Collins, 1999), 174–98. Note also their comment on page 188: "There are circuits in the human brain that are involved in religious experience."

2. The biblical scholar Julia O'Brien puts the problem this way: "The church needs poets, but it also needs critics. It needs those who will challenge its metaphors as well as the ideologies that inform them, trusting that critique can bring new life to theological reflection." O'Brien, *Challenging Prophetic Metaphor: Theology and Ideology in the Prophets* (Louisville, KY: Westminster John Knox, 2008), 177.

3. Tanakh is a Hebrew acronym in which each Hebrew consonant in the word stands for a major section of the Jewish Bible. T stands for Torah, the first five books of the Bible (which Christians often call the Pentateuch); N stands for Neviim or prophets (for Jewish tradition, this part of the Bible also includes the books from Joshua through Kings); and K(h) stands for Ketubim or writings, in other words, the rest of the Jewish Bible.

4. There are many interesting books bearing on this subject. See Denis Lacorne, *Religion in America: A Political History,* trans. George Holoch (New York: Columbia University Press, 2011). See also Eric Michael Mazur and Kate McCarthy, eds., *God in the Details: American Religion in Popular Culture*, 2nd ed. (London/New York: Routledge, 2010).

5. Christians in the United States sometimes speak of a "Judeo-Christian tradition(s)," a term that arguably papers over serious differences between Christians and Jews. For a vivid example of the latter, see the powerful speech that Jesse Jackson gave before the Democratic National convention on July 17, 1984. See Jesse Jackson, "Our Time Has Come," in *The African-American Archive: The History of the Black Experience through Documents*, ed. Kai Wright (New York: Black Dog & Leventhal Publishers, 2001), 699.

6. First cast by the White Chapel Bell Foundry, London, in 1752, the bell was twice recast in Philadelphia by John Pass and John Stow in 1753.

7. Cf. Isaiah 38:7 = 2 Kings 18:22, "in the Lord our God we trusted"; Psalm 40:4, "they trusted in Yahweh"; Psalm 22:5, 6, "In You they trusted"; cf. Psalm 26:1: "In the Lord I have trusted."

8. The speech is often recalled by the line, "I've been to the Mountaintop," which appears at its end. See Clayborne Carson and Kris Shepard, eds., *A Call to Conscience: The Landmark Speeches of Dr. Martin Luther King, Jr.* (New York: IPM in Association with Warner Books, 2001), 201–23, with the line on page 222 and the quotation of Amos on page 213. This occasion was not the first time Dr. King drew on this biblical passage. He had used it in 1963 at the Freedom Rally held in Cobo Hall in Detroit (see *A Call to Conscience*, p. 72) and in his "Letter from a Birmingham Jail," available in *The African-American Archive: The History of the Black Experience through Documents*, ed. Kai Wright (New York: Black Dog & Leventhal Publishers, 2001), 568.

9. See Laurel C. Schneider, *Beyond Monotheism: A Theology of Multiplicity* (New York: Routledge, 2008), 77–78.

10. James Wood, "God in the Quad," *The New Yorker* (August 31, 2009): 75.

11. Walter Kasper, "The Timeliness of Speaking of God: Freedom and Communion as Basic Concepts of Theology," http://www.youtube.com /watch?v=_V7sk5P5MoA. Accessed July 2, 2013. Excerpts of the lecture as delivered at Yale on March 26, 2009, were published as Cardinal Walter Kasper, "The Timeliness of Speaking of God: Freedom and Communion as Basic Concepts of Theology," *Saint Thomas More: The Catholic Chapel & Center at Yale* (Fall 2009): 2–3.

12. Kasper, "The Timeliness of Speaking of God," 3.

13. Janet Martin Soskice, *The Kindness of God: Metaphor, Gender, and Religious Language* (New York: Oxford University Press, 2007), 3.

14. In her book, *Beyond Monotheism*, Laurel C. Schneider criticizes the theological inadequacy of the term monotheism (p. 25). In her striking metaphor, monotheism, for Schneider, is "ontological ice" (p. 91), "the ice in which so much Christian doctrine has become mired, for whom the creeds have become bits of broken glass, beautiful, but still deadly to take in" (p. 10). For Schneider, monotheism—or perhaps really its church advocates—deadens discourse of the divine. I read this book with sympathy, but what I really hear in this book is the limits that religious or church advocates of the term monotheism have placed on it. In this book I get no sense of monotheism for probing reality today. For a vision of biblical monotheism as potentially life giving and life enhancing today, see the wonderful book of Tikva Frymer-Kensky, *In*

the Wake of the Goddesses: Women, Culture, and the Biblical Transformation of Pagan Myth (New York: Free Press, 1992).

15. McFague's book, *Models of God: Theology for an Ecological Age* (Philadelphia: Fortress Press, 1987).

16. *Verbum Domini*, Post-Synodal Apostolic Exhortation of the Holy Father Benedict XVI to the Bishops, Clergy, Consecrated Persons and the Lay Faithful on the Word of God in the Life and the Mission of the Church (Libreria Editrice Vaticana, 2010), Introduction, paragraph 3.

17. Charles Taylor, *Sources of the Self: The Making of Modern Identity* (Cambridge, UK: Cambridge University Press, 1989), 9: "there may be . . . a lack of fit between what people as it were officially and consciously believe, even pride themselves on believing, on one hand, and what they need to make sense of some of their moral reactions, on the other."

18. David Levine, interview, "Learning To Fly," http://nautil.us/issue/2/uncertainty/learning-to-fly. Accessed 28 June 2013. Reference courtesy of David Levine.

19. See Joel S. Burnett, *"Where Is God?" Divine Absence in the Hebrew Bible* (Minneapolis, MN: Fortress Press, 2010). Note also the books by Richard Elliott Friedman, *The Hidden Face of God* (San Francisco: Harper San Francisco, 1996), and by Marjo C. A. Korpel and Johannes C. de Moor, *The Silence of God* (Leiden: Brill, 2012).

20. Barthes's italics. The quote is taken from Jonathan D. Culler, *Barthes: A Very Short Introduction* (New York: Oxford University Press, 2002), 108–9.

21. Lerclerq, *The Love of Learning and the Desire for God: A Study of Monastic Culture,* trans. Catharine Misrahi (New York: Fordham University Press, 1961), 260. French original published in 1957.

22. Weil, *Waiting for God*, trans. Emma Craufurd (New York: HarperCollins, 2009), 50. Originally published in 1951. This is a recurring theme in *Waiting for God*; see also 40, 128, and 138.

23. Weil, *Waiting for God*, 22.

24. For a summary of the scholarly evidence concerning the sins of the Catholic leadership in the Holocaust, see Daniel Jonah Goldhagen, *A Moral Reckoning: The Role of the Catholic Church in the Holocaust and its Unfilled Duty of Repair* (New York: Knopf, 2002).

25. See Marvin A. Sweeney, *Reading the Hebrew Bible After the Shoah: Engaging Holocaust Theology* (Minneapolis, MN: Fortress Press, 2008). I also highly recommend Amy-Jill Levine, *The Misunderstood Jew: The Church and the Scandal of the Jewish Jesus* (San Francisco: HarperSanFrancisco, 2007). Note the recent response on the issue given by Pope Francis on September 11,

2013, http://www.ccjr.us/dialogika-resources/documents-and-statements
/roman-catholic/francis/1252-francis2013sep11, unofficial translation, accessed
September 13, 2013: "you also asked me what we are to say to our Jewish
brothers and sisters about the promise made to them by God: has it been entirely
voided? This, I believe, is a question that radically challenges us, as Christians,
since, with God's help, and especially since the Second Vatican Council, we
have rediscovered that the Jewish people are still, for us, the holy root from
which Jesus came forth. I, too, in the friendship which I have nurtured over all
these years with our Jewish brothers and sisters in Argentina, have many times
in prayer questioned God, particularly when my mind turned to the memory
of the terrible experience of the *Shoah.* What I can tell you—together with the
apostle Paul—is that God's faithfulness to the covenant he established with
Israel has never diminished and that, through all the terrible moments of testing during those centuries, the Jews have clung to their faith in God—and for
this, we will never be able to adequately thank them, both as a church and also
as a human family. For they, precisely by persevering in their faith in the God
of the covenant, recall for all of us—including us Christians—the fact that we,
like pilgrims, are still awaiting the Lord's return and that we ought, therefore,
to be open to him, and never just fall back onto what we have already achieved."
Reference courtesy of Philip Cunningham, with my thanks.

26. Yairah Amit, *Hidden Polemics in Biblical Narrative,* trans. Jonathan
Chapman, Biblical Interpretation Series, vol. 25 (Boston: Brill, 2000), xi.

27. Lawrence Boadt, *Reading the Old Testament: An Introduction,* rev. and
updated by Richard J. Clifford and Daniel Harrington (Mahwah, NJ: Paulist
Press, 2012).

28. Robert McElroy, *Grover Cleveland, the Man and the Statesman; An
Authorized Biography,* vol. 1 (New York: Harper & Brothers, 1923); and
H. Wayne Morgan, *From Hayes to McKinley: National Party Politics, 1877–
1896* (Syracuse: Syracuse University Press, 1969), chapter 5, cited in Martin
E. Marty, "Literalism vs. Everything Else: A Continuing Conflict," *Bible Review*
(April 1994): 38–43, 50, here 41.

Chapter 1—pages 3–24

1. In particular, the "thirteen attributes" of God, based on Exodus 34:7-8.
See also Numbers 14:18; Nehemiah 9:17; Psalm 86:15; 103:8; Joel 2:13; Jonah
4:2; Nahum 1:3.

2. See also Numbers 23:19; Psalm 50:21; compare Isaiah 31:3. See also Ecclesiastes (Qoheleth) 3:18 and 5:1. Cf. Malachi 3:6: "For I the LORD do not change."

3. See Ronald S. Hendel, "Aniconism and Anthropomorphism in Ancient Israel," in *The Image and the Book: Iconic Cults, Aniconism, and the Rise of Book Religion in Israel and the Ancient Near East*, ed. Karel van der Toorn, Biblical Exegesis and Religion Series, vol. 21 (Leuven: Peeters, 1997), 221.

4. *De Principiis* 1.1, in *Anti-Nicene Fathers*, vol. 4 (Peabody, MA: Hendrickson, 1994, originally published 1885), 242. The Latin version of Origen's text refers to God's incorporeal nature. See *Anti-Nicene Fathers*, vol. 4, 377.

5. *Against Celsus* 7.27, in *Anti-Nicene Fathers*, vol. 4 (Peabody, MA: Hendrickson, 1994, originally published 1885), 621. He also cites John 1:18: "No one has ever seen God."

6. J. N. D. Kelly, *Early Christian Doctrines,* 2nd ed. (New York: Harper & Row, 1960), 232.

7. *Adversus Gentes*, paragraphs 11–19, in *Anti-Nicene Fathers*, vol. 6 (Peabody, MA: Hendrickson, 1994, originally published 1886), 467–69.

8. *Adversus Gentes,* paragraph 14.

9. *Encyclopedia Judaica*, 2nd ed., vol. 7, 666.

10. Ibid., 667. For discussion, see Warren Zev Harvey, "Maimonides and Aquinas on Interpreting the Bible," *Proceedings of the American Academy for Jewish Research* 55 (1988): 65–66.

11. For biblical scholarship, see Benjamin Sommer, *The Bodies of God and the World of Ancient Israel* (New York: Cambridge University Press, 2009). For the divine body in rabbinic sources, see Alon Goshen Gottstein, "The Body as Image of God in Rabbinic Literature," *Harvard Theological Review* 87 (1994): 171–95; and David H. Aaron, "Shedding Light on God's Body in Rabbinic Midrashim: Reflections on the Theory of the Luminous Adam," *Harvard Theological Review* 90 (1997): 299–314. For early Jewish and Christian sources on the matter, see Gedaliahu G. Stroumsa, "Form(s) of God: Some Notes on Metatron and Christ," *Harvard Theological Review* 76 (1983): 269–88.

12. For their differences, see Harvey, "Maimonides and Aquinas on Interpreting the Bible," 66–67.

13. Under anthropomorphism are often included ascriptions of human feelings to nonhumans; these properly speaking are "anthropopathisms." See David Stern, "*Imitatio Hominis:* Anthropomorphism and the Character(s) of God," *Prooftexts* 12, no. 2 (1992): 151; and Wesley Williams, "A Body Unlike Bodies: Transcendent Anthropomorphism in Ancient Semitic Tradition and Early Islam," *Journal of the American Oriental Society* 129 (2009): 30.

14. The dictionary of Henry George Liddell and Robert Scott, *A Greek-English Lexicon*, rev. and augmented by Henry Stuart Jones (Oxford, UK: The Clarendon Press, 1968), 141, also notes the word as used by Strabo.

15. For the text, see http://digital.library.wisc.edu/1711.dl/HistSciTech .Cyclopaedia01. Accessed January 23, 2013.

16. *Catechism of the Catholic Church*, 2nd ed. (Washington, DC: United States Catholic Conference, 2000), para. 42; see Soskice, *The Kindness of God*, 119–20.

17. Here Maimonides echoes Deuteronomy 4:12 and 4:15. Actually these biblical verses state that the Israelites did not see any form of God at Horeb, not that God does not have such a form.

18. For discussion, see Sommer, *The Bodies of God*, 4–9.

19. To take only one fine scholar, see Tikva Frymer-Kensky, *In the Wake of the Goddesses: Women, Culture, and the Biblical Transformation of Pagan Myth* (New York: Free Press, 1992) 14 ("cultural projections"), and 32 ("The male/female division of the animal [and human] world was projected onto the cosmic sphere and permeated philosophical reflection").

20. See Piaget's book, *The Child's Conception of the World* (New York: Harcourt Brace, 1929).

21. Jay S. Blanchard, "Anthropomorphism in Beginning Readers," *The Reading Teacher* 35, no. 5 (1982): 586–91, here 587.

22. Justin L. Barrett and Rebekah A. Richert, "Anthropomorphism or Preparedness? Exploring Children's God Concepts," *Review of Religious Research* 44, no. 3 (2003): 300–312.

23. Paschal Boyer, "What Makes Anthropomorphism Natural: Intuitive Ontology and Cultural Representations," *Journal of the Royal Anthropological Institute* 2, no. 1 (1996): 83–97.

24. Ibid., 88.

25. Ibid., 93.

26. Several scholars have made important contributions to the understanding of "God's bodies." Among recent studies with bibliography are: Esther J. Hamori, *"When Gods Were Men": The Embodied God in Biblical and Near Eastern Literature*, Beihefte zur Zeitschrift für die alttestamentliche Wissenschaft Series, vol. 384 (Berlin: de Gruyter, 2008); Benjamin Sommer, *The Bodies of God and the World of Ancient Israel* (New York: Cambridge University Press, 2009); and Andreas Wagner, *Gottes Körper: Zur alttestamentlichen Vorstellung des Menschengestaltigkeit Gottes* (Gütersloh: Gütersloher Verlaghaus, 2010). At the same time, these scholars generally have not distinguished these three types of bodies, nor do they deal much with what I delineate as the first type (except for Hamori).

27. Or, "material" in Sommer's terms. See Sommer, *The Bodies of God*, 2.

28. Wesley Williams, "A Body Unlike Bodies: Transcendent Anthropomorphism in Ancient Semitic Tradition and Early Islam," *Journal of the American*

Oriental Society 129 (2009): 28–44. Williams argues that early Islam also attests to "transcendent anthropomorphism." Note especially Williams's list of scholarly literature on p. 29, n. 70.

29. The miracle of the prophet Elisha in 2 Kings 4:34-35 probably involves an act of resuscitation. According to v. 34, the prophet "lay upon the child, putting his mouth upon his mouth, his eyes upon his eyes, and his hands upon his hands." Only then is there the verb, which is usually translated, "he lay bent over him" (NRSV). We now know, however, that it entails an act involving the mouth. For the evidence, see Mark S. Smith, "Recent Study of Israelite Religion in Light of the Ugaritic Texts," in *Ugarit at Seventy-Five*, ed. K. Lawson Younger Jr. (Winona Lake, IN: Eisenbrauns, 2007), 1–25, and in particular 12–13.

30. For a comparison with Assyrian royal gardens, see Lawrence E. Stager, "Jerusalem as Eden," *Biblical Archaeology Review* 26, no. 3 (2000): 41–43. Depictions of supersized kings relative to other humans constitute a classic motif found in many well-known pieces of iconography. For Egyptian examples, see James B. Pritchard, ed., *The Ancient Near East in Pictures Relating to the Old Testament* (Princeton, NJ: Princeton University Press, 1954; henceforth *ANEP*) #296–297, #312; note also *ANEP* #338. For Mesopotamian examples, see *ANEP* #303 and #309. It is possible that God in this passage is more like the superhuman-sized God (see the next section), perhaps as in the description of God in 2 Samuel 5:24. If so, it would fit the larger social model of humans as royal subjects being received into the palace of God as the divine king (rather than the model of God as a guest in the human home, as we see in the next passage below, Genesis 18).

31. Cf. Genesis 18:22, which refers to the "men" in addition to "the LORD."

32. See the study of Esther J. Hamori, *"When Gods Were Men": The Embodied God in Biblical and Near Eastern Literature*, vol. 384, Beihefte zur Zeitschrift für die alttestamentliche Wissenschaft Series (Berlin: de Gruyter, 2008).

33. My italics. Compare the effect of wine on gods as well as people: wine "cheers gods and mortals" (Judges 9:13).

34. *Pentateuch with Rashi's Commentary: Genesis*, trans. and annotated M. Rosenbaum and A. M. Silberman (Jerusalem: The Silberman Family, 1972), 72.

35. For this view, see Michael Carasik, "The Limits of Omniscience," *Journal of Biblical Literature* 119 (2000): 221–32.

36. The conversations of Moses with God (Exodus 33) and Gideon with God (Judges 6) are also remarkable for the apparent freedom with which they address God and make requests of God.

37. For this discussion, see Nathan MacDonald, "Listening to Abraham— Listening to Yhwh: Divine Justice and Mercy in Genesis 18:16–33," *The Catholic Biblical Quarterly* 66 (2004): 25–43.

38. See MacDonald, "Listening to Abraham—Listening to Yhwh," 40.

39. Joshua 5:13-15 and Judges 13 are two other examples involving angels. The narrative describing the angel that appears to Joshua calls him a "man" (Joshua 5:13). The angel that appears to the unnamed wife of Manoah is reported by her to be "a man of God" (Judges 13:6).

40. See Mark S. Smith, "Remembering God: Collective Memory in Israelite Religion," *The Catholic Biblical Quarterly* 64 (2002): 641–44.

41. I owe this formulation to Michael Coogan, as acknowledged in Smith, "Remembering God," 647.

42. See Ronald S. Hendel, "Sacrifice as a Cultural System: The Ritual Symbolism of Exodus 24:3–8," *Zeitschrift für die alttestamentliche Wissenschaft* 101 (1989): 366–90.

43. The point is nicely captured by Hendel, "Aniconism and Anthropomorphism in Ancient Israel," 220–21. In addition to the passages mentioned here, see also Genesis 16:13 and Isaiah 6:5.

44. Hendel, "Aniconism and Anthropomorphism in Ancient Israel," 220–21.

45. As another (perhaps lesser) possibility, the footprints carved into the sanctuary floor at 'Ain Dara might suggest that the divine feet on the flooring of the divine palace is what is seen in Exod 24:10. For this evidence, see Philip J. King and Lawrence E. Stager, *Life in Biblical Israel* (Louisville, KY: Westminster John Knox Press, 2001), 335–36.

46. Jacob and his kinfolk do similarly in Genesis 31:54. See also 1 Kings 18:42-43, where "Ahab went up to eat and drink," apparently on the mountain of Carmel where, it would appear, Elijah is waiting for God in the storm.

47. R. B. Y. Scott, "The Hebrew Cubit," *Journal of Biblical Literature* 77 (1958): 205–14.

48. For the Baal Cycle section concerning Baal's palace, see Simon B. Parker, ed., *Ugaritic Narrative Poetry*, Society of Biblical Literature Writings from the Ancient World Series, vol. 9 (Atlanta, GA: Scholars, 1997), 129–36. For the elements of the divine palace in the Bible and the Dead Sea Scrolls, see Mark S. Smith, "Biblical and Canaanite Notes to the Songs of the Sabbath Sacrifice from Qumran," *Revue de Qumran* 12 (1987): 585–88. The classic study of the divine mountain is Richard J. Clifford, *The Cosmic Mountain in Canaan and the Old Testament*, Harvard Semitic Monographs Series, vol. 4 (Cambridge, MA: Harvard University Press, 1972).

49. The hope of seeing God is expressed in various psalms, for example, in Psalm 11:7 ("the upright shall behold his face"); Psalm 17:15 ("I shall behold your face in righteousness; when I awake I shall be satisfied beholding your likeness."); Psalm 27:4 ("to behold the beauty of the LORD") and 13 ("I shall see the goodness of the LORD"); Psalm 42:2 ("When shall I come and behold

the face of God?"); and Psalm 63:2 ("So I have looked upon you in the sanctuary, beholding your power and glory"). See also Job 42:5: "I had heard of you by the hearing of the ear, but now my eye sees you."

50. Compare Psalm 139:7-12; Jeremiah 23:23-24; and Amos 9:2.

51. For seraphim, see Friedhelm Hartenstein, "Cherubim and Seraphim in the Bible and in the light of Ancient Near Eastern sources," in *Angels: The Concept of Celestial Beings*, ed. Friedrich V. Reiterer, Tobias Nicklas, and Karin Schöpflin, Deuterocanonical and Cognate Literature Yearbook 2007 (Berlin: de Gruyter, 2007), 155–88, here 163–72.

52. For cherubim here versus seraphim in Isaiah 6, see Hartenstein, "Cherubim and Seraphim in the Bible," 155–88. Hartenstein rightly stresses their role as guardians.

53. For this passage and other examples of the period, see Ryan Stokes, "The Throne Visions of Daniel 7, 1 Enoch 14, and the Qumran Book of Giants (4Q530): An Analysis of Their Literary Relationship," *Dead Sea Discoveries* 15 (2008): 340–58.

54. See James Barr, "Theophany and Anthropomorphism in the Old Testament," in *Congress Volume: Oxford 1959*, Vetus Testamentum Supplements series, vol. 7 (Leiden: Brill, 1960), 38.

55. Genesis 2 and 32 depart from this pattern. As noted above, in Genesis 2, the deity is the host to the humans perhaps more along the lines of the second type of divine body. In Genesis 32 we might say that the hostility of the passage suggests a picture of Jacob as an anti-host, reflecting his worry over meeting his brother, Esau.

56. See Barr, "Theophany and Anthropomorphism in the Old Testament," 38; and Smith, "Like Deities, Like Temples (Like People)," in *Temple and Worship in Biblical Israel: Proceedings of the Oxford Old Testament Seminar*, ed. John Day (New York: T & T Clark, 2005), 3–27.

57. This idea connects with the universe imagined as temple, which is discussed in chapter 5.

58. Baruch Halpern, *From Gods to God: The Dynamics of Iron Age Cosmologies*, ed. Matthew J. Adams, Forschungen zum Alten Testament Series, vol. 63 (Tübingen: Mohr Siebeck, 2009), 429–42; and Christoph Uehlinger and Suzanne Müller Trufaut, "Ezekiel 1, Babylonian Cosmological Scholarship and Iconography: Attempts at Further Refinement," *Theologische Zeitschrift* 57 (2001): 140–71.

59. Uehlinger and Müller Trufaut, "Ezekiel 1," 153.

60. See Alisdair Livingstone, *Mystical and Mythological Explanatory Works of Assyrian and Babylonian Scholars* (Oxford: Clarendon Press, 1986), 86–88. For the important text that he discusses, see Alasdair Livingstone, *Court Poetry*

and Literary Miscellenea (State Archives of Assyria Series, vol. 3; Helsinki: Helsinki University Press, 1989), 100.

61. See Mark S. Smith, *The Origins of Biblical Monotheism: Israel's Polytheistic Background and the Ugaritic Texts* (Oxford, UK: Oxford University Press, 2003).

62. See J. Edward Wright, *The Early History of Heaven* (New York: Oxford University Press, 2000), 98–184.

63. See the Psalm passages mentioned above in endnote 49. Note also Moses' seeing God's form in Numbers 12:8. Compare the form of the spirit in Job 4:16.

64. The quote comes from Einstein's book originally published as *Mein Weltbild*. It appeared in English as *The World As I See It*, trans. Alan Harris (New York: Philosophical Library, 1949), 5.

65. See the theological reflections of David Tracy, "The Hermeneutics of Naming God," *Irish Theological Quarterly* 57 (1991): 253–64, especially 261–64.

Chapter 2—pages 25–41

1. The classic work on the parts of the body and their meanings was Edouard Dhorme's book (originally published in 1923): *L'emploi métaphorique des noms de parties du corps en hébreu et en akkadien* (Paris: Librairie Orientaliste Paul Geuthner, 1963). For reflections on the language of body parts in the Bible, see Robert Alter, *The Five Books of Moses: A Translation with Commentary* (New York/London: W. W. Norton, 2010), xix–xxiii.

2. Here I echo Dhorme, *L'emploi métaphorique*, 161: "Tous les états d'âme, passions, desires, volontés, idées, souvenirs, nous les avons vus localisés dans le coeur et les autres parties internes, puis projetés sur la physionomie . . ."

3. Andreas Wagner, *Gottes Körper: Zur alttestamentlichen Vorstellung des Menschengestaltigkeit Gottes* (Gütersloh: Gütersloher Verlaghaus, 2010), 156.

4. There has been a tremendous amount of scholarly literature devoted to this aspect of *persona*; see Helmuth Plessner, "Zur Anthropologie des Schauspielers," in *Anthropologie*, ed. Gunther Gebauer (Leipzig: Reclam, 1998), 185–202; and Hans Belting, "Toward an Anthropology of the Image," in *Anthropologies of Art*, ed. Mariët Westermann (Williamstown, MA: Sterling and Francine Clark Art Institute, 2005), 47.

5. The term "Trinity" was coined by the third-century author Tertullian, according to J. N. D. Kelly, *Early Christian Doctrines*, 2nd ed. (New York: Harper & Row, 1960), 113.

6. Kelly, *Early Christian Doctrines*, 115. For the modern self, see Charles Taylor, *Sources of the Self: The Making of Modern Identity* (Cambridge/New

York: Cambridge University Press, 1989). For the medieval idea of the self, see Colin Morris, *The Discovery of the Individual 1050–1200*, Medieval Academy Reprints for Teaching Series, vol. 19 (Toronto/Buffalo/London: University of Toronto Press, 1987). For the sense of the person in the biblical context, see Robert A. Di Vito, "Old Testament Anthropology and the Construction of Personal Identity," *The Catholic Biblical Quarterly* 61 (1999): 217–38.

7. See also Psalms 13:2; 30:8; 31:21; 44:25; 51:11; 37:9 = 102:3 = 143:7. For God hiding the divine face, see the book by Richard Elliott Friedman, *The Hidden Face of God* (San Francisco: Harper San Francisco, 1996). Note also the books by Joel S. Burnett *"Where Is God?" Divine Absence in the Hebrew Bible* (Minneapolis, MN: Fortress Press, 2010), and Marjo C. A. Korpel and Johannes C. de Moor, *The Silence of God* (Leiden: Brill, 2012).

8. Psalms 4:6; 44:3; 80:3, 7, 19; 89:15; 90:8.

9. Again, to echo Wagner, *Gottes Körper*, 156.

10. Rabbi Levi in Pesiqta Rabbati, cited from Yochanan Muffs, *Love and Joy: Law, Language and Religion in Ancient Israel* (New York: The Jewish Theological Seminary of America, 1992), 146. Note also from the same discussion of Muffs his citation of the rabbinic tractate *Sopherim* 16:3 about the "faces" of Jewish sources: "The face (i.e., the mood) of Scripture is fearsome; the face of the Mishnah is intermediate (i.e., mild, benign); the face of the Talmud is a smiling one, while the face of the *aggadah* is radiant."

11. For God's thoughts or "purposes," see also Jeremiah 51:29; Micah 4:12.

12. See also Job 14:3; Zechariah 12:4; cf. 1 Kings 8:29 = 2 Chronicles 6:20; 1 Kings 8:52; Nehemiah 1:6; 2 Chronicles 6:40; 7:15.

13. Note also Numbers 11:18; 14:28; 1 Samuel 8:21; Ezekiel 8:18; 2 Kings 19:28 = Isaiah 37:29; Psalm 18:7 = 2 Samuel 22:7; Numbers 11:1.

14. The last two terms are a matter of discussion by some scholars, but it is generally recognized that there is no clear biblical evidence for either one. On the problem of God's phallus, see Howard Eilberg-Schwartz, "The Problem of the Body for the People of the Book," in *Women in the Hebrew Bible*, ed. Alice Bach (New York: Routledge, 1999), 53–73. Eilberg-Schwartz makes this absence into a claim of significance (about avoiding this body part). Perhaps, but see the cautionary remarks of David H. Aaron, *Biblical Ambiguities: Metaphor, Semantics and Divine Imagery*, Brill Reference Library of Judaism Series, vol. 4 (Leiden: Brill, 2001), 184. According to some scholars, the name El Shadday refers to God as having female "breasts." For example, see David Biale, "The God with Breasts: El Shaddai in the Bible," *History of Religions* 21, no. 3 (1982): 240–56. For a more refined treatment of the issue, see Harriett Lutzky, "Shadday as a Goddess Epithet," *Vetus Testamentum* 48 (1998): 15–36. "Breasts and Womb" in Genesis 49:25 is a reference to a goddess, but as Lutzky

notes, the name *'el shadday* has been taken in other ways, for example, "God (El), the one of the mountain." For this view, see Frank Moore Cross, *Canaanite Myth and Hebrew Epic: Essays in the History of the Religion of Israel* (Cambridge, MA/London: Harvard University Press, 1973), 52–60. Lutzsky notes the *shaddayin*-gods in the Deir 'Alla inscription, but these deities who belong to the divine assembly traditionally would meet on the divine mountain, a view that would fit Cross's interpretation. In any case, no biblical narrative presents God with breasts, whether male or female.

15. See also Numbers 20:24; 24:13; 1 Samuel 12:14-15; Isaiah 1:20; 45:23.

16. New Jewish Publication Society Version.

17. My translation attempts to capture the Hebrew phrase's word order, the relative ratio of syllables in its three words, and the syllable initial alliteration as noted by Jerome T. Walsh, *Style and Structure in Biblical Hebrew Narrative* (Collegeville, MN: The Liturgical Press, 2001), 26. Walsh, *Style and Structure*, 26, translates the phrase, "a slender, silent sound." See also Cross, *Canaanite Myth*, 194: "a thin whisper of sound" or an "imperceptible whisper." Cross commented later ("An Interview: Part Two. The Development of Israelite Religion," *Bible Review* 8, no. 5 [October, 1992]: 19): "The Hebrew should be translated 'a silent sound.'" For the semantics, see Gören Eidevall, "Sounds of Silence in Biblical Hebrew: A Lexical Study," *Vetum Testamentum* 62 (2012): 159–74, here 169–72. As commentators note, Job 4:16 contrasts two of the terms here: "there was silence, then I heard a voice." For parallels to the idea of such a "silent" or "quiet" divine voice or whisper, compare Job 4:16 and 26:14.

18. See Ezra 7:6, 28; 8:22, 31; used also with "good" in Ezra 7:9; 8:18; and Nehemiah 2:8, 18.

19. Compare the writing on the wall by the fingers of the other disembodied human hand (Daniel 5:5), which was sent by God (Daniel 5:24).

20. 1 Chronicles 28:2; Psalms 99:5; 132:7; Isaiah 60:13; see also Lamentations 2:1; Ezekiel 43:7.

21. Heinz-Josef Fabry, "*leb; lebab*," in *Theological Dictionary of the Old Testament. Volume VII*, ed. G. Johannes Botterweck, Helmer Ringgren, and Heinz-Josef Fabry, trans. David E. Green (Grand Rapids, MI: Eerdmans, 1995), 434. See also Dhorme, *L'emploi métaphorique*, 109–30.

22. For the "thinking heart," see Michael Carasik, *Theologies of the Mind in Biblical Israel*, Studies in Biblical Literature Series, vol. 85 (New York: Peter Lang, 2005), 104–10.

23. Ibid., 93.

24. Ibid., 120.

25. See Dhorme, *L'emploi métaphorique*, 43. Compare Richard J. Clifford, *Proverbs: A Commentary*, Old Testament Library Series (Louisville, KY:

144   *How Human Is God?*

Westminster John Knox, 1999), 239–40; and Michael V. Fox, *Proverbs 10–31: A New Translation with Introduction and Commentary*, Anchor Bible Series, volume 18B (New Haven, CT/London: Yale University Press, 2009), 812–13.

26. For consideration of the narrative context, see Yairah Amit, *Hidden Polemics in Biblical Narrative*, trans. Jonathan Chapman, Biblical Interpretation Series, vol. 25 (Leiden/Boston/Köln: Brill, 2000), 54, 89.

27. Cf. Jeremiah 4:28: "I have not relented nor will I turn back." In the verse's context, this is a possibility that God refuses to undertake.

28. Compare 1 Samuel 1:13, where Hannah talking to herself literally "speaks on her heart." This sounds like persons addressing their *nepesh*, discussed below, but might the preposition "on" (*'al*) denote the burden "on her heart" (compare the expression in Numbers 30:5, 6, 7, 8, 9, 10, 11, 12)?

29. The issues are difficult. See David H. Aaron, *Biblical Ambiguities: Metaphor, Semantics and Divine Imagery*, Brill Reference Library of Judaism Series, vol. 4 (Leiden: Brill, 2001), 101–24.

30. For an older survey, see Daniel Lys, *Nèpèsh: Histoire de l'âme dans le révélation d'Israël au sein des religions proche-orientales* (Paris: Presses Universitaires de France, 1959). For a more recent discussion, see Bernd Janowski, "Die lebendige *næpæš*: Das Alte Testament und die Frage nach der »Seele«," in *Gott—Seele—Welt: Interdisziplinäre Beiträge zur Rede von der Seele*, ed. B. Janowski and B. C. Schwöbel (Neukirchen: Neukirchener-Verlag, 2013), 12–43. The discussion here also relies on Horst Seebass, "*nepesh*," in *Theological Dictionary of the Old Testament. Volume IX*, ed. G. Johannes Botterweck, Helmer Ringgren, and Heinz-Josef Fabry (Grand Rapids, MI: Eerdmans, 1998), 497–519.

31. Here I echo Lys, *Nèpèsh*, 38.

32. See Lys, *Nèpèsh*, 69. Or, in the words of Edouard Dhorme (*L'emploi métaphorique*, 8), "le principe de vie," understanding that *nepesh* is in the blood (Genesis 9:4-5; Leviticus 17:11; and Deuteronomy 12:23).

33. Lys, "The Israelite Soul According to the LXX," *Vetus Testamentum* 16 (1966): 182.

34. See further Avigdor Hurowitz, "A Forgotten Meaning of *Nepesh* (Isaiah LVIII 10)," *Vetus Testamentum* 47 (1997): 43–52. The texts where Hurowitz translates *nepesh* as "sustenance" may involve a semantic extension of the word's basic meaning.

35. Gruber, *The Motherhood of God*, 185–92, on dryness of *nepesh*, suggests that *nepesh* can literally mean "throat," based on parallelism of *nepesh* with mouth in Isaiah 5:14 and instances of parallelism involving other words.

36. For Septuagint translations of Hebrew *nepesh* by Greek *psyche*, see Lys, "The Israelite Soul According to the LXX," 181–228; and Seebass, "*nepesh*,"

503. Lys emphasizes that *psyche* in the Septuagint does not refer to an individual immortal soul. For early Christian notions and their complexities, see John Cooper, "Biblical Anthropology and the Body-Soul Problem," in *Soul, Body and Survival: Essays on the Metaphysics of Human Persons*, ed. Kevin Corcoran (Ithaca, NY: Cornell University Press, 2001), 218–28; Julia Konstantinovsky, "Soul and Body in Early Christian Thought: A Unified Duality?" *Studia Patristica* 44 (2010): 349–54; Stefanie Frost, "How the Early Christians Discovered the Soul," *Studia Patristica* 44 (2010): 355–59; and Clare K. Rothschild and Trevor W. Thompson, eds., *Christian Body, Christian Self: Concepts of Early Christian Personhood*, Wissenschaftliche Untersuchungen zum Neuen Testament Series, vol. 284 (Tübingen: Mohr Siebeck, 2011).

37. For the Greek notion of the soul, see the classic essay of Jan N. Bremmer, *The Early Greek Concept of the Soul* (Princeton, NJ: Princeton University Press, 1983).

38. Note the discussion of Nancey Murphy, *Bodies and Souls, or Spirited Bodies?* Current Issues in Theology Series (Cambridge, UK/New York: Cambridge University Press, 2006).

39. Di Vito, "Old Testament Anthropology," 218. See also Judges 12:3, "I took my life in my hand."

40. For other priestly passages, see Genesis 9:10, 12, 15, 16; Leviticus 11:10, 46; Ezekiel 47:9. For a case of a nonpriestly passage, note Genesis 2:19. This is discussed in Seebass, "*nepesh*," 516.

41. Carasik (*Theologies of the Mind*, 77–78) suggests that the expression here "may be a frozen form for the reflexive 'myself,'" but he also notes that "all that is in me" in verse 1 is "an explicit reference of the interior life."

42. Hannah prays (1 Samuel 1:10, 12) with "a sad heart" (as seen by her husband in 1 Samuel 1:8) and being "bitter of *nepesh*" (1 Samuel 1:10). Her prayer is "pouring out my *nepesh* before the Lord" (1:15). The narrator also describes this prayer as Hannah praying "silently" (New Revised Standard Version), literally "speaking to her heart" (1 Samuel 1:13). This expression is rarely, if ever, used elsewhere for communicating with oneself; it is usually used for one person "speaking to the heart" of someone else, in other words, for purposes of speaking tenderly or intimately to another person (see Genesis 34:3; 50:21; Judges 19:3; Ruth 2:13; 2 Samuel 19:8; 2 Chronicles 30:22; 32:6; Isaiah 40:23; Hosea 2:16).

43. Seebass, "*nepesh*," 509.

44. Compare the image of sleep as a "second self" in Shakespeare's Sonnet 73: "Death's second self that seals up all in rest." The literary study of the "second self" is an old subject; see C. F. Keppler, *The Literature of the Second Self* (Tucson, AR: The University of Arizona Press, 1972). Keppler's examples

focus on literary characters or "selves" and do not include the "praying second self," and his definition of a second self mostly excludes what is purely internal of a person (Keppler, *The Literature of the Second Self,* 3). However, he recognizes the linguistic phenomenon of language addressed to the self "when under severe stress" (pp. 4–5), an observation that is of help for thinking about the "praying second self."

45. Note "I do not know myself (literally, my *nepesh*)" in Job 9:21 (cf. Song of Songs 6:12). See also the idiom "to bind/afflict one's *nepesh*," used eleven times in Numbers 30:3-12. Cf. "my self" as used by Shakespeare in his sonnets, as noted by the Shakespeare scholar Helen Vendler, *The Art of Shakespeare's Sonnets* (Cambridge, MA/London: The Belknap Press of Harvard University Press, 1997), xviii: "*My self* is the separable self objectified" as opposed to "myself," which "can substitute for 'I' or 'me.'"

46. Compare the motif of speaking in one's heart, for example in Psalm 14:1 = Psalm 53:2: "The fool says in his heart, 'There is no god.'" Carasik (*Theologies of the Mind,* 103 and 116) emphasizes the idea that the speech said in the heart is designed from the speaker's perspective to remain secret. Cf. the Egyptian text known as "The Debate between a Man and His Soul," for which there is a recent edition by James P. Allen, *The Debate between a Man and His Soul* (Leiden/Boston: Brill, 2011).

47. For discussion of God's *nepesh*, see Seebass, "*nepesh*," 516–17.

48. Baruch A. Levine, *Numbers 1–20: A New Translation with Introduction and Commentary,* Anchor Bible Series, vol. 4 (New York: Doubleday, 1993), 367.

49. The usage is ambiguous, since the idiom can denote either impatience or being worn down. The latter seems to be supported by the parallel expression in Judges 16:16, that because of Delilah's nagging, Samson's *nepesh* was worn down even to the point of death. It could mean (to use more colloquial language) that God "ran out of gas" because of the trouble that Israel gave God. For discussion, see Robert D. Haak, "A Study and New Interpretation of QSR NPS," *Journal of Biblical Literature* 101 (1982): 161–67.

50. The context is ambiguous as to whether it is the prophet or God who is speaking here. One might think it is the prophet, since Yahweh is mentioned in the third person in the same verse. However, this is not a necessary view. For the merits of the differing positions, see David Bosworth, "The Tears of God in the Book of Jeremiah," *Biblica* 94 (2013): 24–46, especially 36–38.

51. Stern, *Midrash and Theory: Ancient Jewish Exegesis and Contemporary Legal Studies* (Evanston, IL: Northwestern University Press, 1996), 79–83. See also Stern's article, "*Imitatio Hominis:* Anthropomorphism and the Character(s) of God," *Prooftexts* 12, no. 2 (1992): 151–74.

52. For example, note how they are used together in Isaiah 26:9: "My soul (*nepesh*) yearns for you in the night, my spirit (*ruah*) within me earnestly seeks you."

53. For an older survey, see Daniel Lys, *Rûach: Le souffle dans l'Ancient Testament* (Paris: Presses Universitaires de France, 1962). Note also John R. Levison, *Filled with the Spirit* (Grand Rapids, MI: Eerdmans, 2009), and his article, "Holy Spirit," in *The New Interpreter's Dictionary of the Bible*, ed. Katherine Doob Sackenfeld, et al., vol. 2 (Nashville, TN: Abingdon Press, 2007), 859–79; and the fine article by Carol A. Newsom, "Flesh, Spirit, and the Indigenous Psychology of the *Hodayot*," in *Prayer and Poetry in the Dead Sea Scrolls and Related Literature: Essays in Honor of Eileen Schuller on the Occasion of Her 65th Birthday*, ed. Jeremy Penner, Ken M. Penner, and Cecilia Wassen, Studies on the Texts of the Desert of Judah Series, vol. 98 (Boston: Brill, 2012), 338–54.

54. For the idiom, see Hayyim Tawil, *An Akkadian Lexical Companion for Biblical Hebrew* (Jersey City, NJ: KTAV, 2009), 290.

55. Note the statement of Newsom, "Flesh," 347: "in the biblical texts in which the spirit sent by God is conceptualized as an agent that overrides the subject's autonomy for better or for worse, it is represented as an external phenomenon that is metonymically related to the subject, whether this changed condition is temporary or lasting." By "metonymically related," Newsom ("Flesh," p. 347) means, "external but contiguous."

56. Compare Lyes, *Rûach*, 341–48. There is further background for the notion of the divine wind or breath in Mesopotamian literature. For example, the god Marduk is called "the god of sweet breath" in the Epic of Marduk (also called The Epic of Creation or in Akkadian, Enuma Elish), tablet VII, line 20. For this passage, see Benjamin R. Foster, *Before the Muses: An Anthology of Akkadian Literature*, 3rd ed. (Bethesda, MD: CDL Press, 2005), 477. Note also The Babylonian Theodicy, line 241, for gods in general having "kindly wind," in W. G. Lambert, *Babylonian Wisdom Literature* (Clarendon Press, 1960; reprinted, Winona Lake, IN: Eisenbrauns, 1996), 84–85. For more evidence, see Erica Reiner, ed., *The Assyrian Dictionary. Volume 17: Sh Part II* (Chicago: The Oriental Institute, Chicago, 1992), 138.

57. For details, see Arthur Everett Sekki, *The Meaning of Ruah at Qumran*, SBL Dissertation Series, vol. 100 (Atlanta: Scholars Press, 1989); and Newsom, "Flesh," 338–54. Newsom, "Flesh," 349–50, suggests that the Hodayot (4:29; 5:36; 8:29; 20:15; 21:34) show a conceptual shift from the paradigm inherited from the Bible: "What had been seen as an external spirit applied to a fundamentally autonomous self is no longer the operative model. Rather, the originally external spirit from God becomes conceptualized as moving from outside

to inside. Nor is the self construed any longer as a simply autonomous subject." See also the surveys of F. W. Horn, "Holy Spirit," in *Anchor Bible Dictionary, Volume III*, ed. David Noel Freedman (New York: Doubleday, 1992), 261–80; and John R. Levison, "Holy Spirit," in *The New Interpreter's Dictionary of the Bible*, ed. Katherine Doob Sackenfeld, et al., vol. 2 (Nashville, TN: Abingdon Press, 2007), 859–79. For biblical and Christian tradition, see Anthony C. Thiselton, *The Holy Spirit—in Biblical Teaching through the Centuries, and Today* (Grand Rapids MI: Eerdmans, 2013). "God's "holy spirit" is also a long-standing motif in rabbinic and later Jewish literature.

58. See also Jeremiah 23:23-24.

59. See the groundbreaking article of Robert Di Vito ("Old Testament Anthropology") as well as the important book by Andreas Wagner, *Gottes Körper: zur alttestamentlichen Vorstellung des Menschengestaltigkeit Gottes* (Gütersloh: Gütersloher Verlaghaus, 2010). This subject has also become an important one in Mesopotamian studies. See Ulrike Steinert, *Aspekte des Menschseins im Alten Mesopotamie: Eine Studie zu Person und Identität im 2. und 1. Jt. v. Chr.*, Cuneiform Monographs Series, vol. 44 (Leiden: Brill, 2012).

60. The human person has various operative centers, according to recent research in cognitive psychology and neuroscience. Multiple brain centers are involved in seemingly simple acts, such as perception. Oliver Sacks (*An Anthropologist on Mars: Seven Paradoxical Tales* [New York: Vintage Books, 1995], xvii) comments: "That the brain is minutely differentiated is clear: there are hundreds of tiny areas crucial for every area of perception and behavior . . . The miracle is how they all cooperate, are integrated together, in the creation of a self." Researchers dispute whether people constitute a single, central "self." For example, according to Ramachandran and Blakeslee (pages 227–28), "the notion of a unified self 'inhabiting' the brain may indeed be an illusion. Everything I have learned from the intensive study of both normal people and patients who have sustained damage to various parts of their brains points to an unsettling notion: that you create your own 'reality' from mere fragments of information, that what you 'see' is a reliable—but not always accurate—representation of what exists in the world, that you are completely unaware of the vast majority of events going on in your brain. Indeed, most of your actions are carried out by a host of unconscious zombies who exist in peaceful harmony along with you (the 'person') inside your body!" Sacks, in *An Anthropologist on Mars*, 226–27, disputes this view. For more, see Ramachandran and Blakeslee, *Phantoms in the Brain*, 61, 80–84, 134–37, and 227–54; on 247–57, they speak of different selves: "the embodied self," "the passionate self," "the executive self," "the mnemonic self," "the unified self," "the vigilant self," "the conceptual self," and "the social self." Note also the entertaining and accessible book on the

unconscious by Leonard Mlodinow, *Subliminal: How Your Unconscious Mind Rules Your Behavior* (New York: Pantheon Books, 2012).

61. See the valuable comparative study of Beate Pongratz-Leisten, "When the Gods are Speaking: Toward Defining the Interface between Polytheism and Monotheism," in *Propheten in Mari, Assyrien und Israel,* ed. Matthias Köckert and Martti Nissinen, Forschungen zur Religion und Literatur des Alten und Neuen Testaments Series, vol. 201 (Göttingen: Vandenhoeck & Ruprecht, 2003), 162–68.

62. Di Vito, "Old Testament Anthropology," 233.

63. Contrast what Tikva Frymer-Kensky says about ancient goddesses as generic figures. See Frymer-Kensky, *In the Wake of the Goddesses: Women, Culture, and the Biblical Transformation of Pagan Myth* (New York: Free Press, 1992), 24. Comparative study of deities on this score remains a major area for scholarly research. To my mind, the development of monotheism in Israel in the seventh and sixth centuries correlates not only with Israel's most difficult historical experience but also with its strongest expressions of divine emotions. See the following chapter for more discussion.

64. See also Proverbs 20:27: "The lamp of God is the lifebreath of humanity, revealing all the inner rooms." Author's translation.

Chapter 3—pages 42–54

1. For example, Jan Assman, *Of God and Gods: Egypt, Israel, and the Rise of Monotheism,* George L. Mosse Series in Modern European Cultural and Intellectual History (Madison, WI: The University of Wisconsin Press, 2008). I have discussed the issues in Assman's earlier work on the Bible in a book entitled *God in Translation: Deities in Cross-Cultural Discourse in the Biblical World,* Forschungen zum Alten Testament Series 1, vol. 57 (Tübingen: Mohr Siebeck, 2008, Grand Rapids, MI: Eerdmans, 2010).

2. See also the expressions of divine wrath in Romans 2:5; 3:5; 9:22; 12:19; 13:4-5; 1 Thessalonians 1:10; Revelation 6:16-17; 11:18; 16:19. God is a force of violent judgment also according to Matthew 13:41-43, 49; and 18:34-35.

3. See also Jesus issuing words of woe against towns that do not accept him in Matthew 11:20-24. Note also Jesus' cursing of a tree, even though "it was not the time for figs" (Mark 11:12-14, 20-21; Matthew 21:18-19).

4. For a good survey of the question in Mesopotamian literature, see Karel van der Toorn, *Sin and Sanction in Israel and Mesopotamia: A Comparative Study,* Studia Semitica Neerlandica Series, vol. 22 (Assen: Van Gorcum, 1985), 56–93.

5. Carvalho, "The Beauty of the Bloody God: The Divine Warrior in Prophetic Literature," in *Aesthetics of Violence in the Prophets,* ed. Chris Franke and Julia M. O'Brien, Library of Hebrew Bible/Old Testament Studies Series,

vol. 517 (New York: T & T Clark, 2010), 151. There is a huge literature offering theological reflection on God's violence. See the recent book of J. Denny
Weaver, *The Nonviolent God* (Grand Rapids, MI: Eerdmans, 2013).

6. Carvalho, "The Beauty of the Bloody God," 152.

7. There is a list of twelve ways in which biblical scholars have approached
the problem of divine violence in the Bible in Gerlinde Baumann's book, *Got-
tesbilder der Gewalt im Alten Testament verstehen* (Darmstadt: Wissenschaftliche Buchgesellschaft, 2006).

8. For this notion, see the essays in *Cultural Models in Language and
Thought*, eds. Dorothy Holland and Naomi Quinn (New York: Cambridge
University Press, 1987).

9. This social model and the evidence for it cited here derive from the
important study of Deena Grant, "Wrath of God," in *The New Interpreter's
Dictionary of the Bible,* eds. Katharine Doob Sakenfeld et al., vol. 5 (Nashville,
TN: Abingdon Press, 2009), 932–37, especially 933–35. See also her book,
Divine Anger in Biblical Literature, The Catholic Biblical Quarterly Monograph
Series, vol. 20 (Washington, DC: The Catholic Biblical Association of America,
2014). The discussion of the first social model here is highly dependent on her
article. For some comments on this social model, see also the article of Ellen
van Wolde, "Sentiments as Culturally Constructed Emotions: Anger and Love
in the Hebrew Bible," *Biblical Interpretation* 16 (2008): 1–24.

10. For these references as well as examples outside of the Bible, see James
M. Lindenberger, *The Aramaic Proverbs of Ahiqar*, The Johns Hopkins Near
Eastern Studies (Baltimore/London: The Johns Hopkins University, 1983), 81.

11. Grant notes that even the two passages where a subordinate does appear
to get angry at his superior are quite telling. These are Jonathan's anger when
he discovers Saul's intent to kill David (1 Samuel 20:34) and David's anger
over God's execution of Uzzah (2 Samuel 6:8). Even in these cases, Grant
observes, the Bible seems to avoid describing the subordinate as angry at his
superior; instead, they describe the angry parties as angry at the situation.

12. Author's translation.

13. Julia M. O'Brien, *Challenging Prophetic Metaphor: Theology and
Ideology in the Prophets* (Louisville, KY: Westminster John Knox, 2008), 123.

14. Exodus 15:7-8; Jeremiah 50:13; Ezekiel 25:14; cf. Psalm 1:2.

15. See Mark S. Smith, *Poetic Heroes: The Literary Commemoration of
Warriors and Warrior Culture in the Early Biblical World* (Grand Rapids, MI:
Eerdmans, 2014). Contrast the amusing claim of Stephen D. Moore that when
Yahweh is the angry, violent warrior, Yahweh is on steroids. See Moore, "Gi-
gantic God: Yahweh's Body." *Journal for the Study of the Old Testament* 70
(1996): 108–10.

16. For further discussion as it applies to biblical material (and with reference to psychological literature), see Mark S. Smith, "The Heart and Innards in Israelite Emotional Expressions: Notes from Anthropology and Psychobiology," *Journal of Biblical Literature* 117, no. 3 (1998): 427–36.

17. For human and divine anger in the Hebrew Bible, see Smith, "The Heart and Innards in Israelite Emotional Expressions," 427–36; Paul A. Kruger, "A Cognitive Interpretation of the Emotion of Anger in the Hebrew Bible," *Journal of Northwest Semitic Languages* 26, no. 1 (2000): 181–93; Zacharias Kotzé, "A Cognitive Linguistic Methodology for the Study of Metaphor in the Hebrew Bible," *Journal of Northwest Semitic Languages* 31, no. 1 (2005): 101–17; Reinhard G. Kratz and Hermann Spieckermann, eds., *Divine Wrath and Divine Mercy in the World of Antiquity*, Forschungen zum Alten Testament Series II, vol. 33 (Tübingen: Mohr Siebeck, 2008).

18. Smith, "The Heart and Innards in Israelite Emotional Expressions," 427–36. For comparable expressions in English, see the discussion of George Lakoff and Zoltán Kövecses, "The Cognitive Model of Anger Inherent in American English," in *Cultural Models in Language and Thought*, ed. Dorothy Holland and Naomi Quinn (New York: Cambridge University Press, 1987), 195–221.

19. Cf. divine *rûah* in Isaiah 30:28, with *ʾap* and *zaʿam* in verse 27.

20. Accordingly, this image for the divine warrior may provide conceptual backdrop to the "force" (*ruah*) that comes upon a warrior from the deity at the outset of conflict (Judges 3:10; 6:34; 11:29; 14:6; 19; 15:14; 1 Samuel 11:6; 16:3-34; cf. Judges 13:25; Job 33:4). According to Baruch A. Levine, infusion of *ruah* "ultimately originated in the heroic tradition, where we read that the divine spirit infuses the hero (Judges 3:10; 11:29; 13:25)." See Levine, *Numbers 21–36: A New Translation with Introduction and Commentary*, Anchor Bible Series, vol. 4A (New York: Doubleday, 2000), 354; for further discussion, see pp. 191 and 350.

21. Compare Isaiah 59:17; Ezekiel 23:25; Psalm 79:5-6. Note also Phinehas's fury in Numbers 25:13 when he wields the spear in Numbers 25:7-8.

22. This verse is of further interest as it represents divine fury in the context of the fury of human warriors; in addition, the following verse 12 mentions the practice of repaying military vows. The vows made seem to concern the divine gift of battle fury given to human warriors. It seems similar to the *ruah* that the deity gives to warriors.

23. For the semantics of the Hebrew terms, see Paul A. Kruger, "A Cognitive Interpretation of the Emotion of Anger in the Hebrew Bible," *Journal of Northwest Semitic Languages* 26, no. 1 (2000): 181–93; Zacharias Kotzé, "A Cognitive Linguistic Methodology for the Study of Metaphor in the Hebrew

Bible," *Journal of Northwest Semitic Languages* 31, no. 1 (2005): 101–17; and Ellen van Walde, "Sentiments as Culturally Constructed Emotions," 1–24.

24. Cf. "the worthless and volatile" (or "unstable") men hired by Abimelekh in Judges 9:4. For another view of the second word, see Aaron D. Rubin, "Genesis 49:4 in Light of Arabic and Modern South Arabian," *Vetus Testamentum* 59 (2009): 499–502.

25. Cf. the *ruah* in Judges 8:3 for the post-battle animus of the Ephraimites who felt left out of the fight.

26. Note also the family as the agent of the covenant with its capacity to punish with violence, as discussed by Caryn A. Reeder, *The Enemy in the Household: Family Violence in Deuteronomy and Beyond* (Grand Rapids, MI: Baker Academic, 2012), 22–23.

27. See the classic study by William L. Moran, "The Ancient Near Eastern Background of the Love of God in Deuteronomy," *The Catholic Biblical Quarterly* 25 (1963): 77–87, reprinted in Moran, *The Most Magic Word*, ed. Ronald S. Hendel, The Catholic Biblical Quarterly Monograph Series 35 (Washington, DC: The Catholic Biblical Association of America, 2002), 170–81. Note also Jacqueline E. Lapsley, "Feeling Our Way: Love for God in Deuteronomy," *The Catholic Biblical Quarterly* 65 (2003): 350–69.

28. Frank M. Cross, *From Epic to Canon: History and Literature in Ancient Israel* (Baltimore/London: The Johns Hopkins University, 1998), 11. See also Paul Kalluveettil, *Declaration and Covenant: A Comprehensive Review of Covenant Formulae from the Old Testament and the Ancient Near East*, Analecta Biblica Series, vol. 88 (Rome: Pontifical Biblical Institute, 1982) 7–16 and 205.

29. See also 1 Samuel 20:17.

30. Moran, "The Love of God," in *Most Magic Word*, 173.

31. Moran, "The Love of God," in *Most Magic Word*, 174.

32. O'Connor, *Jeremiah: Pain and Promise* (Minneapolis, MN: Fortress Press, 2011).

33. Kalmanofsky, "Israel's Baby: The Horror of Childbirth in the Biblical Prophets," *Biblical Interpretation* 16 (2008): 78.

34. Irene Nowell has written a beautiful little book, *Pleading, Cursing, Praising: Conversing with God through the Psalms* (Collegeville, MN: Liturgical Press, 2013). It provides concrete advice about how to use the psalms for expressing pain and for dealing with people who seem to be the source of our suffering.

35. For a recent, fresh reading of the *Magnificat*, see Richard J. Dillon, *The Hymns of Saint Luke: Lyricism and Narrative Strategy in Luke 1–2*, The Catholic Biblical Quarterly Monograph Series, vol. 50 (Washington, DC: The Catholic Biblical Association of America, 2013), 15–48.

36. Yohanan Muffs comments in this regard: "We must consider not only YHWH's love, but also His anger and the human capacity to mollify it." See Muffs, "On Biblical Anthropomorphism," in *Bringing the Hidden to Light: The Process of Interpretation. Studies in Honor of Stephen A. Geller*, ed. Kathryn F. Kravitz and Diane M. Sharon (Winona Lake, IN: Eisenbrauns, 2007), 165.

37. Because the picture of God crying seems too human, some scholars have preferred to see these verses as a depiction of the prophet's weeping. However, several scholars have recently stressed that it is God here weeping for Israel. For a recent discussion, see David Bosworth, "The Tears of God in the Book of Jeremiah," *Biblica* 94 (2013): 24–46.

38. See David R. Blumenthal, *Facing the Abusive God: A Theology of Protest* (Louisville, KY: Westminster John Knox, 1993).

39. Compare the reflection on love and hate in Ecclesiastes (Qoheleth) 9:1, how human actions, including love and hate, are "in the hand of God."

40. Among the many books on this subject, see Gerlinde Baumann, *Love and Violence: Marriage as Metaphor for the Relationship between YHWH and Israel in the Prophetic Books*, trans. Linda M. Maloney (Collegeville, MN: Liturgical Press, 2003).

41. Author's translation.

42. Yochanan Muffs comments: "It is clear, then, that we are dealing with a most human God." Muffs, "On Biblical Anthropomorphism," in *Bringing the Hidden to Light: Studies in Honor of Stephen J. Geller*, ed. Kathryn F. Kravitz and Diane M. Sharon (Winona Lake, IN: Eisenbrauns, 2007), 168.

Chapter 4—pages 55–71

1. Soskice, *The Kindness of God: Metaphor, Gender, and Religious Language* (Oxford/New York: Oxford University Press, 2007), 45.

2. See Marc Zvi Brettler, *God is King: Understanding an Israelite Metaphor*, Journal for the Study of the Old Testament Supplement Series, vol.76 (Sheffield: Sheffield Academic Press, 1989); and Shawn W. Flynn, *YHWH is King: The Development of Divine Kingship in Ancient Israel*, Vetus Testamentum Supplements Series, vol.159 (Leiden: Brill, 2013).

3. For a survey of the Queen of Heaven, see Susan Ackerman, "'And the Women Knead Dough': The Worship of the Queen of Heaven in Sixth-Century Judah," in *Gender and Difference in Ancient Israel*, ed. Peggy L. Day; Minneapolis, MN: Fortress Press, 1989), 109–24; and Saul Olyan, "Some Observations Concerning the Identity of the Queen of Heaven," *Ugarit Forschungen* 19 (1988): 161–74.

4. See the older survey of Phyllis Trible, *God and the Rhetoric of Sexuality*, Overtures to Biblical Theology (Philadelphia: Fortress Press, 1978), 31–71. Compassion in the ancient Near East is not always a female attribute (see Psalm 103:13), as noted by Trible, *God and the Rhetoric of Sexuality*, 34, and Meyer I. Gruber, *The Motherhood of God and Other Studies*, South Florida Studies in the History of Judaism Series, vol. 57 (Atlanta, GA: Scholars, 1992), 6–7: Isaiah 49:13; Jeremiah 31:20; Hosea 2:19 (verse 21 in the Hebrew text); 2:23 (verse 25 in the Hebrew text). Trible's arguments relating a woman's *rehem*, "womb," and divine *rahamim*, "compassion," suffer at times from the "root fallacy" (in which words belonging to the same root are assumed to bear the meaning of one another); on this problem, see James Barr, *The Semantics of Biblical Language* (Oxford: Oxford University Press, 1961), 100–106; and Arthur Gibson, *Biblical Semantic Logic: A Preliminary Analysis*, 2nd ed., The Biblical Seminar, vol. 75 (Sheffield: Sheffield Academic Press, 2001), 18, 20, n. 30, 33, and 177–89.

5. Deuteronomy 32:6; Isaiah 63:16; 64:7 [E 8]; Jeremiah 3:4, 19; 31:9; Malachi 1:6; 2:10; Wisdom of Solomon 14:3; Ben Sira 23:1, 4; cf. Exodus 4:22; Jeremiah 1:8; Hosea 11:1.

6. For the following, see David E. Bokovoy, "Did Eve Acquire, Create, or Procreate with Yahweh? A Grammatical and Contextual Reassessment of *qnh* in Genesis 4:1," *Vetus Testamentum* 63 (2013): 19–35.

7. Bokovoy ("Did Eve Acquire," p. 34) points to Genesis 15:16 as another example of the latter. Note also the story of Hannah in 1 Samuel 1–3. The god El answers prayer for conception in the Canaanite stories of Kirta and Aqhat. These two stories are presented in a handy book by Michael D. Coogan and Mark S. Smith, *Stories from Ancient Canaan*, 2nd rev. and expanded ed. (Louisville, KY: Westminster John Knox, 2012).

8. Gerlinde Baumann, *Love and Violence: Marriage as Metaphor for the Relationship between YHWH and Israel in the Prophetic Books*, trans. Linda M. Maloney (Collegeville, MN: Liturgical Press, 2003). See also Michael David Coogan, *God and Sex: What the Bible Really Says* (New York/Boston: Twelve, 2010), 186. See also chapter 3.

9. See Julia M. O'Brien, *Challenging Prophetic Metaphor: Theology and Ideology in the Prophets* (Louisville, KY: Westminster John Knox, 2008); and Corrine Carvalho, "The Beauty of the Bloody God: The Divine Warrior in Prophetic Literature," in *Aesthetics of Violence in the Prophets*, ed. Chris Franke and Julia M. O'Brien, Library of Hebrew Bible/Old Testament Studies Series, vol. 517 (New York: T & T Clark, 2010), 131–52.

10. Trible, *God and the Rhetoric of Sexuality*, 62–64. See also Soskice, *The Kindness of God*, 2, 79, and 181–82. The first verb might be taken as the paternal role of "begetting," but as Jeffrey H. Tigay (*The JPS Commentary:*

Deuteronomy [Philadelphia: The Jewish Publication Society, 1996], 307 and 404, n. 99) notes, it applies more often to mothers (about 208 times, versus 22 times for males), and here it is in parallelism with a clear maternal role. For a parallel example for the second line, see Isaiah 51:2; cf. Psalm 51:7.

11. Gruber, *The Motherhood of God*, 8–9. See also Hanne Løland, *Silent or Salient Gender: The Interpretation of Gendered God-Language in the Hebrew Bible Exemplified in Isaiah 42, 46, and 49*, Forschungen zum Alten Testament Series 2, vol. 32 (Tübingen: Mohr Siebeck, 2008).

12. The best overall treatment of poetic parallelism is Adele Berlin's book, *The Dynamics of Biblical Parallelism*, rev. ed., Biblical Resources Series (Grand Rapids, MI: Eerdmans, 2008).

13. See Phyllis A. Bird, "'Male and Female He Created Them': Gen 1:27b in the Context of the Priestly Creation Account." *Harvard Theological Review* 74, no. 2 (1981): 129–59; and the important studies of W. Randall Garr, "'Image' and 'Likeness' in the Inscription from Tell Fakhariyeh," *Israel Exploration Journal* 50 (2000): 227–34, and *In His Own Image and Likeness: Humanity, Divinity, and Monotheism*, Culture and History of the Ancient Near East Series, vol. 15 (Leiden/Boston: Brill, 2003). Note also Thomas Gudbergsen, "God consists of both the Male and the Female Genders: A Short Note on Gen 1:27," *Vetus Testamentum* 62 (2012): 450–53.

14. For the primary sources and scholarly literature on these two goddesses, see Mark S. Smith, *Poetic Heroes: The Literary Commemoration of Warriors and Warrior Culture in the Early Biblical World* (Grand Rapids, MI: Eerdmans, 2014).

15. For these inscriptions, see the important volume of Ze'ev Meshel, *Kuntillet ʿAjrud (Horvat Teman): An Iron Age II Religious Site on the Judah-Sinai Border* (Jerusalem: Israel Exploration Society, 2012), and also F. W. Dobbs-Allsopp, J. J. M. Roberts, C. L. Seow, and R. E. Whitaker, *Hebrew Inscriptions: Texts from the Biblical Period of the Monarchy with Concordance* (New Haven, CT/London: Yale University Press, 2005), 277–79. For the inscriptions and their broader significance, see Judith Hadley, *The Cult of Asherah in Ancient Israel and Judah: Evidence for a Hebrew Goddess* (University of Cambridge Oriental Publications, vol. 57; Cambridge, UK: Cambridge University Press, 2000).

16. See Shmuel Ahituv, *Echoes from the Biblical Past: Hebrew and Cognate Inscriptions from the Biblical Period* (Jerusalem: Carta, 2008), 221–24; Frank Moore Cross, "The Phoenician Ostracon from Acco, the Ekron Inscriptions and החרשא," *Eretz Israel* 29 (2009 = Ephraim Stern Festschrift): 20*-22*; Mark S. Smith, "The Blessing God and Goddess: A Longitudinal View from Ugarit to 'Yahweh and . . . his asherah' at Kuntillet 'Ajrud," in *Enigmas and Images: Studies in Honor of Tryggve N. D. Mettinger*, ed. Göran Eidevall and Blazenka Scheuer, Coniectana Biblica Old Testament Series, vol. 58 (Winona Lake, IN: Eisenbrauns, 2011), 213–26; and Shmuel Ahituv, Esther Eshel and Ze'ev Meshel,

in Ze'ev Meshel, *Kuntillet 'Ajrud (Horvat Teman): An Iron Age II Religious Site on the Judah-Sinai Border* (Jerusalem: Israel Exploration Society, 2012), 127, 130–32, and 138, n. 36. See also Stephen A. Geller, *Sacred Enigmas: Literary Religion in the Hebrew Bible* (New York: Routledge, 1996), 189.

17. A female figure has been noted in the drawings found at this site; in one instance she is next to a male figure, and it has been thought this might be Asherah (Coogan, *God and Sex,* 169).

18. I owe this point to my friend, the late Anthony Ceresko, who suggested it to me orally many years ago.

19. Frymer-Kensky, *In the Wake of the Goddesses*, 189. Contrast the fun but extravagant claim of Stephen D. Moore: "The God of Israel is an androgyne, a hermaphrodite, a she-male." See Moore, "Gigantic God: Yahweh's Body," *Journal for the Study of the Old Testament* 70 (1996): 104.

20. Soskice, *The Kindness of God*, 63.

21. For Leviathan, see also Isaiah 27:1; Psalms 74:14; 104:26; Job 3:8; 40:25; cf. 1 Enoch 50:7-9, 24; 2 Apocalypse of Baruch 29:4; 4 Ezra 6:49-52; Apocalypse of Abraham 21:4; see Christoph Uehlinger, "Leviathan," in *Dictionary of Deities and Demons in the Bible*, ed. Karel van der Toorn, Bob Becking, and Pieter W. van der Horst, 2nd ed. (Leiden/Boston/Köln: Brill; Grand Rapids, MI/Cambridge, UK: Eerdmans, 1999), 511–15.

22. Bloch-Smith, personal communication.

23. Weatherall, *Gender, Language and Discourse* (Women and Psychology Series; New York: Routledge, 2002), 156.

24. Weatherall, *Gender, Language and Discourse*, 121.

25. See the mention of this passage at the outset of this chapter.

26. *Catechism of the Catholic Church*, 2nd ed. (Washington, DC: United States Catholic Conference, 2000), para. 255; see Soskice, *The Kindness of God*, 119–20.

27. See *Catechism of the Catholic Church*, para. 239, 252, and 255. For the Trinity, see also the essays in Volker Henning Drecoll, ed., *Trinität* (Tübingen: Mohr Siebeck, 2011).

28. For example, Elisabeth Schussler Fiorenza, *The Power of the Word: Scripture and the Rhetoric of Empire* (Minneapolis, MN: Fortress Press, 2007), 221.

29. Soskice, *The Kindness of God*, 112–14.

30. In the Dead Sea Scrolls and the New Testament, the "holy spirit" cleanses and drives away evil spirits; it also has the means for humans to gain spiritual knowledge. See Sekki, *The Meaning of Ruah at Qumran*, 70–93; and also Menahem Kister, "Demons, Theology and Abraham's Covenant (CD 16:4-6 and Related Texts)," in *The Dead Sea Scrolls at Fifty: Proceedings of the 1997 Society of Biblical Literature Qumran Section Meetings*, ed. Robert

A. Kugler and E. M. Schuller (Atlanta: Scholars Press, 1999), 178 (reference courtesy of Miryam Brand).

31. For a recent discussion of the Holy Spirit, see Najeeb Awad, *God Without a Face? On the Personal Individuation of the Holy Spirit* (Tübingen: Mohr Siebeck, 2011).

32. The messiah seems to be called "my son" by God in line 18 of the so-called "Gabriel Revelation," a text dating to the turn of the millennium. See the views of the different scholars in Matthias Henze, ed., *Hazon Gabriel: New Readings of the Gabriel Revelation*, Early Judaism and Its Literature Series, vol. 29 (Atlanta: Society of Biblical Literature, 2011), 33, 34, 41 (especially note 10), 102, and 176.

33. Soskice (*The Kindness of God*, p. 83) emphasizes that God is only Father because "only the Son can show us the Father." Her further claim, however, would not work for Jewish readers of their Hebrew Scriptures for the biblical images of God as Father: "Without the Son 'the Father' is not God, but an idol." Here Soskice is taking a Christian view. A different formulation and consideration would be needed from a Jewish perspective.

34. John 1:18; 5:19-23; 6:40, 45-46; 8:19, 38, 54; 10:25, 38; 12:26, 49; 14:10-13, 23-24, 26-28, 31; 15:8-10, 15, 23-24; 16:10, 15, 23, 26-27; see also 3:16-17, 35-36; 5:17; 20:17.

35. Awad, *God Without a Face?*

36. Soskice, *The Kindness of God, 123.*

37. Ibid., 124.

38. See Schneider, *Beyond Monotheism*, 71. See also the remarks in this vein by David Tracy, "The Hermeneutics of Naming God," *Irish Theological Quarterly* 57 (1991): 253–64, especially 253 and 255. Note Shakespeare's Sonnet 105 for a reflection on human love in relation to the notion of the Trinity, as noted by Helen Vendler, *The Art of Shakespeare's Sonnets* (Cambridge, MA/London: The Belknap Press of Harvard University Press, 1997), 444–47.

39. So see Brevard S. Childs, *Old Testament Theology in a Canonical Context* (Philadelphia: Fortress Press, 1985), 40.

40. Kune Biezeveld, "One Unique God for All Parts of Life: Reconsidering an Exclusive Tradition," in *The Boundaries of Monotheism: Interdisciplinary Explorations into the Foundations of Western Monotheism*, ed. Anne-Marie Korte and Maaike de Haardt, Studies in Theology and Religion Series, vol. 13 (Boston: Brill, 2009), 154–73: Biezeveld sees theological possibilities for working out issues of divine gender and sexuality in the context of Christian monotheism. By contrast, Laurel Schneider, *Beyond Monotheism: A Theology of Multiplicity* (London: Routledge, 2008) sees monotheism as inherently

incapable of addressing diversity of divinity. For various approaches to gendered language for God in the Bible, see also Dille, *Mixing Metaphors*; Løland, *Silent or Salient Gender*; and O'Brien, *Challenging Prophetic Metaphor*.

41. Soskice, *The Kindness of God*, 81–83.

42. In this context, perhaps we do well to hear Martin Luther King's words to the church, available in Kai Wright, ed., *The African-American Archive: The History of the Black Experience through Documents* (New York: Black Dog & Leventhal Publishers, 2001), 569: "In deep disappointment, I have wept over the laxity of the church. But be assured that my tears have been tears of love. There can be no deep disappointment where there is no deep love. Yes, I love the church. How could I do otherwise? . . .Yes, I see the church as the body of Christ. But oh! How we have blemished and scarred that body through social neglect and through fear of being non-conformists."

Chapter 5—pages 75–90

1. See George Lakoff and Mark Johnson, *Metaphors We Live By* (Chicago: The University of Chicago Press, 2004); and George Lakoff and Mark Turner, *More Than Cool Reason: A Field Guide to Poetic Metaphor* (Chicago/London: The University of Chicago Press, 1987). Note also the essays in Andrew Ortony, ed., *Metaphor and Thought*, 2nd ed. (Cambridge/New York: Cambridge University Press, 1993). The volume includes an essay by Lakoff, entitled "The Contemporary Theory of Metaphor," on 202–51. For discussion of various approaches to biblical metaphor, see Andrea L. Weiss, *Figurative Language in Biblical Prose Narrative: Metaphor in the Book of Samuel*, Vetus Testamentum Supplements Series, vol. 107 (Leiden: Brill, 2006), 5–34. Note also David H. Aaron, *Biblical Ambiguities: Metaphor, Semantics and Divine Imagery*, Brill Reference Library of Judaism Series, vol. 4, (Leiden: Brill, 2001), 101–24.

2. George Lakoff and Mark Turner, *More Than Cool Reason: A Field Guide to Poetic Metaphor* (Chicago: The University of Chicago Press, 2004), 3.

3. For further details, see Mark S. Smith, *The Priestly Vision of Genesis 1* (Minneapolis, MN: Fortress Press, 2010). See also the fine surveys of creation texts by Paul Beauchamp, *Création et separation: Étude exégétique du chapitre premier de la Genèse*, Lectio Divina (Paris: Cerf, 2005, first published in 1969), 346–73; and Richard J. Clifford, *Creation Accounts in the Ancient Near East and in the Bible*, The Catholic Biblical Quarterly Monograph Series, vol. 26 (Washington, DC: The Catholic Biblical Association of America, 1994), 137–97. For the ancient Near Eastern material, see also Jean Bottéro and S. N. Kramer, *Lorsque les dieux faisaient l'homme: mythologie mésopotamienne* (Paris: Gallimard, 1993). W. G. Lambert wrote several important works on

creation, including: "A New Look at the Babylonian Background of Genesis," in *Babylonien und Israel: Historische, religiöse und sprachliche Beziehungen*, ed. H. P. Müller (Darmstadt: Wissenschaftliche Buchgesellschaft, 1991), 94–113; "The Relationship of Sumerian and Babylonian Myth as seen in Accounts of Creation," in *La circulation des biens, des personnes et des idées dans le Proche-Orient Ancien: Actes de la XXXVIIIᵉ Rencontre Assyriologique Internationale* (Paris, 9–10 juillet 1991), ed. D. Charpin and F. Joannès (Paris: Éditions Recherche sur les Civilisations, 1992), 129–35; and "Mesopotamian Creation Stories," in *Imagining Creation*, ed. M. J. Geller and M. Schipper (Leiden/Boston: Brill, 2008), 15–59.

4. See the emphasis on this point by Cardinal Joseph Ratzinger, *"In the Beginning . . .": A Catholic Understanding of the Story of Creation and the Fall*, trans. Boniface Ramsey (Huntington, IN: Our Sunday Visitor Publishing Division, 1990), 24.

5. For Genesis 1, I am thinking primarily of the cosmological pairs such as heaven and earth. This pairing occurs also in the Ugaritic texts and in biblical poetry (see Genesis 27:28 and 39; compare Genesis 49:25). Pairs such as heaven and earth go back to the idea of creation of pairs of cosmic components imagined as successive generations of parents giving birth. See Frank Moore Cross, "The 'Olden Gods' in Ancient Near Eastern Creation Myths and in Israel," in Cross, *From Epic to Canon: History and Literature in Ancient Israel* (Baltimore/London: The Johns Hopkins University Press, 1998), 72–83; and Othmar Keel, *The Symbolism of the Biblical World: Ancient Near Eastern Iconography and the Book of Psalms*, trans. Timothy J. Hallett (New York: Crossroad, 1985), 30–31 and 36.

6. The comments of Tikva Frymer-Kensky on Genesis 1 suggest a distance between this chapter and other biblical passages that draw on the model of creation as divine birth. See Frymer-Kensky, *In the Wake*, 93.

7. For examples in the ancient Near Eastern context, see my book, *God in Translation: Deities in Cross-Cultural Discourse in the Biblical World*, Forschungen zum Alten Testament series 1, vol. 57 (Tübingen: Mohr Siebeck, 2008; Grand Rapids, MI: Eerdmans, 2010), 14, 48, 69, and 298–99.

8. The linkage of cosmic battle and creation has been undermined in recent discussions of divine conflict, for example, in David Toshio Tsumura, *Creation and Destruction: A Reappraisal of the Chaoskampf Theory in the Old Testament* (Winona Lake, IN: Eisenbrauns, 2005). The linkage, however, is evident in Psalm 74, and the effort to dismiss this case is unconvincing. To be sure, the assumption that images of cosmic waters point to divine conflict has been overstated; in this, Tsumura is correct.

9. Author's translation.

10. The classic formulation of this worldview is by Frank Moore Cross, *Canaanite Myth and Hebrew Epic: Essays in the History of the Religion of Israel* (Cambridge, MA/London: Harvard University Press, 1973), 91–111. For the deity's march back from battle, see Psalm 68 in addition to royal psalms (see the following note). For divine enthronement following divine victory and recognized in the temple, see Psalm 29. For the reading of the iconography of the Jerusalem Temple as representing divine victory and enthronement (as in Psalm 29), see Elizabeth M. Bloch-Smith, "'Who is the King of Glory': Solomon's Temple as Symbol" in *Scripture and Other Artifacts: Essays on the Bible and Archaeology in Honor of Philip J. King*, ed. Michael Coogan, Cheryl Exum, and Lawrence Stager (Louisville, KY: Westminster John Knox, 1994), 18–31; and "Solomon's Temple: The Politics of Ritual Space," in *Sacred Place-Sacred Time: Archaeology and the Religion of Israel*, ed. Barry Gitlin (Winona Lake, IN: Eisenbrauns, 2001), 83–94. In these essays, Bloch-Smith discusses Psalm 29 and other relevant texts. The divine temple could be expressed equally as the heavenly abode of the God (see Psalm 68:29-30).

11. Psalm 89, with its creation references in verses 10-12 (Hebrew text, verses 11-13), requests divine help for the Judean king against his enemies. For another dramatic example of divine punishment, which opens with a call to the earth to listen, see Isaiah 34; note its use of "void" (*tohu*) in verse 11 (see this term used in Genesis 1:2). See Smith, *The Priestly Vision of Genesis 1*, chapter 2.

12. For the worldview of Psalm 89, see Paul Mosca, "Ugarit and Daniel 7: A Missing Link," *Biblica* 67 (1986): 496–517. For a more recent study of Psalm 89 and its royal worldview, see Robert Couffignal, *Les psaumes royaux de la Bible: Étude littéraire*, Cahiers de la Revue Biblique Series, vol. 54 (Paris: Gabalda, 2003), especially 94–112. For a general study of the royal worldview, see Tryggve N. D. Mettinger, *King and Messiah: The Civil and Sacral Legitimation of the Israelite Kings*, Coniectanea Biblica, Old Testament Series, vol. 8 (Lund: C. W. K. Gleerup, 1976). For divine kingship, see the essays in *Religion and Power: Divine Kingship in the Ancient World and Beyond*, Oriental Institute Studies Series, vol. 4 (Chicago: The Oriental Institute of the University of Chicago, 2008). As we will see in the discussion below, the model of divine power is attested also in Psalm 74:12-17.

13. Author's translation. See the insightful study of Paul Mosca, "Ugarit and Daniel 7," *Biblica* 67 (1986): 496–517, here 509, 512. As Mosca and others have noted, this verse reflects the idea of the cosmic enemies of Sea and River(s) as in the Ugaritic texts (presented in *Ugaritic Narrative Poetry*, ed. Simon B. Parker, Society of Biblical Literature Writings from the Ancient World Series, vol. 9 [Atlanta: Society of Biblical Literature, 1997] 103–4, 111, and 141).

14. Note also wisdom in the creation texts of Job 38:1-11, especially verses 5-6; and Job 28:25-27. Scholars often compare the Egyptian god Re in his role as creator by wisdom. See also Nili Shupak, *Where Can Wisdom Be Found? The Sage's Language in the Bible and in Ancient Egyptian Literature*, Orbis Biblicus et Orientalis Series, vol. 130 (Fribourg: University Press; Göttingen: Vandenhoeck & Ruprecht, 1993), 225 and 398, n. 46. Closer to Israel, the figure of El in the Ugaritic texts is the preeminent, wise creator deity (for his wisdom, see KTU 1.3 V 30-31 and 1.4 IV 41-43, presented in *Ugaritic Narrative Poetry*, pp. 117, 128). For another version of divine wisdom, see the following note.

15. Author's translation.

16. For the use of the verb, "to stretch out," also presupposing this model, see Isaiah 42:5; 44:24; 51:13; Jeremiah 10:12; 51:15; Zechariah 12:1; and Job 9:8.

17. The word *raqia'* in Genesis 1:6-7, often translated "firmament," stands in parallelism with "the heavens" in Psalm 19:1 (verse 2 in the Hebrew text). In Psalm 150:1, the same word is parallel to "his holy place" and in apposition to "his strong place." From these comparisons, the firmament is located in the heavens, and it is the site of divine enthronement in the heavens. For comparative evidence from Mesopotamia, see chapter 1.

18. For this passage, see the recent study of Alan Lenzi, *Secrecy and the Gods: Secret Knowledge in Ancient Mesopotamia and Biblical Israel* (State Archives of Assyria Studies Series, vol. 19 (Helsinki: Neo-Assyrian Text Corpus Project, 2008), 339–62.

19. Adele Berlin remarks of Psalm 104:35: "sinners undermine God's favor to the world: they may cause God to hide his face." See Berlin, "The Wisdom of Creation in Psalm 104," in *Seeking Out the Wisdom of the Ancients: Essays Offered to Honor Michael V. Fox on the Occasion of His Sixty-Fifth Birthday*, ed. Ronald L. Troxel, Kelvin G. Friebel, and Dennis R. Magary (Winona Lake, IN: Eisenbrauns, 2005), 83. See also Psalm 1:6, discussed at the end of chapter 3.

20. See also Isaiah 40:22; 57:15; note also Ezekiel 1, discussed in chapter 1.

21. The New Revised Standard Version translation takes the verbs as simple past (perhaps on the theory that these are short past prefix forms), while the New Jewish Publication Society translation takes them as simple future. The verbs might be taken as durative past in keeping with the usage of verse 16.

22. Beyond this importance given to the word is the matter of the degree to which the production of the Bible itself represented a form of textual devotion of the "word." Compare the suggestion by Stephen A. Geller that "biblical religion is an essentially literary faith." See Geller, *Sacred Enigmas: Literary*

162   *How Human Is God?*

Religion in the Hebrew Bible (London/New York: Routledge, 1996), 168. For this notion, see further Geller's discussion on 170–71.

23. Among the expressions denoting the divine presence, one may also note the term "glory, effulgence" (*kabod*), or more precisely, "gravitas," which fits with the root meaning of the word, "to be heavy" (compare *kabod* used of a human person in Genesis 49:6). This term may be less a separate term for divine presence than a word that characterizes that presence; compare "the *kabod* of his name" in Psalm 29:2. *Kabod* perhaps captures the palpable sense of that presence as marked by these terms for presence. Still, the distinction is perhaps not to be drawn too finely. For *kabod*, see Tryggve N. D. Mettinger, *The Dethronement of Sabaoth: Studies in the Shem and Kabod Theologies*, Coniectanea Biblica, Old Testament Series, vol. 18 (Lund: Gleerup, 1982), 80–115 and 116–23; and the discussion in chapter 1.

24. This idea connects with the third body of God discussed in chapter 1.

25. Ecclesiasticus (Ben Sira) 33:8 views the creation of Genesis 1 as a matter of divine wisdom. In this presentation, this later wisdom text of the second model offers a wisdom interpretation of an earlier example of the third model.

26. This is also true of texts that do not specifically discuss creation. In Psalm 29 and Isaiah 35 the appearance of God as a warrior is characterized with language of holiness (see Psalm 29:2; Isaiah 35:8). Or, a biblical passage that is grounded in the wisdom model can draw on the idea of God's nearness in a sanctuary (Psalm 73).

27. See the analysis of the "cult of distraction" by Chris Rojek, *Celebrity* (London: Reaktion Books, 2001), 33–34, discussed by Chris Hedges, *Empire of Illusion: The End of Literacy and the Triumph of Spectacle* (New York: Nation Books, 2009), 37–38.

28. So the title of the critique of American university in Chris Hedges, *Empire of Illusion*, 89–114.

29. See also Job 4:19; 10:8-12; 27:3; and 30:19 for various aspects of this idea; cf. Isaiah 41:25; 45:9.

30. See Old Babylonian Atrahasis, tablet I, lines 203 and 210–34, in W. G. Lambert and A. R. Millard, *Atra-Hasis: The Babylonian Story of the Flood* (Oxford, UK: Clarendon, 1969; reprint edition, Winona Lake, IN: Eisenbrauns, 1999), 56–59.

31. See Benjamin R. Foster, *Before the Muses: An Anthology of Akkadian Literature*, 3rd ed. (Bethesda, MD: CDL Press, 2005), 496. This is also the method of creation used by the chief god El to make the female figure who cures King Kirta of his illness in KTU 1.16 V 28-30: "He fills his hands [with soil], With good soil fills his [fingers]. He pinches off some clay." For this

translation as well as an English transcription of the Ugaritic letters, see Edward L. Greenstein, "Kirta," in *Ugaritic Narrative Poetry*, ed. Simon B. Parker, Society of Biblical Literature Writings from the Ancient World Series, vol. 9 (Atlanta: Society of Biblical Literature, 1997), 38. The element mixed with this clay varies in these accounts. In some instances, it is a component that links human life with divinity in some manner, for example, divine spirit or *ruah* in the case of Genesis 2; in Atrahasis it is the flesh and blood of the slain god that contains his "spirit," as *etemmu* is translated by Lambert and Millard, and also by Benjamin R. Foster, *Before the Muses: An Anthology of Akkadian Literature*, 3rd ed. (Bethesda, MD: CDL Press, 2005), 236.

32. Author's translation.

33. The miracle of the prophet Elisha in 2 Kings 4:34-35 probably involves an act of resuscitation. According to verse 34, the prophet "lay upon the child, putting his mouth upon his mouth, his eyes upon his eyes, and his hands upon his hands." Only then is there *wayyighar* in verses 34–35, the waw-consecutive form suggesting the next action in the sequence. The verb does not mean, "he lay bent over him" (New Revised Standard Version). Instead, it entails an act involving the mouth, now known, thanks to the Ugaritic attestation of the root (RS 92.2014.11). The resulting picture in 2 Kings 4:34-35 seems to be mouth-to-mouth resuscitation. For the evidence, see Mark S. Smith, "Recent Study of Israelite Religion in Light of the Ugaritic Texts," in *Ugarit at Seventy-Five*, ed. K. Lawson Younger Jr. (Winona Lake, IN: Eisenbrauns, 2007), 1–25, here 12–13.

34. Author's translation.

35. See Abou Assaf, A. Pierre Bordreuil, and Alan R. Millard, *La statue de Tel Fekherye et son inscription bilingue assyro-araméenne*, Etudes assyriologiques, Cahiers Series, vol. 10 (Paris: Éditions Recherche sur les civilisations, 1982), 23–25; W. Randall Garr, "'Image' and 'Likeness' in the Inscription from Tell Fakhariyeh," *Israel Exploration Journal* 50 (2000): 227–34, and *In His Own Image and Likeness: Humanity, Divinity, and Monotheism*, Culture and History of the Ancient Near East Series, vol. 15 (Leiden/ Boston: Brill, 2003); and Bernd Janowski, "Die lebendige Statue Gottes: zur Anthropologie der priesterlichen Urgeschichte," in *Gott und Mensch im Dialog. Volume I* (Berlin/New York: de Gruyter, 2004), 183–214.

36. Critics may rightly object to my rendering the pronoun "her" when its gender is patently masculine in Hebrew. However, this would miss the point that the meaning of its antecedent *'adam*, "human being," is male and female, as Genesis 1:27 shows. For this reason, I have balanced "her" and "him" in my translation of verses 5 and 6 here.

37. Cited in V. S. Ramachandran and Sandra Blakeslee, *Phantoms in the Brain: Probing the Mysteries of the Human Mind*, Quill edition (New York: HarperCollins, 1999), 256–57, italics mine.

38. Ibid., 257.

39. See also the various sentiments along these lines in Proverbs 18:4; 20:5; 25:3. Note the statement that "no one knows man," is an Aramaic proverb presented in James M. Lindenberger, *The Aramaic Proverbs of Ahiqar*, The Johns Hopkins Near Eastern Studies Series (Baltimore/London: The Johns Hopkins University, 1983), 104. Cf. Ecclesiastes (Qoheleth) 7:24. Cf. the Sumerian-Akkadian proverb, "People do not by themselves know their doing." See Bendt Alster, *Wisdom of Ancient Sumer* (Bethesda, MD: CDL Press, 2005), 325.

40. Psalm 145:3; Job 5:9; 9:10; 11:7; 30:3-4; 36:26; Ecclesiastes 8:17; Isaiah 40:28. See also the sentiments as expressed in Mesopotamian literature, e.g., the Sumerian proverb, "The will of a god cannot be understood, the way of a god cannot be known, Anything of a god [is difficult] to find out." See Wilfred G. Lambert, *Babylonian Wisdom Literature* (Oxford, UK: Clarendon Press, 1960; reprinted, Winona Lake, IN: Eisenbrauns, 1996), 266 (lines 7–8).

Chapter 6—pages 91–109

1. *Catechism of the Catholic Church*, 2nd ed. (Washington, DC: United States Catholic Conference), para. 2850. This line of the "Our Father" in Matthew 6:13 is not included in the parallel version of the "Our Father" in Luke 11:4.

2. This translation of *ponerou* in this line in the "Our Father" in Matthew 6:13 is not uncommon, but the translation "evil" is possible. The grammatical issue turns on whether the word is to be understood as masculine or neuter. The neuter translation is favored by Ulrich Lutz, *Matthew 1–7: A Commentary*, ed. Helmut Koester, trans. James E. Crouch (Minneapolis, MN: Fortress Press, 2007), 323. For a more nuanced view of this "evil" as possibly associated with Satan, see Hans Dieter Betz, *The Sermon on the Mount: A Commentary on the Sermon on the Mount, including the Sermon on the Plain (Matthew 5:3–7:27 and Luke 6:20-49)*, ed. Adela Yarbro Collins, Hermeneia (Minneapolis, MN: Fortress Press, 1995), 411–13. My thanks go to Matteo Crimella for help on this point.

3. The *New York Times*, Saturday, March 16, 2013, p. A5.

4. See Elaine Pagels, *The Origin of Satan: How Christians Demonized Jews, Pagans, and Heretics* (New York: Vintage, 1995), especially xviii–xx and 37. This approach does not apply to the satan in the Hebrew Bible (Pagels, *The Origin of Satan*, 35–44). See the discussion below.

5. See the discussion below for New Testament references to Satan and the devil.

6. See the similar expression in Genesis 8:21 and Sirach 37:3, and note also 2 Esdras 4:30-31. It is not uncommon in the Dead Sea Scrolls. For scholarship on this subject as well as the early sources for this idea, see the recent survey of Miryam T. Brand, *Evil Within and Without: The Source of Sin and Its Nature as Portrayed in Second Temple Literature* (Göttingen: Vandenhoeck & Ruprecht, 2013), 19–22, 46–48, 138–42, and 280–83.

7. For references in early Jewish sources, see Louis Isaac Rabinowitz, "Satan," in *Encyclopedia Judaica: Second Edition*, ed. Fred Skolnik and Michael Berenbaum (Detroit/New York: Thomas Gale, 2007), vol. 18, p. 72.

8. Armin Lange, "Satanic Verses: The Adversary in the Qumran Manuscripts and Elsewhere," *Revue de Qumrân* 93 (2009): 35–48, here 47.

9. So Victor P. Hamilton, "Satan," in *Anchor Bible Dictionary*, ed. David Noel Freedman (New York: Doubleday, 1992), vol. 5, 987. See also Lange, "Satanic Verses," 48.

10. See the book-length works on the subject cited below and listed in the Recommended Reading listed for this chapter at the end of this book. Readers interested in further details are encouraged to consult these works.

11. See the surveys with references to secondary literature in Miryam T. Brand, *Evil Within and Without: The Source of Sin and Its Nature as Portrayed in Second Temple Literature* (Göttingen: Vandenhoeck & Ruprecht, 2013); and Derek R. Brown, "The Devil in the Details: A Survey of Research on Satan in Biblical Studies," *Currents in Biblical Research* 9, no. 2 (2011): 205–8. Other named figures (such as Belial and Mastema) are the major leaders of demons in the world.

12. Jubilees 10:11. Except for "the satan," this translation follows *The Old Testament Pseudepigrapha. Volume 2*, ed. James H. Charlesworth (Garden City, NY: Doubleday, 1985), 76, which instead translates "Satan." Jubilees 10.11 uses the definite article (compare "the satan" in Job 1–2, discussed below). The translation "the satan" for Jubilees 10:11 can be found in James C. VanderKam, *The Book of Jubilees* (Sheffield: Sheffield Academic Press, 2001), 43 and 128; for his critical edition of the Ethiopic text, see VanderKam, *The Book of Jubilees: A Critical Text* (Louvain: Peeters, 1989), 62. In context, the figure of "the satan" is identified with another demonic figure named Mastema (see Jubilees 10:7-9). "The satan" here may serve as a title for Mastema.

13. For the etymology and meaning for the word, see Day, *An Adversary*, 17–43. As Day's study makes clear and we will see, the two operative meanings more broadly are (legal) "accuser" and (political) "adversary." To my mind, "opponent" or "adversary" seems to be the broader meaning, and "accuser" a specific legal manifestation.

14. The satan is identified here with the demonic power in the universe named Mastema, according to Michael Segal, *The Book of Jubilees: Rewritten Bible, Redaction, Ideology and Theology* (Atlanta: Society of Biblical Literature, 2007), 176, n. 19; and Brand, *Evil Within*, 180 (my thanks go to Segal and Brand for their comments on this matter). It seems possible that the satan might not be identified as Mastema, and if so, the satan is the earthly worker for Mastema or an earthly demonic manifestation of his. The name of Mastema, which goes back to a common noun for "animosity" (Hosea 9:7-8), has been thought to be related etymologically to the title "the satan," despite the difference in their last consonants. Jubilees also predicts that there "will be neither a satan nor any evil one who will destroy" (23:29 and also 50:5).

15. George W. E. Nickelsburg and James C. VanderKam, *1 Enoch 2*, ed. Klaus Baltzer, Hermeneia (Minneapolis, MN: Fortress Press, 2012), 130. See also *The Old Testament Pseudepigrapha*, vol. 1, 32. The section of Enoch containing these verses (Enoch 37–71, called the "Book of Parables") is thought to date to around the turn of the era. See George W. E. Nickelsburg, "Enoch, Books of," in *Encyclopedia of the Dead Sea Scrolls*, vol. 1, ed. Lawrence H. Schiffman and James C. VanderKam (Oxford/New York: Oxford University Press, 2000), 250.

16. It occurs only five times in Hebrew texts and once in an Aramaic text. See the survey with considerable information by Lange, "Satanic Verses," 38. According to Lange, the word occurs once in Aramaic, in Aramaic Levi Document 3:9, in Jonas C. Greenfield, Michael E. Stone, and Esther Eshel, *The Aramaic Levi Document: Edition, Translation, Commentary*, Studia in Veteris Testamenti Pseudepigrapha Series, vol. 19 (Leiden: Brill, 2004), 62–63; on this Aramaic attestation, see below in note 21.

17. See similarly, Kelly, *Satan*, 41–50.

18. Cave 11 Psalms scroll, ms. a (11QPs^a = 11Q5), column 19, line 15, in *Poetic and Liturgical Texts*, The Dead Sea Scrolls Reader, vol. 5, ed. Donald W. Parry and Emanuel Tov (Leiden/Boston: Brill 2005), 192–93. See the parallel in 4QTestament of Levi, ms. b. (= Aramaic Levi Document 3:9, in Greenfield, Stone, and Eshel, *The Aramaic Levi Document*, 60–61 = 4Q213a, fragment 1, line 17, in *Parabiblical Texts*, The Dead Sea Scrolls Reader, vol. 3, ed. Donald W. Parry and Emanuel Tov (Leiden/Boston: Brill, 2005), 390–91. The parallel was noted first by David Flusser, "Qumrân and Jewish 'Apotropaic' Prayers," *Israel Exploration Journal* 16 (1966): 194–205, especially 197–200: "And let not any satan have power over me." See also Jonas C. Greenfield, "Two Notes on the Apocryphal Psalms," in *"Sha'arei Talmon": Studies in the Bible, Qumran, and the Ancient Near East presented to Shemaryahu Talmon*, ed. Michael Fishbane and Emanuel Tov, with the assistance of Weston W. Fields (Winona Lake, IN: Eisenbrauns, 1992), 310–12. A similar formulation seems also to inform a very dam-

aged passage in the Blessings (1QSb = 1Q28b, column 1, lines 7–8: "[may he de]liver you from all . . . you hate . . . a satan . . ."), in James H. Charlesworth and Loren T. Stuckenbruck, "Blessings (1QSb)," in *Hebrew, Aramaic, and Greek Texts with English Translations: Volume 1: Rule of the Community and Related Documents*, ed. James H. Charlesworth (Tübingen: Mohr Siebeck; Louisville: Westminster John Knox, 1994), 122–23. However, the context is fragmentary and no further information can be derived from this attestation.

19. Psalms scroll, ms. a (11Q5), column 19, line 15–16, in *Poetic and Liturgical Texts*, The Dead Sea Scrolls Reader, vol. 5, ed. Donald W. Parry and Emanuel Tov (Leiden/Boston: Brill 2005), 192–93. For the meaning of this line, see Jonas Greenfield, "Two Notes on the Apocryphal Psalms," 310–12; note also Brand, *Evil Within*, 208–10.

20. Brand, *Evil Within*, 210. Brand's italics.

21. Brand, *Evil Within*, 209.

22. Matthew 4:10; 12:26 [2 times]; 16:23; Mark 1:13; 3:23 [2 times], 26; 4:15; 8:33; Luke 10:18; 11:18; 13:16; 22:3, 31; John 13:27; Acts 5:3; 26:18; Romans 16:20; 1 Corinthians 5:5; 7:5; 2 Corinthians 2:11; 11:14; 12:7; 1 Thessalonians 2:18; 2 Thessalonians 2:9; 1 Titus 1:20; 5:15; Revelation 2:9, 13, 24; 3:9; 12:9; 20:2, 7). We also have this figure in his Greek form as "the devil" (for example, in Matthew 4:1, 5, 8, 11; Luke 4:2, 3, 5, and 8:12; John 6:70 and 8:44; Ephesians 4:27 and 6:11; 1 Timothy 3:6; Hebrews 2:14; James 4:7; 1 Peter 5:8; 1 John 3:8.

23. For Satan in the Marcan account, see S. R. Garrett, *The Temptations of Jesus in Mark's Gospel* (Grand Rapids, MI: Eerdmans, 1998). For the Lucan account, see S. R. Garrett, *The Demise of the Devil: Magic and the Demonic in Luke's Writings* (Minneapolis, MN: Fortress Press, 1989). Note also the older study of Henry Ansgar Kelly, "The Devil in the Desert," *The Catholic Biblical Quarterly 26* (1964): 190–220. For further discussion of Satan in scholarly literature on Matthew, Mark, and Luke (commonly called "the Synoptic Gospels"), see Brown, "The Devil in the Details," 209–11.

24. The story is commonly assigned to the source thought to lie behind and shared by Matthew and Luke (called the "Q source").

25. Author's translation.

26. For the grammar, see Joseph A. Fitzmyer, *The Gospel According to Luke (X–XXIV): Introduction, Translation, and Notes*, Anchor Bible Series, vol. 28A (New York: Doubleday, 1985), 1012.

27. The word is without the definite article in Luke 22:3, but with the definite article in John 13:27.

28. For this type of language, see also 1 John 3:8.

29. See Joshua Trachtenberg, *The Devil and the Jews: The Medieval Conception of the Jew and Its Relation to Modern Anti-Semiticism* (Philadelphia:

Jewish Publication Society, 1986); and Daniel Jonah Goldhagen, *A Moral Reckoning: The Role of the Catholic Church in the Holocaust and its Unfilled Duty of Repair* (New York: Knopf, 2002).

30. For this passage, see the discussion of Pagels, *The Origin of Satan*, 103–4. Pagels suggests a considerably wider group of passages that contribute to the demonization of Jews, even if these are not as explicit as John 8:44. Note also the (rather illogical) accusation represented about Jesus in Matthew 12:24 that he casts out demons by the ruler of demons. For this passage, see the discussion of Pagels, *The Origin of Satan*, 82–83. Pagels notes that Christian demonization of other Jews is found also in the Dead Sea Scrolls.

31. For a good probing of the problem, see Amy-Jill Levine, *The Misunderstood Jew: The Church and the Scandal of the Jewish Jesus* (San Francisco: HarperOne, 2007), 102–10.

32. For the god Baal in this role as enemy of the serpent, see *Ugaritic Narrative Poetry*, 141–42.

33. See Fitzmyer, *The Gospel According to Luke*, 858–61.

34. See also the psychological interpretation of spirits in the Dead Sea Scrolls Rule of the Community as "good" and "bad" inclinations, in Kelly, *Satan*, 46. To be sure, Kelly (*Satan*, p. 93) sees "a sophisticated Devil" in Matthew.

35. Elaine Pagels, *The Origin of Satan: How Christians Demonized Jews, Pagans, and Heretics* (New York: Vintage, 1995) 14. Pagels also comments on page 33: "Furthermore, what Mark merely implies—that Jesus' opponents are energized by Satan—Luke and John will state explicitly."

36. The basic survey for the evidence in the Hebrew Bible is Peggy L. Day, *An Adversary in Heaven: Satan in the Hebrew Bible*, Harvard Semitic Museum Series, vol. 43 (Atlanta: Scholars Press, 1988). See also Josef Wehrle, "Wesen und Wandel der Satansvorstellung im Alten Testament," *Münchener Theologische Zeitschrift* 52 (2001): 194–207; and Derek R. Brown, "The Devil in the Details: A Survey of Research on Satan in Biblical Studies." *Currents in Biblical Research* 9, no.2 (2011): 200–227, here 203–5.

37. Baruch A. Levine, *Numbers 21–36: A New Translation with Introduction and Commentary*, Anchor Bible Series, vol. 4b (Garden City, New York: Doubleday, 2000), 155.

38. Author's translation.

39. For this passage, see Peggy L. Day, "Abishai the *śāṭān* in 2 Samuel 19:17-24," *The Catholic Biblical Quarterly* 49 (1987): 543–47.

40. See also Zechariah 3:1, discussed below (compare "to stand against," used of Satan in 1 Chronicles 21:1, also discussed below). For the legal context, see Raymond Westbrook and Bruce Wells, *Everyday Law in Biblical Israel:*

An Introduction (Louisville, KY: Westminster John Knox, 2009), 41. Compare the idea of the opponent in court in Isaiah 50:8 and Proverbs 18:17; cf. the two false witnesses seated before the accused and testifying against him in 1 Kings 21:11-13 (cf. Deuteronomy 19:15-20). For these passages, see Tikva Frymer-Kenski, "Israel," in *A History of Ancient Near Eastern Law*, vol. 2, ed. Raymond Westbrook (Leiden/Boston: Brill, 2003), 995.

    41. See Erhard S. Gerstenberger, *Psalms, Part 2, and Lamentations*, The Forms of the Old Testament Series, vol. 14 (Grand Rapids, MI/Cambridge, UK: Eerdmans, 2001), 257–63; and David P. Wright, "Ritual Analogy in Psalm 109," *Journal of Biblical Literature* 113 (1994): 385–404. See also verses 20 and 29, as well as "my adversaries" in Psalm 38:20 and "my accusers" in Psalm 71:13. This legal sense of the word also pops up with the related noun *sitnâ*, meaning "accusation" (Ezra 4:6), which was drawn up by "the adversaries of Judah and Benjamin" (verse 1). A related meaning of this word is used as a place-name, based on a dispute between Isaac's herders and the herders of Gerar in Genesis 26:21: "Then they dug another well, and they quarreled over that one also; so he [Isaac] called it Sitnah." Here Sitnah denotes "quarrel."

    42. This part of the Balaam story seems to be a secondary addition to the larger complex of Numbers 22–24. This is indicated by the editorial technique of secondary addition known as "resumptive repetition" in Numbers 22:21 ("he went with the officials of Moab") and 22:35 ("So Balaam went on with the officials of Moab."), as seen in Levine, *Numbers 21–36*, 159. So this passage may reflect a later usage of the word; Levine (*Numbers 21–36*, 155) suggests comparison with late, pre-exilic historical books.

    43. For this passage, see John W. Wright, "The Innocence of David in 1 Chronicles 21," *Journal for the Study of the Old Testament* 60 (1993): 87–105; Pancratius Beentjes, "Satan, God, and the Angel(s) in 1 Chronicles," in *Angels: The Concept of Celestial Beings—Origins, Development and Reception*, ed. Friedrich V. Relterei, Tobias Nicklas, and Karin Schöpflin, Deuterocanonical and Cognate Literature Yearbook 2007 (Berlin/New York: Walter de Gruyter, 2007), 139–54; Dominic Rudman, "Zechariah and the Satan Tradition in the Hebrew Bible," in *Tradition in Transition: Haggai and Zechariah 1–8 in the Trajectory of Hebrew Theology*, ed. Mark J. Boda and Michael H. Floyd, Library of Hebrew Bible/Old Testament Studies, Journal for the Study of the Old Testament Supplement Series, vol. 475 (New York/London: T & T Clark, 2008), 205–8; and Ryan Stokes, "The Devil Made David Do It . . . Or Did He? The Nature, Identity, and Literary Origins of the *Satan* in 1 Chronicles 21," *Journal of Biblical Literature* 128 (2009): 91–106.

    44. For the second view, see Day, *An Adversary*, 128 and 143–44. Otherwise, Satan is not a name until the later texts of Jubilees 23:29 and Assumption

of Moses 10:1, as noted by Day and also by Pancratius Beentjes, "Satan, God, and the Angel(s) in 1 Chronicles," 140. See the discussion above.

45. It is because of the nature of this replacement that one may doubt the view that a human satan is involved in 1 Chronicles 21:1 (along the lines of human satans noted above). For this view, see the discussion of Derek R. Brown, "The Devil in the Details: A Survey of Research on Satan in Biblical Studies," *Currents in Biblical Research* 9, no. 2 (2011): 200–227, here 205.

46. According to Peggy L. Day (*An Adversary*, 137), the reason is more specific: it is in order to downplay Yahweh's disapproval of David, a most beloved figure in the books of Chronicles.

47. Compare Fitzmyer, *The Gospel According to Luke (X–XXIV)*, 862.

48. See C. L. Seow, *Job 1–21: Interpretation and Commentary*, Illuminations Series (Grand Rapids, MI/Cambridge, UK: Eerdmans, 2013), 273. For the idea that divine anger functions as a force acting on its own, see McCarter, "When Gods Lose Their Temper," 90–91.

49. Karel van der Toorn (personal communication) also suggests possible comparison with Akkadian *ezzu*, "angry, fierce, terrible," used with weapons, in *The Chicago Assyrian Dictionary Volume 4: E* (Chicago: The Oriental Institute, 1958), 43. In this approach, the satan would be God's weapon.

50. Here I echo a comment made by Karel van der Toorn about "humanized" Mesopotamian demons: "The humanization of evil implied by this development can be viewed as an attempt to rationalize evil." See van der Toorn, "The Theology of Demons in Mesopotamia and Israel: Popular Belief and Scholarly Speculation," in *Die Dämonen—Demons: Die Dämonologie der israelitisch-jüdischen und frühchristlichen Literatur im Kontext ihrer Umwelt—The Demonology of Israelite-Jewish and Early Christian Literature in Context of Their Environment*, ed. Armin Lange, Hermann Lichtenberger, and K. F. Diethard Römheld (Tübingen: Mohr Siebeck, 2003), 67.

51. "He" in 3:1 in context goes back to the angel mentioned in 2:3. Zechariah 3 has been thought to be a secondary interpolation. For this issue, see Thomas Pola, "Form and Meaning in Zechariah 3," in *Yahwism after the Exile: Perspectives on Israelite Religion in the Persian Era. Papers Read at the First Meeting of the European Association for Biblical Studies Utrecht, 6–9 August 2000*, ed. Rainer Albertz and Bob Becking, Theology and Religion Series, vol. 5 (Assen: Van Gorcum, 2003), 156–67, here 159–60; Martin Hallaschka, "Zechariah's Angels: Their Role in the Night Visions and in the Redaction History of Zech 1, 7-6, 8," *Scandinavian Journal of the Old Testament* 24 (2010): 13–27, here 16–17. For another approach, see Danie F. O'Kennedy, "Zechariah 3–4: Core of Proto-Zechariah," *Old Testament Essays* 16 (2003): 635–53.

52. For this scene, see Thomas Pola, "Form and Meaning in Zechariah 3," 156–67; Marvin Sweeney, "Targum Jonathan's Reading of Zechariah 3," in *Tradition in Transition: Haggai and Zechariah 1–8 in the Trajectory of Hebrew Theology*, ed. Mark J. Boda and Michael H. Floyd, Library of Hebrew Bible/ Old Testament Studies, Journal for the Study of the Old Testament Supplement Series, vol. 475 (New York/London: T & T Clark, 2008), 271–90. For the satan in this divine council scene, see Dominic Rudman, "Zechariah and the Satan Tradition in the Hebrew Bible," in *Tradition in Transition: Haggai and Zechariah 1–8 in the Trajectory of Hebrew Theology*, ed. Mark J. Boda and Michael H. Floyd, Library of Hebrew Bible/Old Testament Studies, Journal for the Study of the Old Testament Supplement Series, vol. 475 (New York/London: T & T Clark, 2008), 191–209. For scenes of what have been called the divine assembly or council, see E. Theodore Mullen, *The Assembly of the Gods: The Divine Council in Canaanite and Early Hebrew Literature* (Harvard Semitic Monographs Series, vol. 24 (Chico, CA: Scholars Press, 1908); and Ellen White, *The Council of Yahweh: Its Structure and Membership* Forschungen zum Alten Testament, second series (Tübingen: Mohr Siebeck, 2014).

53. The Satan here is commonly called a "prosecuting attorney," but this distinct legal role is unknown in ancient Israel and apparently it is also missing in Mesopotamia. See Day, *An Adversary*, 39–43; and Shalom E. Holtz, *Neo-Babylonian Court Procedure*, Cuneiform Monographs Series, vol. 38, (Leiden/ Boston: Brill, 2009). The accuser is one who brings a suit against the accused or a witness who offers testimony against the accused. See also the material cited in note 38 above. In addition, the situation of Psalm 109 has been compared with a legal dispute in one of the Elephantine papyri; see Bezalel Porten, *Archives from Elephantine: The Life of an Ancient Jewish Military Colony* (Berkeley/Los Angeles: University of California, 1968), 156–57.

54. On the details of the apparel here as well as the shifts evident in the Septuagintal rendering, see Patricia Ahearne-Kroll, "LXX/OG Zechariah 1–6 and the Portrayal of Joshua Centuries after the Restoration of the Temple," in *Septuagint Research: Issues and Challenges in the Study of the Greek Jewish Scriptures*, ed. Wolfgang Kraus and R. Glenn Wooden, Septuagint and Cognate Studies Series, vol. 53 (Atlanta: Society of Biblical Literature, 2006), 179–92, here 180–83. For further details, see Michael Segal, "The Responsibilities and Rewards of Joshua the High Priest according to Zechariah 3:7," *Journal of Biblical Literature* 126 (2007): 717–34.

55. See W. A. M. Beuken, *Haggai—Sacharja 1–8* (Studia Semitica Neerlandica Series, vol. 10 (Assen: van Gorcum, 1967), 284 and 299. For the association of "filth" and sin, see Isaiah 4:4 and Proverbs 30:12; compare Job

9:30-31 and 14:4. For further discussion, see Rudman, "Zechariah and the Satan Tradition in the Hebrew Bible," 193–97; and Lena-Sofia Tiemeyer, "The Guilty Priesthood (Zech 3)," in *The Book of Zechariah and its Influence*, ed. Christopher Tuckett (Burlington, VT/Aldershot: Ashgate, 2003), 1–19. Such purity issues are classic priestly concerns, and so the divine voices in Zechariah 3 may be giving voice to an inner-priestly disagreement: on one side are perhaps some priests in Judah represented by the satan, and on the other side is Joshua, representing another priestly subgroup or line, perhaps one more recently arrived from Babylonia (perhaps alluded to by the phrase, "plucked from the fire" in verse 2). Compare Day, *An Adversary*, 120–21 ("certain factions within the restoration community"); and James VanderKam, *From Joshua to Caiaphas: High Priests after the Exile* (Minneapolis, MN: Fortress Press; Assen: van Gorcum, 2004), 25; cf. Jeremiah W. Cataldo, *Breaking Monotheism: Yehud and the Material Formation of Monotheistic Identity*, Library of Hebrew Bible/Old Testament Studies 565 (London: Bloomsbury, 2012), 60. For priestly issues in this context, see the important book by Stephen L. Cook, *Prophecy and Apocalypticism: The Postexilic Social Setting* (Minneapolis: Fortress Press, 1995), 123–61, especially 136, 144, 160, and 161, n. 48; and Deborah W. Rooke, *Zadok's Heirs: The Role and Development of the High Priesthood in Ancient Israel* (Oxford Theological Monographs Series (Oxford/New York: Oxford University Press, 2000), 140.

56. Seow (*Job 1–21*, 273) suggests that the satan in Zechariah "seems to be a projection of the divine will to condemn, a will held in tension with the possibility of divine deliverance, as represented by the *mal'ak yhwh*."

57. This discussion of Job 1–2 is informed by David J. A. Clines, "False Naivety in the Prologue of Job," *Hebrew Annual Review* 9 (1985): 127–36; and Alan Cooper, "Reading and Misreading the Prologue to Job," *Journal for the Study of the Old Testament* 46 (1990): 67–79. For a reliable guide to the book, see C. L. Seow, *Job 1–21: Interpretation and Commentary*, Illuminations Series (Grand Rapids, MI/Cambridge, UK: Eerdmans, 2013). For the figure of the satan in this scene, see also Rudman, "Zechariah and the Satan Tradition in the Hebrew Bible," 197–204; and Raik Heckl, "Die Figur des Satan in der Rahmenerzählung des Hiobbuches," *leqach* 10 (2012): 45–57.

58. Compare Seow, *Job 1–21*, 250. Seow (*Job 1–21*, 298) also notes how the verb "they met together" in 2:11 suggests "an assembly on earth," recalling the gathering of the divine beings in heaven in 1:6 and 2:1.

59. For further appreciation of the description of Job and how it relates to God's characterization of Job in 1:8 and 2:3, see the fine work of Adele Berlin, *Poetics and Interpretation of Biblical Literature* (Winona Lake, IN: Eisenbrauns, 1994), 41–42.

60. For the suggestion that the offerings made in verse 5 are to invoke the blessing of *haʾelohim* as they meet in judgment of humans in heaven in verse 6, see Alan Cooper and Bernard R. Goldstein, "Exodus and *Maṣṣôt* in History and Tradition," *Maarav* 8 = *Let Your Colleagues Praise You: Studies in Memory of Stanley Gevirtz: Volume 2*, ed. Robert J. Ratner, Lewis M. Barth, Marianne Luijken Gevirtz, and Bruce Zuckerman (Rolling Hill Estates, CA: Western Academic Press, 1992), 33, n. 62.

61. So A. L. Oppenheim, "The Eyes of the Lord," *Journal of the American Oriental Society* 88 (1968): 173–80, followed by many commentators such as F. Rachel Magdalene, *On the Scales of Righteousness: Neo-Babylonian Trial Law and the Book of Job*, Brown Judaic Studies Series, vol. 348 (Providence, RI: Brown University Judaic Studies, 2007), 72–74 and 101–2 (reference courtesy of Bruce Wells).

62. A related motif involves God hearing the cry of humans and coming down in response, for example, in Exodus 3:7-8.

63. See Akkadian *izišubbû*, "stroke of lightning," derived from the Sumerian i z i. š u b. b a, meaning literally, "fire fell down from heaven" (*The Assyrian Dictionary Volume 7: I and J* [Chicago: The Oriental Institute, 1960], 319; information courtesy of Christopher Frechette). Compare also the sort of omen-text from Mesopotamia (especially the second clause): "If Adad thunders, and lightning which is like fire flashes towards the south, there will be sick people in Akkad, the children will die at the behest of Lamashtu." See Erlend Gehlken, *Weather Omens of Enûma Anu Enlil: Thunderstorms, Wind and Rain (Tablets 44–49)*, Cuneiform Monographs Series, vol. 43 (Leiden/Boston: Brill, 2012), 28–29. The examples could be multiplied.

64. Note the omen with the result that "the south wind will spring up and destroy houses" (Gehlken, *Weather Omens of Enûma Anu Enlil*, 64). Note also the death of the children in the omen-text cited in the preceding footnote.

65. Compare the omens cited in the preceding two footnotes.

66. NRSV translates, "Curse God and die." The use of Hebrew **brk*, "to bless," seems to be "antiphrastic, that is, used in a sense opposite to its normal sense," according to Seow, *Job 1–2*, 254–55, 270–71, and 305; note also Cooper, "Reading and Misreading," 76–77, n. 17, who defends a literal translation.

67. Cooper, "Reading and Misreading," 73.

68. This is discussed in chapter 1, with what is called there the second body of God.

69. For the "whirlwind," see Aloysius Fitzgerald, F.S.C., *The Lord of the East Wind*, The Catholic Biblical Quarterly Monograph Series, vol. 34 (Washington, DC: The Catholic Biblical Association of America, 2002), 136–39. Fitzgerald (*The Lord of the East Wind*, p. 139) concludes: "In sum, the evidence

174 *How Human Is God?*

indicates that *sᶜr/sᶜrh* is a strong wind, frequently the scirocco. It is very doubt-
ful that it can be a rainstorm." As Fitzgerald notes, this type of wind comes
from the eastern desert; perhaps God's appearance in the whirlwind then echoes
"the mighty wind that comes from the wilderness" in Job 1:19.

70. Some recent commentators have reacted with good reason to pious
readings of God, issuing in interpretations of God's speeches that, to my mind,
somewhat overreact. According to Bart Ehrman (*God's Problem*, p. 188), "God
does not explain why Job suffers. He simply asserts that he is the Almighty,
and as such, cannot be questioned." While the first sentence is right, the second
is not: God does not simply assert his Almighty status and criticize Job for
questioning the divine; on the contrary, God affirms that Job has "spoken of
(to?) me what is right" (see Job 42:7).

71. In this summary, I cannot address the text's many philological difficulties. The range of views both on the details and on the book of Job as a whole
perhaps suggests that it mirrors back to readers their thoughts about the problems that it raises (perhaps the writers were little better off).

72. Here I draw on Berlin, "What is the Book of Job about?" 113–21. For
these speeches, see also Othmar Keel and Françoise Smyth, *Dieu répond à
Job: Une interprétation de Job 38–41 à la lumière de l'iconographie du Proche-
Orient ancien*, Lectio Divina Commentary Series, vol. 2 (Paris: Éditions du
Cerf, 1993).

73. See above note 71. This approach fits with the context of Job; it is not
evident in Zechariah 3.

74. See the probing comments on this score by Cooper, "Reading and
Misreading," 69–73.

75. I take this expression from the helpful and insightful discussion of David
H. Aaron, *Biblical Ambiguities: Metaphor, Semantics and Divine Imagery*,
Brill Reference Library of Judaism Series, vol. 4 (Leiden: Brill, 2001), 101–24,
here 112.

76. Cross, quoted in "Contrasting Insights of Biblical Giants: BAR Inter-
views Elie Wiesel and Frank Moore Cross," *Biblical Archaeology Review* 30,
no. 4 (July/August 2004): 32.

77. The Persian period is the setting for Job 1–2 according to many interpreters: H. L. Ginsberg, "Job the Patient and Job the Impatient," *Conservative Judaism* 21, no. 3 (1967): 12–28, here 24; Edward L. Greenstein, "The Language of
Job and its Poetic Function," *Journal of Biblical Literature* 122 (2003): 652, n. 6.

78. See Martin Rösel and Uwe Glessmer, "God," in *Encyclopedia of the
Dead Sea Scrolls*, ed. Lawrence H. Schiffman and James C. VanderKam, vol.
1 (Oxford/New York: Oxford University Press, 2000), 317.

79. Seow, *Job 1–21*, 105, 299, 553–54, 558. It is sometimes thought that the satan versus God is a reflection of Persian dualism, specifically of Zoroastrian dualism between Ahura Mazda and Angra Mainyu (attributed good and light on the one hand, and evil and darkness on the other). Isaiah 45:7 assigns both sets of attributes to God. As God's subordinate in Job 1–2 and Zechariah 3, the satan does not reflect a dualistic theology with God. In Zechariah 3, the satan would reflect at most part of a theology of angelic benefit (the other angel, in verses 1, 3-5, 6) versus angelic accusation (the satan), both under God and subordinate to God. In Job 1–2, the other "sons of God" (verses 1:6; 2:1) likewise check on human beings. See Seow, *Job 1–21*, 273.

80. Pope, *Job*, xxxviii: "A practical monotheism seems implicit throughout the Book of Job"; xxxix: "The alleged monotheism of Job is not explicit, as it is in Second Isaiah."

81. Otherwise, one might be led to think that God is "sadistic," an "abusive victimizer," as suggested by Edward L. Greenstein, "The Problem of Evil in the Book of Job," in *Mishneh Todah: Studies in Deuteronomy and Its Cultural Environment in Honor of Jeffrey H. Tigay*, ed. Nili Sacher Fox, David A. Glatt-Gilad, and Michael James Williams (Winona Lake, IN: Eisenbrauns, 2009), 342. For a more constructive and balanced reading, see Adele Berlin, "What is the Book of Job about?" in *A Common Cultural Heritage: Studies on Mesopotamia and the Biblical World in Honor of Barry L. Eichler*, ed. Grant Frame, Erle Leichty, Karen Sonik, Jeffrey Tigay, and Steve Tinney (Bethesda, MD: CDL Press, 2011), 113–21

82. See Day, *An Adversary in Heaven*, 21.

83. Commentators have stressed this point, explored in some detail by Lowell K. Handy, "The Authorization of Divine Power and the Guilt of God in the Book of Job: Useful Ugaritic Parallels," *Journal for the Study of the Old Testament* 60 (1993): 107–18.

84. See van der Toorn, "The Theology of Demons in Mesopotamia and Israel," 65–67. For examples of spells against demons for health, see Foster, *From Distant Days*, 411–32; for spells for various life problems, see Foster, *From Distant Days*, 412–32.

85. For this point also for the writings of Ignatius of Antioch (died 107 CE/AD) and Polycarp of Smyrna (died about 156 CE/AD), see Jeffrey Burton Russell, *Satan: The Early Christian Tradition* (Ithaca, NY: Cornell University Press, 1982), 34–35 and 41–43.

86. In his autobiography Mark Twain recounts how kindly his mother was to people and animals. Pressed to finally admit that Satan is evil, she also responded: "would any claim that he [Satan] had been fairly treated? A sinner

176   *How Human Is God?*

was but a sinner; Satan was just like the rest. What saves the rest? Their efforts alone? No—or none might ever be saved. To their feeble efforts is added the mighty help of pathetic, appealing imploring prayers . . . But who prays for Satan?" *The Autobiography of Mark Twain*, ed. Charles Neider (New York: Washington Square Press, 1961), 28.

Chapter 7—pages 110–27

1. Kushner, *When Bad Things Happen to Good People* (New York: Random House, 1978). The book was republished in 2001 with a new preface.

2. See the older survey of John Hicks, *Evil and the God of Love* (San Francisco: Harper & Row, 1978).

3. In what follows, the discussion takes up several of the biblical arguments covered in Anti Laato and J. C. de Moor, eds., *Theodicy in the World of the Bible* (Leiden: Brill, 2003), listed on p. xx; Elizabeth Boase, "Constructing Meaning in the Face of Suffering: Theodicy in Lamentations." *Vetus Testamentum* 58 (2008): 449–68; and Bart Ehrman, *God's Problem: How the Bible Fails to Answer our Most Important Question—Why We Suffer* (New York: Harper-One, 2008). These are discussed also by Neil Gillman, *Sacred Fragments: Recovering Theology for the Modern Jew* (Philadelphia: Jewish Publication Society, 1990), 187–214; and Marvin A. Sweeney, *Reading the Hebrew Bible After the Shoah: Engaging Holocaust Theology* (Minneapolis, MN: Fortress Press, 2008), 5–17. Gilman and Sweeney survey some Jewish theological positions on suffering offered in response to the Holocaust. For the problem of divine anger and theodicy in Mesopotamian literature, see Karel van der Toorn, *Sin and Sanction in Israel and Mesopotamia: A Comparative Study*, Studia Semitica Neerlandica Series, vol. 22 (Assen: Van Gorcum, 1985), 56–93. Note also his article on the problem of demons and humans suffering: "The Theology of Demons in Mesopotamia and Israel: Popular Belief and Scholarly Speculation," in *Die Dämonen—Demons: Die Dämonologie der israelitisch-jüdischen und frühchristlichen Literatur im Kontext ihrer Umwelt—The Demonology of Israelite-Jewish and Early Christian Literature in Context of Their Environment*, ed. Armin Lange, Hermann Lichtenberger, and K. F. Diethard Römheld (Tübingen: Mohr Siebeck, 2003), 61–83.

4. This is a major problem for New Testament scholar Bart Ehrman. Because Ehrman expects to get an answer from the Bible, he says that he gave up his faith in God (as he recounts in his book, *God's Problem*). One problem with Ehrman's book is that it does not take sufficient note of the fact that the biblical writers often do not agree with what he takes to be the Bible's answers to suffering or that even within specific books the arguments are met by counter-

considerations or arguments. Instead, he picks away at a number of arguments one by one. Given his rejection of God based on physical and personal evil in the world, logically Ehrman might have arrived at a dualistic view of divine good and evil in the world. Instead, he rejects theism in general, which is not necessarily the logical conclusion to be drawn from his arguments.

5. Ehrman (*God's Problem*, 21–90) discusses passages about people suffering because of divine punishment for sin, largely in the biblical prophets, Deuteronomy, and the historical books. See also Job 4:7-8; 11:6; 18:5-21; 22:5-11. For the New Testament, see among many passages 1 Thessalonians 2:16 and 2 Thessalonians 1:6-10. Potentially more difficult variations on this idea are that humans cannot be righteous before God or are inherently prone to sin, views voiced, for example, by Eliphaz in Job 4:17-21 and 5:7 (the former voiced also by Job in Job 9:2, by Eliphaz in 15:14 and note his question in 22:2, and by Bildad in 25:4).

6. Verse 24; compare the verb "to take" in the sense "to take to heaven" with Elijah in 2 Kings 2:11-12, and "to take" (to be with God) with Enoch (Genesis 5:24).

7. See Chapter Two concerning *nepesh*.

8. Note the communal lament of Jeremiah 14:2-9, followed by the divine word to the prophet in 14:11-12a, "Do not pray for the welfare of this people. Although they fast, I do not hear their cry . . ." This is preceded by communal laments in Jeremiah 8:14-15, 18-21; 9:18, 21; 14:2-9, as well as the divine word to the prophet in 11:14: "do not pray for this people, or lift up a cry or prayer on their behalf, for I will not listen when they call to me in the time of their trouble."

9. See Ehrman, *God's Problem*, 91–123, especially 120: suffering comes from other human beings. He notes the problem that if God is in charge of all, how then can unrighteous people afflict righteous or innocent people?

10. On this score, I am reminded of the heightened awareness of satanic power in the writings of early Christian martyrs such as Ignatius of Antioch (died 107 AD/CE) and Polycarp of Smyrna (died about 156). See Jeffrey Burton Russell, *Satan: The Early Christian Tradition* (Ithaca, NY: Cornell University Press, 1982), 34–35, 41–43. Note also the many sixteenth-century Anabaptist expressions of the need for their suffering. This theological concern seems closely tied to the suffering and persecution that they faced from both Catholics and Protestants. In other words, the historical situation and the theological response went hand in hand, much as we see for ancient Israel in the seventh to sixth centuries and for early Christianity. For Anabaptist suffering, see C. Arnold Snyder, *Anabaptist History and Theology: An Introduction* (Kitchener, Ontario: Pandora Press; Scottdale, PA/Waterloo, Ontario: Herald Press, 1995), 77, 93–94, 106, 169–70.

11. Elizabeth Boase, "Constructing Meaning in the Face of Suffering: Theodicy in Lamentations," *Vetus Testamentum* 58 (2008): 449–68.

12. Boase, "Constructing Meaning in the Face of Suffering," 460.

13. See Ehrman, *God's Problem*, 197–227.

14. See Ehrman, *God's Problem*, 228–60.

15. See the reflections of Richard B. Hays and Stefan Alkier, "Introduction," in *Revelation and the Politics of the Apocalyptic Interpretation*, ed. Richard B. Hays and Stefan Alkier (Waco, TX: Baylor University Press, 2012), 1–8.

16. Overall, God and most gods and goddesses in the ancient world were generally about providing blessing, benefit, and prosperity. They could get angry at their people for ritual infractions or poor behavior, but this does not normally issue in natural disaster, but in defeat by enemy forces or the like. Instead, the source of natural catastrophe tended to be found less in such deities than in malevolent forces, sometimes considered divine as well. For example, the manifestation of death in Jeremiah 9:20 in the form of pestilence: "Death has come up into our window . . ." For other examples, with discussion, see Karel van der Toorn, "The Theology of Demons in Mesopotamia and Israel: Popular Belief and Scholarly Speculation," in *Die Dämonen—Demons: Die Dämonologie der israelitisch-jüdischen und frühchristlichen Literatur im Kontext ihrer Umwelt—The Demonology of Israelite-Jewish and Early Christian Literature in Context of Their Environment*, ed. Armin Lange, Hermann Lichtenberger, and K. F. Diethard Römheld (Tübingen: Mohr Siebeck, 2003), 61–83.

17. Edward L. Greenstein, "The Problem of Evil in the Book of Job," in *Mishneh Todah: Studies in Deuteronomy and Its Cultural Environment in Honor of Jeffrey H. Tigay*, ed. Nili Sacher Fox, David A. Glatt-Gilad, and Michael James Williams (Winona Lake, IN: Eisenbrauns, 2009), 333–62, here 342. If this view were correct, one might compare the "demonic side" of some deities in Mesopotamian religion, as discussed by van der Toorn, "The Theology of Demons in Mesopotamia and Israel," 79–81.

18. Ehrman (*God's Problem*, 276–78) rightly emphasizes this point.

19. For the Septuagint of Genesis 22, see Heinrich Seesemann, *"peira, perao, peiraso, peirasmos, ekpeiraso,"* in *Theological Dictionary of the New Testament*, ed. Gerhard Friedrich, trans. Geoffrey W. Bromiley (Grand Rapids, MI: Eerdmans, 1968), vol. 6, 25. It is noted that this depiction influences later Greco-Roman passages, such as Sirach 44:20; 1 Maccabees 2:52; and Judith 8:25-27. See F. J. Helfmeyer, *"nissah,"* in *Theological Dictionary of the Old Testament. Volume IX*, ed. G. Johannes Botterweck, Helmer Ringgren, and Heinz-Josef Fabry, trans. David E. Green (Grand Rapids, MI/Cambridge, UK: Eerdmans, 1998), 450.

20. For problems with this assumption in the Bible, see Michael Carasik, "The Limits of Omniscience," *Journal of Biblical Literature* 119 (2000): 221–32. See also Carasik, *Theologies of the Mind in Biblical Israel*, Studies in Biblical Literature Series, vol. 85 (New York: Peter Lang, 2005), 112–14, with discussion of Genesis 22 on 113.

21. See Helfmeyer, *"nissah,"* 453; and Seeseman, *"peira,"* 26. Sesseman stresses the Hellenistic model of testing as education for Sirach 2:1; 33:1; and Wisdom of Solomon 3:5 and 11:9.

22. For these New Testament usages, see Seeseman, *"peira,"* 28–36. See also Mark 13:22; Matthew 5:4; 10-12; and Luke 6:22f.

23. See the older discussion of Henry Ansgar Kelly, "The Devil in the Desert," *The Catholic Biblical Quarterly 26* (1964): 196–97.

24. This passage is discussed in the preceding chapter.

25. Exodus 15:25; 16:4; 20:20; Deuteronomy 8:2, 16; see also Deuteronomy 33:8; Wisdom of Solomon 18:20-25.

26. Exodus 17:2, 7; Numbers 14:22; Deuteronomy 6:16; Psalms 78:18, 41, 56; 95:9; 106:14; 1 Corinthians 10:9: Hebrew 3:8-9. See Helfmeyer, *"nissah,"* 446–48.

27. For other cases of God testing, see the testing of the Israelites in Deuteronomy 13:3; Judges 2:22; and 3:1, 4; of Hezekiah in 2 Chronicles 32:31; and of the psalmist in Psalm 26:2. The root also means to try or attempt something; see Deuteronomy 4:34; 28:56; and 1 Samuel 17:39; and note Job 4:2. See Helfmeyer, *"nissah,"* 445.

28. For tests to friendship, see also Sirach 6:8-17; 9:10; 19:13; 15; 22:19-22; 27:16-21; and 37:1-6.

29. The Greek word *peiraterion* appears in the Septuagint of Job. For details, see Sesseman, *"peira,"* 25.

30. See chapter 6 for this point.

31. See Ehrman, *God's Problem*, 263–64. See also John Hicks, *Evil and the Evidence for God* (Philadelphia: Temple University Press, 1995).

32. See Ehrman, *God's Problem*, 125–57. In this category, Ehrman includes the Joseph story, but the text does not include the idea that the suffering was caused by God for this purpose. See my comments above.

33. I refer to the process of resilience in the face of trauma, drawing on David Bosworth, "Faith and Resilience: King David's Reaction to the Death of Bathsheba's Firstborn," *The Catholic Biblical Quarterly* 73 (2011): 691–707.

34. See Gillman, *Sacred Fragments*, 201–10. Gillman specifically discusses Richard Rubenstein's "Death of God" theology, Martin Buber's "Eclipse of God" (reminiscent of the biblical idea of God hiding the divine face), and

Abraham Joshua Heschel's "Suffering God" (reminiscent of biblical passages describing God's emotional response to Israel's plight, such as Jeremiah 14:17). For these biblical ideas, see chapter 2 above.

35. For an example of a "process theodicy," see David Ray Griffin, *God, Power, and Evil: A Process Theodicy* (Louisville, KY: Westminster John Knox, 1976).

36. Ehrman, *God's Problem*, 8.

37. Translation from the New Jewish Publication Society.

38. Frank Moore Cross, *Canaanite Myth and Hebrew Epic: Essays in the History of the Religion of Israel* (Cambridge, MA/London: Harvard University, 1973), 191–94.

39. See chapter 2 for God's voice, with discussion of this specific instance.

40. Quoted in an interview with David Levine, "Learning To Fly," http://nautil.us/issue/2/uncertainty/learning-to-fly (accessed 28 June 2013). Reference courtesy of David Levine.

Epilogue—pages 128–31

1. https://en.wikipedia.org/wiki/St._Elsewhere. This episode was episode 9 in season five.

2. See the helpful and insightful discussion of David H. Aaron, *Biblical Ambiguities: Metaphor, Semantics and Divine Imagery*, Brill Reference Library of Judaism Series, vol. 4 (Leiden: Brill, 2001), 101–24, especially 112.

3. See David Tracy, *The Analogical Imagination: Christian Theology and the Culture of Pluralism* (New York: Crossroad Publishing Company, 1981).

4. Here (as in chapter 3), I draw on Corrine Carvalho, "The Beauty of the Bloody God: The Divine Warrior in Prophetic Literature," in *Aesthetics of Violence in the Prophets*, ed. Chris Franke and Julia M. O'Brien, Library of Hebrew Bible/Old Testament Studies Series, vol. 517 (New York/London: T & T Clark, 2010), 152.

5. For the impact of our own modern and post-modern settings on our sense of divine mystery, see the reflections of David Tracy, "The Hermeneutics of Naming God," *Irish Theological Quarterly* 57 (1991): 253–64.

Recommended Readings

Prologue: Invitation to Thinking about God in the Hebrew Bible

Kaspar, Walter. "The Timeliness of Speaking of God: Freedom and Communion as Basic Concepts of Theology." Uploaded March 9, 2010, accessed July 2, 2013, http://www.youtube.com/watch?v=_V7sk5P5MoA.

Leclerq, Jean. *The Love of Learning and the Desire for God: A Study of Monastic Culture.* Translated by Catharine Misrahi. New York: Fordham University Press, 1961. This work was originally published as *L'Amour des lettres et le désir de Dieu: Initiation aux auteurs monastiques du moyen âge.* Paris: Les Éditions du Cerf, 1957.

Levine, Amy-Jill. *The Misunderstood Jew: The Church and the Scandal of the Jewish Jesus.* San Francisco: HarperSanFrancisco, 2007.

O'Brien, Julia M. *Challenging Prophetic Metaphor: Theology and Ideology in the Prophets.* Louisville, KY: Westminster John Knox, 2008.

Soskice, Janet Martin. *The Kindness of God: Metaphor, Gender, and Religious Language.* New York: Oxford University Press, 2007.

Weil, Simone. *Waiting for God.* Translated by Emma Craufurd. New York: HarperCollins, 2009; originally published in 1951.

Chapter 1: Why Does God in the Bible Have a Body?

Frymer-Kensky, Tikva. *In the Wake of the Goddesses: Women, Culture, and the Biblical Transformation of Pagan Myth.* New York: Free Press, 1992.

Halpern, Baruch. *From Gods to God: The Dynamics of Iron Age Cosmologies*. Edited by Matthew J. Adams. Forschungen zum Alten Testament Series, volume 63. Tübingen: Mohr Siebeck, 2009.

Hamori, Esther J. *"When Gods Were Men": The Embodied God in Biblical and Near Eastern Literature*. Beihefte zur Zeitschrift für die alttestamentliche Wissenschaft Series, volume 384. Berlin: de Gruyter, 2008.

Hendel, Ronald S. "Aniconism and Anthropomorphism in Ancient Israel." In *The Image and the Book: Iconic Cults, Aniconism, and the Rise of Book Religion in Israel and the Ancient Near East*. Edited by Karel van der Toorn. Biblical Exegesis and Religion Series, volume 21. Leuven: Peeters, 1997.

Kamionkowski, S. Tamar and Wonil Kim, eds. *Bodies, Embodiment, and Theology of the Hebrew Bible*. New York: T & T Clark, 2010.

Smith, Mark S. "Like Deities, Like Temples (Like People)." In *Temple and Worship in Biblical Israel: Proceedings of the Oxford Old Testament Seminar*. Edited by John Day. Library of Hebrew Bible/Old Testament Studies, formerly Journal for the Study of the Old Testament Supplement Series, volume 422. New York: T & T Clark, 2005.

Sommer, Benjamin. *The Bodies of God and the World of Ancient Israel*. New York: Cambridge University Press, 2009.

Stern, David. "*Imitatio Hominis:* Anthropomorphism and the Character(s) of God." *Prooftexts* 12, no. 2 (1992): 151–74.

Tracy, David. *The Analogical Imagination: Christian Theology and the Culture of Pluralism*. New York: Crossroad Publishing Company, 1981.

Uehlinger, Christoph, and Suzanne Müller Trufaut. "Ezekiel 1, Babylonian Cosmological Scholarship and Iconography: Attempts at Further Refinement." *Theologische Zeitschrift* 57 (2001): 140–71.

Williams, Wesley. "A Body Unlike Bodies: Transcendent Anthropomorphism in Ancient Semitic Tradition and Early Islam." *Journal of the American Oriental Society* 129 (2009): 19–44.

Wolfson, Elliot R. *Through a Speculum That Shines: Vision and Imagination in Medieval Jewish Mysticism*. Princeton, NJ: Princeton University Press, 1994.

Wright, J. Edward. *The Early History of Heaven*. New York: Oxford University Press, 2000.

Chapter 2: What Do God's Body Parts in the Bible Mean?

Bosworth, David. "The Tears of God in the Book of Jeremiah." *Biblica* 94 (2013): 24–46.

Burnett, Joel S. *"Where Is God?" Divine Absence in the Hebrew Bible.* Minneapolis, MN: Fortress Press, 2010.

Carasik, Michael. *Theologies of the Mind in Biblical Israel.* Studies in Biblical Literature Series, volume 85. New York: Peter Lang, 2005.

Di Vito, Robert A. "Old Testament Anthropology and the Construction of Personal Identity." *The Catholic Biblical Quarterly* 61 (1999): 217–38.

Friedman, Richard Elliott. *The Hidden Face of God.* San Francisco: Harper San Francisco, 1996.

Korpel, Marjo C. A., and Johannes C. de Moor. *The Silence of God.* Leiden: Brill, 2012.

MacDonald, Paul S. *History of the Concept of Mind: Speculations about Soul, Mind, and Spirit from Homer to Hume.* Burlington, VT: Ashgate, 2003.

Seebass, Horst. *"nepesh."* In *Theological Dictionary of the Old Testament, Volume IX.* Edited by G. Johannes Botterweck, Helmer Ringgren, and Heinz-Josef Fabry. Grand Rapids, MI: Eerdmans, 1998.

Whitlock, Glenn E. "The Structure of Personality in Hebrew Psychology." *Interpretation* 14 (1960): 3–13.

Chapter 3: Why Is God Angry in the Bible?

Baumann, Gerlinde. *Love and Violence: Marriage as Metaphor for the Relationship between YHWII and Israel in the Prophetic Books.* Translated by Linda M. Maloney. Collegeville, MN: Liturgical Press, 2003.

Carvalho, Corrine. "The Beauty of the Bloody God: The Divine Warrior in Prophetic Literature." In *Aesthetics of Violence in the Prophets.* Edited by Chris Franke and Julia M. O'Brien. Library of Hebrew Bible/Old Testament Studies Series, volume 517. New York: T & T Clark, 2010.

Frymer-Kensky, Tikva. *In the Wake of the Goddesses: Women, Culture, and the Biblical Transformation of Pagan Myth.* New York: Free Press, 1992.

Geller, Stephen A. "The One and the Many: An Essay on the God of the Covenant." In *One God or Many? Concepts of Divinity in the Ancient World*. Edited by Barbara N. Porter. Transactions of the Casco Bay Assyriological Institute, vol. 1; Bethesda, MD: CDL Press, 2000.

Grant, Deena. "Wrath of God," in *The New Interpreter's Dictionary of the Bible*. Edited by Katharine Doob Sakenfeld et al. Five volumes. Nashville, TN: Abingdon Press, 2009. Volume 5, pp. 932–37.

———. *Divine Anger in Biblical Literature*. The Catholic Biblical Quarterly Monograph Series, vol. 20. Washington, DC: The Catholic Biblical Association of America, 2014.

Kalmanofsky, Amy. "Israel's Baby: The Horror of Childbirth in the Biblical Prophets." *Biblical Interpretation* 16 (2008): 60–82.

Korte, Ann-Marie. "A Unique Instability? Exploring the Boundaries of Monotheism Introduction." In *The Boundaries of Monotheism: Interdisciplinary Explorations into the Foundations of Western Monotheism*. Edited by Anne-Marie Korte and Maaike de Haardt. Studies in Theology and Religion Series, vol. 13. Boston: Brill, 2009.

Lapsley, Jacqueline E. "Feeling Our Way: Love for God in Deuteronomy." *The Catholic Biblical Quarterly* 65 (2003): 350–69.

Mermelstein, Ari. "Love and Hate at Qumran: The Social Construction of Sectarian Emotion." *Dead Sea Discoveries* 20 (2013): 237–63.

Moran, William L. "The Ancient Near Eastern Background of the Love of God in Deuteronomy." *The Catholic Biblical Quarterly* 25 (1963): 77–87. Reprinted in Moran, *The Most Magic Word*. Edited by Ronald S. Hendel. The Catholic Biblical Quarterly Monograph Series, vol. 35. Washington, DC: The Catholic Biblical Association of America, 2002.

Muffs, Yochanan. *Love and Joy: Law, Language and Religion in Ancient Israel*. New York: The Jewish Theological Seminary of America, 1992.

———. *The Personhood of God: Biblical Theology, Human Faith and the Divine Image*. Woodstock, VT: Jewish Lights Publishing, 2005.

———. "On Biblical Anthropomorphism." In *Bringing the Hidden to Light: The Process of Interpretation. Studies in Honor of Stephen A. Geller*. Edited by Kathryn F. Kravitz and Diane M. Sharon. Winona Lake, IN: Eisenbrauns, 2007.

Nowell, Irene. *Pleading, Cursing, Praising: Conversing with God through the Psalms.* Collegeville, MN: Liturgical Press, 2013.

O'Brien, Julia M. *Challenging Prophetic Metaphor: Theology and Ideology in the Prophets.* Louisville, KY: Westminster John Knox, 2008.

O'Connor, Kathleen. *Jeremiah: Pain and Promise.* Minneapolis, MN: Fortress Press, 2011.

Smith, Mark S. "The Heart and Innards in Israelite Emotional Expressions: Notes from Anthropology and Psychobiology." *Journal of Biblical Literature* 117, no. 3 (1998): 427–36.

———. *Poetic Heroes: The Literary Commemoration of Warriors and Warrior Culture in the Early Biblical World.* Grand Rapids, MI: Eerdmans, 2014.

Van Wolde, Ellen. "Sentiments as Culturally Constructed Emotions: Anger and Love in the Hebrew Bible." *Biblical Interpretation* 16 (2008): 1–24.

Chapter 4: Does God in the Bible Have Gender or Sexuality?

Biezeveld, Kune. "One Unique God for All Parts of Life. Reconsidering an Exclusive Tradition." In *The Boundaries of Monotheism: Interdisciplinary Explorations into the Foundations of Western Monotheism.* Edited by Anne-Marie Korte and Maaike de Haardt. Studies in Theology and Religion Series, vol. 13. Boston: Brill, 2009.

Brettler, Marc Zvi. *God is King: Understanding an Israelite Metaphor.* Journal for the Study of the Old Testament Supplement Series, volume 76. Sheffield, UK: Sheffield Academic Press, 1989.

Carvalho, Corrine. "The Beauty of the Bloody God: The Divine Warrior in Prophetic Literature." In *Aesthetics of Violence in the Prophets.* Edited by Chris Franke and Julia M. O'Brien. Library of Hebrew Bible/Old Testament Studies Series, vol. 517. New York: T & T Clark, 2010.

Childs, Brevard S. *Old Testament Theology in a Canonical Context.* Philadelphia: Fortress Press, 1985.

Coogan, Michael David. *God and Sex: What the Bible Really Says.* New York/Boston: Twelve, 2010.

Dille, Sarah. *Mixing Metaphors: God as Mother and Father in Deutero-Isaiah.* London: T & T Clark, 2004.

Frymer-Kensky, Tikva. *In the Wake of the Goddesses: Women, Culture, and the Biblical Transformation of Pagan Myth*. New York: Free Press, 1992.

Geller, Stephen A. *Sacred Enigmas: Literary Religion in the Hebrew Bible*. New York: Routledge, 1996.

Gerstenberger, Erhard. *Yahweh the Patriarch: Ancient Images of God and Feminist Theology*. Translated by F. J. Gaiser. Minneapolis, MN: Fortress Press, 1996.

Gruber, Mayer I. *The Motherhood of God and Other Studies*. South Florida Studies in the History of Judaism Series, vol. 57. Atlanta, GA: Scholars, 1992.

Hadley, Judith. *The Cult of Asherah in Ancient Israel and Judah: Evidence for a Hebrew Goddess*. University of Cambridge Oriental Publications, vol. 57. Cambridge, UK: Cambridge University Press, 2000.

Keel, Othmar, and Christoph Uehlinger. *Gods, Goddesses, and Images of God in Ancient Israel*. Translated by Thomas Trapp. Minneapolis, MN: Fortress Press, 1998.

Løland, Hanne. *Silent or Salient Gender: The Interpretation of Gendered God-Language in the Hebrew Bible Exemplified in Isaiah 42, 46, and 49*. Forschungen zum Alten Testament Series 2, vol. 32. Tübingen: Mohr Siebeck, 2008.

O'Brien, Julia M. *Challenging Prophetic Metaphor: Theology and Ideology in the Prophets*. Louisville, KY: Westminster John Knox, 2008.

Smith, Mark S. *God in Translation: Deities in Cross-Cultural Discourse in the Biblical World*. Forschungen zum Alten Testament Series I, vol. 57. Tübingen: Mohr Siebeck, 2008; Grand Rapids, MI: Eerdmans, 2010.

Soskice, Janet Martin. *The Kindness of God: Metaphor, Gender, and Religious Language*. New York: Oxford University Press, 2007.

Trible, Phyllis. *God and the Rhetoric of Sexuality*. Overtures to Biblical Theology. Philadelphia: Fortress Press, 1978.

Chapter 5: What Can Creation Tell Us about God?

Bird, Phyllis. "Gen 1:27b in the Context of the Priestly Account of Creation." *Harvard Theological Review* 74 (1981): 138–44.

Clifford, Richard J. *Creation Accounts in the Ancient Near East and in the Bible*. The Catholic Biblical Quarterly Monograph Series, vol. 26. Washington, DC: The Catholic Biblical Association of America, 1994.

Garr, W. Randall. "'Image' and 'Likeness' in the Inscription from Tell Fakhariyeh," *Israel Exploration Journal* 50 (2000): 227–34.

———. *In His Own Image and Likeness: Humanity, Divinity, and Monotheism*. Culture and History of the Ancient Near East Series, vol. 15. Leiden/Boston: Brill, 2003.

Keel, Othmar, and Silvia Schroer. *Creation: Biblical Theology in the Context of Ancient Near Eastern Religion*. Winona Lake, IN: Eisenbrauns, 2008.

Smith, Mark S. *God in Translation: Deities in Cross-Cultural Discourse in the Biblical World*. Forschungen zum Alten Testament Series I, vol. 57. Tübingen: Mohr Siebeck, 2008; Grand Rapids, MI: Eerdmans, 2010.

———. *The Priestly Vision of Genesis 1*. Minneapolis, MN: Fortress Press, 2010.

Chapter 6: Who—or What—Is the Satan?

Berlin, Adele. "What is the Book of Job about?" In *A Common Cultural Heritage: Studies on Mesopotamia and the Biblical World in Honor of Barry L. Eichler*. Edited by Grant Frame, Erle Leichty, Karen Sonik, Jeffrey Tigay, and Steve Tinney. Bethesda, MD: CDL Press, 2011.

Bernstein, Alan E. *Formation of Hell: Death and Retribution in the Ancient and Early Christian Worlds*. Ithaca, NY: Cornell University Press, 1993.

Brand, Miryam T. *Evil Within and Without: The Source of Sin and Its Nature as Portrayed in Second Temple Literature*. Göttingen: Vandenhoeck & Ruprecht, 2013.

Brown, Derek R. "The Devil in the Details: A Survey of Research on Satan in Biblical Studies." *Currents in Biblical Research* 9, no. 2 (2011): 200–227.

Day, Peggy L. *An Adversary in Heaven: Satan in the Hebrew Bible*. Harvard Semitic Museum Series, vol. 43. Atlanta: Scholars Press, 1988.

Forsyth, Neil. *The Old Enemy: Satan and the Combat Myth*. Princeton, NJ: Princeton University Press, 1987.

Kelly, Henry Ansgar. *Satan: A Biography*. Cambridge, UK: Cambridge University Press, 2006.

Lange, Armin. "Satanic Verses: The Adversary in the Qumran Manuscripts and Elsewhere." *Revue de Qumrân* 93 (2009): 35–48.

✝ Pagels, Elaine. *The Origin of Satan: How Christians Demonized Jews, Pagans, and Heretics*. New York: Vintage, 1995.

Patella, Michael. *Angels and Demons: A Christian Primer of the Spiritual World*. Collegeville, MN: Liturgical Press, 2012.

Russell, Jeffrey Burton. *Satan: The Early Christian Tradition*. Ithaca, NY: Cornell University Press, 1982.

Stokes, Ryan. "The Devil Made David Do It . . . Or Did He? The Nature, Identity, and Literary Origins of the *Satan* in 1 Chronicles 21." *Journal of Biblical Literature* 128 (2009): 91–106.

Van der Toorn, Karel. "The Theology of Demons in Mesopotamia and Israel: Popular Belief and Scholarly Speculation." In *Die Dämonen—Demons: Die Dämonologie der israelitisch-jüdischen und frühchristlichen Literatur im Kontext ihrer Umwelt—The Demonology of Israelite-Jewish and Early Christian Literature in Context of Their Environment*. Edited by Armin Lange, Hermann Lichtenberger, and K. F. Diethard Römheld. Tübingen: Mohr Siebeck, 2003.

Wright, J. Edward. *The Early History of Heaven*. Oxford, UK: Oxford University Press, 2000.

Chapter 7: Why Do People Suffer According to the Hebrew Bible?

Boase, Elizabeth. "Constructing Meaning in the Face of Suffering: Theodicy in Lamentations." *Vetus Testamentum* 58 (2008): 449–68.

Ehrman, Bart. *God's Problem: How the Bible Fails to Answer Our Most Important Question—Why We Suffer*. New York: HarperOne, 2008.

Gutiérrez, Gustavo. *On Job: God-talk and the Suffering of the Innocent*. Maryknoll, NY: Orbis Books, 1987.

Hays, Richard B., and Stefan Alkier, eds. *Revelation and the Politics of the Apocalyptic Interpretation*. Waco, TX: Baylor University Press, 2012.

Laato, A., and J. C. de Moor, eds. *Theodicy in the World of the Bible.* Leiden: Brill, 2003.

Safire, William. *The First Dissident: The Book of Job in Today's Politics.* New York: Random House, 1992.

Tambasco, Anthony J. *The Bible on Suffering: Social and Political Implications.* Mahwah, NJ: Paulist Press, 2001.

Acknowledgments

I happily begin my acknowledgments with my gratitude to Liturgical Press, and in particular, to Peter Dwyer, Hans Christoffersen, Patrick McGowan, Colleen Stiller, and Mary Stommes. They have been enthusiastic about this project, and the press has been most helpful. Julie Deluty, a doctoral student at New York University, assisted me with proofreading and editing.

The chapters of this book originated as talks. Five of them were presented before the 48th Annual Georgetown University Institute on Sacred Scripture, held on 21–25 June 2011. I am grateful to Professor Alan Mitchell for his invitation and kind hospitality. The Institute's fellow faculty, Professor Mitchell and Professor Thomas Stegman, as well as its devoted following, posed many thoughtful questions. It was also a particular pleasure for me to roam the site of some of my early memories as a child when my mother worked at the university in the early 1960s.

Over the ten days of 21–31 May 2012, I delivered five talks at the Minzu University of China in Beijing. My host, Professor You Bin, was most gracious. I also appreciate the help provided by my student host, Xu Zhiyan, as well as Xue Lijie; the three of us spent a delightful day at the Great Wall. The audience, composed mostly of students studying religion at the university, was challenging. It was a dream for me to travel to China, to learn of its history and culture at close range, and to talk to so many friendly people there.

In the spring term of 2013, I developed these chapters for classes for a freshman seminar at New York University. The students were smart and engaged, and the course was inspiring for me.

On 23–24 June 2013, Mundelein Seminary hosted three of the talks. I am grateful to my host, Elizabeth Nagel, for her gracious invitation, and to Megan Deichl for her work in arranging for these talks. Preparing for these talks helped me to think once again about the issues. In July of 2013, I had the opportunity to live and work at the Ecole Biblique in Jerusalem, long a home for me in earlier summers. This project benefitted from the time there.

I with to thank the Anabaptist Menonite Biblical Seminary for most graciously hosting me in March 2014. On this occasion, I was given an opportunity to deliver three of the talks in this book and to reflect further on them. I am particularly grateful to my hosts, Dean Rebecca Slough and Professors Ben Ollenburger and Safwat Marzouk.

For help with this study, it has given me great pleasure to turn to the works of many of my teachers: Brevard Childs, Michael Coogan, Frank Cross, Joseph Fitzmyer, Jonas Greenfield, P. Kyle McCarter, William Moran, and Marvin Pope. In addition, I would mention an older master, Edouard Dhorme, whose mark has also been most helpful to this study. Some of these names, now perhaps forgotten, should be remembered today, as our work is built, knowingly or not, on the foundations provided by these figures and others of their times.

My work has also benefitted enormously from the published studies of three wonderful scholars (also former students of mine): Corrine Carvalho, Miryam Brand, and Deena Grant. As is well known, students such as these are very important teachers. In Chapter 3, I am particularly indebted to Deena Grant for her work on divine anger. Many colleagues and friends have also helped me: Paul Aspan, Kune Biezeveld, Matteo Crimella, Philip

Cunningham, Bob Di Vito, David Goldenberg, Ron Hendel, Wayne Horowitz, Bernd Janowski, Peter Kearney (to whom I am thankful for his suggestion for the book's main title), David Levine, Riccardo Lufrani, Peter Machinist, Irene Nowell, Julia O'Brien, Kathleen O'Connor, Benjamin Sommer, David Stern, Karel van der Toorn, Christoph Uehlinger, Andreas Wagner, Bruce Wells, Ed Wright, and Jacob Wright. I have also had many conversations with people over the past few years, and often the topics in this book have come up. As a result, I have found myself going back and rethinking and rewording various points. To all of you (unfortunately too many to name), I express my thanks.

Family, as always, has been very important for this work. My younger brother, Jeffrey Smith (publisher of *The Word Among Us*), provided helpful advice, as did my daughters, Rachel and Shula, and my son, Benjamin. My wife, Liz Bloch-Smith, has also been crucial in my efforts to find a way to express the matters discussed in this book. I am eternally grateful to Liz and our children (and now, thanks to Ben and his Elizabeth, our granddaughter, Addison Elizabeth!). Finally, I thank my parents, Donald Eugene Smith and Mary Elizabeth Reichert Smith, my first teachers of God (cf. Job 36:22, "who is a teacher like him?").

This work is dedicated in love to the memory of Charles (Charlie) Jay Smith, the son of my nephew, David Smith-Watts, and his wife, Barbara Gutierrez Smith. Born prematurely this past November, Charlie lived a mere four days on this earth. We bear the memory of his tiny, vulnerable life in our hearts.